Reading, Writing & Language

INSIDE

LANGUAGE • LITERACY • CONTENT

PROGRAM AUTHORS

Deborah J. Short

Josefina Villamil Tinajero

Acknowledgments

Grateful acknowledgment is given to the authors, artists, photographers, museums, publishers, and agents for permission to reprint copyrighted material. Every effort has been made to secure the appropriate permission. If any omissions have been made or if corrections are required, please contact the Publisher.

Photographic Credits
Cover (front): Royal Bengal Tiger, Ranthambore National Park, Rajasthan, India, Danita Delimont. Photograph © Danita Delimont/Gallo Images/Getty Images.
Cover (back): Royal Bengal Tiger, Ranthambore National Park, Rajasthan, India, Aditya Singh. Photograph © Aditya Singh/Getty Images.

Acknowledgments continue on page 399.

For product information and technology asistance, contact us at
Cengage Learning Customer & Sales Support, 1-800-354-9706

For permission to use material from this text or product, submit all requests online at **www.cengage.com/permissions**
Further permissions questions can be emailed to
permissionrequest@cengage.com

National Geographic Learning | Cengage Learning
1 Lower Ragsdale Drive
Building 1, Suite 200
Monterey, CA 93940

Cengage Learning is a leading provider of customized learning solutions with office locations around the globe, including Singapore, the United Kingdom, Australia, Mexico, Brazil, and Japan. Locate your local office at **www.cengage.com/global**.

Visit National Geographic Learning online at **ngl.cengage.com**
Visit our corporate website at **www.cengage.com**

Printer: Quad/Graphics, Versailles, KY

ISBN: 9781285439440

Printed in the United States of America
18 19 20 21 22
10 9 8 7 6 5 4 3 2

Contents at a Glance

| Unit | Vocabulary | Language & Grammar | | Reading | | Writing |
		Function	Grammar	Phonics/Decoding	Comprehension	
1	Time	Tell What May Happen	Phrases with *Have To* and *Need To* Possessive Adjectives	Long Vowels (*ie, igh, ui, ue*)	Cause and Effect	Friendly Letter
2	Direction Words Civil Rights Words	Give Information Give Directions Express Wants and Feelings	Irregular Past Tense Verbs	*R*-controlled Vowels	Sequence Classify	Personal Narrative
3	Opinion Words Animals and Habitats Plants and Habitats	Give Your Opinion Describe Places Make a Suggestion	Sensory Adjectives	*R*-controlled Syllable Types	Details	Fact-and-Opinion Article
4	History and Historical Records	Have a Discussion Make Comparisons	Nouns Present and Past Tense Verbs Object Pronouns	Words with *y*	Comparisons	Comparison Paragraph
5	Opposites Phrases for Times and Places	Ask for and Give Advice Ask for and Accept a Favor Describe Actions	Commands Prepositional Phrases	Diphthongs and Variant Vowels	Character Traits Story Elements	Short Story
6	The Body Sports	Ask for and Give Information Express Thanks	Present Tense Verbs Pronouns	Variant Vowels and Consonants	Main Idea and Details	Procedure
7	American History Landforms and Bodies of Water	Ask and Answer Questions Give Directions	Questions with *How?* and *Why?* Capitalization: Proper Nouns	Multisyllabic Words	Classify	Biography
8	Farming	Buy or Sell an Item Give Information	Subjects and Predicates Word Order in Sentences	Prefixes and Suffixes	Comparisons	Report
9	Idioms Space	Agree and Disagree Give Information	Future Tense Verbs Contractions Verb Tenses	Multisyllabic Words	Goal and Outcome	Diamante Poem

Reviewers

We gratefully acknowledge the many contributions of the following dedicated educators in creating a program that is not only pedagogically sound, but also appealing to and motivating for middle school students.

Teacher Reviewers

Idalia Apodaca
English Language Development Teacher
Shaw Middle School
Spokane, WA

Pat E. Baggett-Hopkins
Area Reading Coach
Chicago Public Schools
Chicago, IL

Judy Chin
ESOL Teacher
Arvida Middle School
Miami, FL

Sonia Flores
Teacher Supporter
Los Angeles Unified School District
Los Angeles, CA

Brenda Garcia
ESL Teacher
Crockett Middle School
Irving, TX

Kristine Hoffman
Teacher on Special Assignment
Newport-Mesa Unified School District
Costa Mesa, CA

Dr. Margaret R. Keefe
ELL Contact and Secondary Advocate
Martin County School District
Stuart, FL

Julianne Kosareff
Curriculum Specialist
Paramount Unified School District
Paramount, CA

Lore Levene
Coordinator of Language Arts
Community Consolidated School District 59
Arlington Heights, IL

Natalie M. Mangini
Teacher/ELD Coordinator
Serrano Intermediate School
Lake Forest, CA

Laurie Manikowski
Teacher/Trainer
Lee Mathson Middle School
San Jose, CA

Patsy Mills
Supervisor, Bilingual-ESL
Houston Independent School District
Houston, TX

Juliane M. Prager-Nored
High Point Expert
Los Angeles Unified School District
Los Angeles, CA

Patricia Previdi
ESOL Teacher
Patapsco Middle School
Ellicott City, MD

Dr. Louisa Rogers
Middle School Team Leader
Broward County Public Schools
Fort Lauderdale, FL

Rebecca Varner
ESL Teacher
Copley-Fairlawn Middle School
Copley, OH

Hailey F. Wade
ESL Teacher/Instructional Specialist
Lake Highlands Junior High
Richardson, TX

Cassandra Yorke
ESOL Coordinator
Palm Beach School District
West Palm Beach, FL

Program Authors

Deborah J. Short, Ph.D.

Dr. Deborah Short is a co-developer of the research-validated SIOP Model for sheltered instruction. She has directed quasi-experimental and experimental studies on English language learners funded by the Carnegie Corporation of New York, the Rockefeller Foundation, and the U.S. Dept. of Education. She recently chaired an expert panel on adolescent ELL literacy and coauthored a policy report: *Double the Work: Challenges and Solutions to Acquiring Language and Academic Literacy for Adolescent English Language Learners*. She has also conducted extensive research on secondary level newcomer programs. Her research articles have appeared in the *TESOL Quarterly*, the *Journal of Educational Research*, *Educational Leadership*, *Education and Urban Society*, *TESOL Journal*, *Social Education*, and *Journal of Research in Education*.

Josefina Villamil Tinajero, Ph.D.

Dr. Josefina Villamil Tinajero specializes in staff development and school-university partnership programs, and consulted with school districts in the U.S. to design ESL, bilingual, literacy, and biliteracy programs. She has served on state and national advisory committees for standards development, including the English as a New Language Advisory Panel of the National Board of Professional Teaching Standards. She is currently Professor of Education and Associate Dean at the University of Texas at El Paso, and was President of the National Association for Bilingual Education, 1997–2000.

Unit 1

HERE to HELP

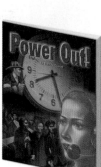

THEME BOOK

Unit 2

Make a Difference!

THEME BOOK

Unit 3

Our Living Planet

THEME BOOK

Unit 6

PERSONAL BEST

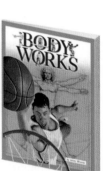

THEME BOOK

Unit 7

This Land Is Our Land

THEME BOOK

Unit 8

HARVEST TIME

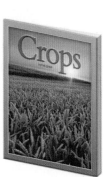

THEME BOOK

Unit 9

Superstars

THEME BOOK

Resources

Handbook

Genres at a Glance

Plants and animals are important to each other. ▶

▲ Skiers must be in great shape to compete.

These women
help to bring
food to people.

HERE to HELP

Look at the pictures. These women work as a team to get people what they need. Tell what is happening in each picture. Then work in a small group. Think of 3 other workers who depend on one another to get people what they need. Draw a picture to show how they work together.

In This Unit

▶ **Language Development**

▶ **Language and Literacy**

▶ **Language and Content**
Language Arts

▶ **Writing Project**

Vocabulary
- Time
- Local Government
- Key Vocabulary

Language Functions
- Tell What May Happen

Grammar
- Verbs (*may, might, could*)
- Phrases with *Have to* and *Need to*
- Possessive Adjectives

Reading
- Long Vowels: *ie, igh; ui, ue*
- High Frequency Words
- Comprehension: Identify Cause and Effect
- Text Features: Paragraphs

Writing
- Friendly Letter

I Could Help

▶ **Language: Tell What May Happen**

Listen and chant. CD

I think I'll be a paramedic
In the town of West McCheswick.
Someone may fall.
A man might call,
And I could get there quick.

If I could be a paramedic
In the town of West McCheswick,
I might save lives.
I'd get to drive
A big, white mobile clinic.

> **Verbs**
> Sometimes you aren't sure if something will happen. Use helping verbs *may, might,* or *could* with another verb to tell about it.
>
> Someone **may fall**.
> A man might **call**.
> I could **be** a paramedic.

EXPRESS YOURSELF ▶ TELL WHAT MAY HAPPEN

Work with a partner. Read each question. Then have your partner answer with **may, might,** or **could**. Then switch roles.

EXAMPLE **1.** What kind of job could you have?
I could be a police officer.

1. What kind of job could you have?
2. What might you do in your work?
3. Where might you work?
4. How may you help your community?

<u>5.–7.</u> Interview a partner. What might he or she be? Use *may, might,* or *could* to tell about it. Then switch roles.

EXAMPLE **5.** Jasmine may be a firefighter.

They All Work in Our City

▶ **Vocabulary: Time**
▶ **Language: Tell What May Happen**

7:00 a.m.

It's seven o'clock.

9:30 a.m.

It's nine thirty.
It's half past nine.

12:00 p.m.

It's noon.
It's twelve o'clock.

4:15 p.m.

It's four fifteen.
It's a quarter after four.
It's fifteen after four.

5:50 p.m.

It's five fifty.
It's ten to six.
It's ten of six.

12:00 a.m.

It's midnight.
It's twelve o'clock.

ORAL LANGUAGE PRACTICE ▶ TELL WHAT MAY HAPPEN

<u>1.–3.</u> **Who's talking?** CD
Listen. Who is talking? Point to the correct person.
Say what time it is. Tell what the person may do.

WRITTEN PRACTICE

Read each clock. Write a sentence. Tell something
that you may do at that time.

EXAMPLE **4.** At seven thirty, I may call you.

4.
(a.m.)

5.
(p.m.)

6.
(p.m.)

7.
(p.m.)

8.
(a.m.)

9.
(a.m.)

Language Development

We Have to Help

▶ Phrases With *Have To* and *Need To*

Use a verb to complete a phrase with *have to* or *need to*.

have to + verb

They **have to hurry.**

He **has to hold** the hose.

> Use *has* with
> *he, she,* or *it.*

need to + verb

They **need to stop** the fire.

He **needs to spray** the water.

> Use *needs* with
> *he, she,* or *it.*

BUILD SENTENCES

Look at each picture. Read the sentence. Add the correct form of *have to* or *need to*. Say the new sentence.

EXAMPLE **1.** He needs to recycle the trash.

1.

He _____ recycle the trash.

2.

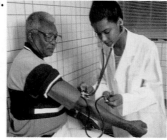

She _____ help the sick.

3.

They _____ fight the fire.

4.

They _____ fix the road.

5.

They _____ work on the wires.

6.

He _____ deliver the mail.

WRITE ABOUT JOBS

7.–9. Work with a partner. Act out 3 jobs. Your partner guesses what you *need to* or *have to* do. Write the sentence.

EXAMPLE **7.** You need to drive the bus.

What Is Your Job?

▶ **Possessive Adjectives**

These **possessive adjectives** tell who or what owns something.

Adjective	Example
my	I am in this picture. **My** hand is on Malcolm's chin.
your	You can see Mark. He is on **your** left.
his	He has **his** hand on Malcolm's shoulder.
her	Sally is lifting Malcolm's legs on **her** shoulder.
its	The ocean is rough. **Its** waves almost knocked us down.
our	We are practicing **our** rescue plan.
your	Did your team practice **your** rescue plan, too?
their	Our supervisors are watching from **their** towers on the beach.

BUILD SENTENCES

Read each sentence. Add the missing adjective. Say the new sentence.

EXAMPLE **1.** This young man fell and hurt his arm.

1. This young man fell and hurt ____**(his/your)**____ arm.
2. We called his parents. They are waiting for ____**(its/their)**____ son at the hospital.
3. We need to get this man into ____**(our/its)**____ ambulance.
4. I have tightened all the straps around ____**(his/her)**____ body.
5. Are you ready to lift the stretcher, Tom? Are you holding ____**(their/your)**____ side?
6. Is Joanne ready? Does she have ____**(his/her)**____ equipment?
7. One, two, three lift! Do you all still have ____**(your/my)**____ sides of the stretcher?
8. OK. The ambulance is ready to go. It has ____**(my/its)**____ sirens on. Everything will be all right!

WRITE CAPTIONS

9.–12. Talk with a group. List some things people own. Draw 4 things and write captions. Use the correct possessive adjective.

EXAMPLE **9.**

his flashlight

Listen and Read Along

FOCUS ON GENRE

Realistic Fiction   Realistic fiction tells a story that could actually happen. The characters and events could be real. This story shows how a community works together when the power is lost.

FOCUS ON VOCABULARY

Words About Community Workers
You have been learning words like the ones below. Use these words as you talk about *Power Out!* Collect more words to put in the web.

THEME BOOK

Read this realistic fiction about a community's emergency.

People use power for things like lights, heat, and clocks.

Think About *Power Out!*

IDENTIFY CAUSE AND EFFECT

**Make a cause-and-effect chart for *Power Out!*
Follow these steps.**

1 Draw a box like the one below. What important event happens in the beginning of the story? Write it in the box.

> **Cause:** The power goes out.

2 What happens because the power goes out? Draw 4 boxes. Draw a picture of the effect in each box. Write about it, too.

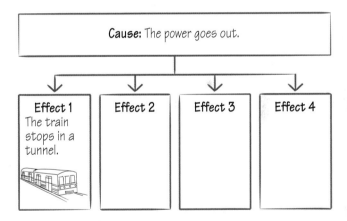

> **Cause:** The power goes out.

Effect 1	Effect 2	Effect 3	Effect 4
The train stops in a tunnel.			

3 Compare your chart with a partner. Did you choose the same effects?

4 Use your finished chart to retell the story to your partner.

High Frequency Words

▲ These people help during a flood.

REVIEW HIGH FREQUENCY WORDS

Read the words aloud. Which word goes in the sentence?

river	picture
only	important
were	water

1. The _____ is rising fast.
2. It is _____ to work together.
3. The sandbags will hold back the _____.

LEARN NEW WORDS

Study these words. Say them as whole words when you read.

been	Mina has **been** in India since 1992.
four	**Four** years ago, there was an earthquake.
sound	Mina heard a loud **sound**.
caused	The earthquake **caused** her house to fall down.
between	Mina was trapped **between** a wall and a table.

PRACTICE

Put the words in alphabetical order. Then, answer the questions.

4. Which word comes after **caused**?
5. Which word comes first?
6. Which word comes last?

Where does each new word fit in the chart?
Say the word and spell it.

EXAMPLE 7. *caused*
c-a-u-s-e-d

What to Look For	Word
7. ends in **ed**	_ _ _ _ _ _
8. ends in **nd**	_ _ _ _ _
9. is a number	_ _ _ _
10. has **tw**	_ _ _ _ _ _ _
11. has one syllable and **ee**	_ _ _ _

More High Frequency Words

▶ **How to Learn a New Word**
- Look at the word.
- Listen to the word.
- Listen to the word in a sentence. What does it mean?
- Say the word.
- Spell the word.
- Say the word again.

REVIEW HIGH FREQUENCY WORDS

Read the words aloud. Which word goes in the sentence?

enough	through
above	on
always	world

1. People can help each other get _____ an emergency.
2. Turn _____ a flashlight during a blackout.
3. Rescue workers are _____ there to help.

LEARN NEW WORDS

Study these words. Say them as whole words when you read.

could	Mina **could** not move.
almost	She **almost** didn't get out, but she did.
life	A rescue team saved her **life**.
often	Mina **often** tells her story.
never	We **never** get tired of hearing it.

PRACTICE

Put the words in alphabetical order. Then, take turns saying the words with a partner. After you have both said the words aloud, answer the questions.

4. Which word has the word *most*?
5. Which word has the word *ever*?
6. Which word rhymes with *wife*?

Where does each new word fit in the chart? Say the word and spell it.

EXAMPLE 7. *almost*
a-l-m-o-s-t

What to Look For	Word
7. begins with **al**	_ _ _ _ _ _
8. means "many times"	_ _ _ _ _
9. has a long **i** sound	_ _ _ _
10. rhymes with **good**	_ _ _ _ _
11. is the opposite of **always**	_ _ _ _ _

Reading and Spelling

▶ **Long Vowels:** *ie, igh; ui, ue*

Listen and learn. CD

Night Watch

The night watchman at the museum
wears a suit of blue,
a bright red tie, a badge, a belt,
and shiny leather shoes.

The night watchman at the museum
works the whole night through.
He checks the lights, the doors, the locks,
each painting, and the statues.

CONNECT SOUNDS AND LETTERS

What letters stand for the vowel sound in each word?

1.

t**ie**

n**igh**t

2.

s**ui**t

bl**ue**

Follow these steps to read a word.

1 Look for a pattern of letters.

blue These two vowels make one sound: **long u**.

high These three letters make one sound: **long i**.

2 Start at the beginning. Blend the sounds in your head. Then say the word.

blue **b + l + ue = blue**

high **h + igh = high**

READING PRACTICE

Look for a pattern to read these words.

1. lights **2.** suit **3.** blue **4.** tie **5.** Sue **6.** high

Use what you learned to read the sentences.

7. Sue fixes street lights between 6 and 9 at night.

8. One night, she did not tie her safety belt.

9. The belt opened. Sue almost fell from a high pole!

10. Her blue suit got stuck on the pole. That saved her life.

11. "I might die if I don't tie my belt right," Sue said.

SPELLING PRACTICE

12.–16. Now write the sentences that your teacher reads.

WORD WORK

17. Write each of these words on a card.

tie	high	true	sight	fried	right	clue
pie	fruit	blue	die	sigh	suit	glue

Say each word. Sort the words by vowel sound. Make 2 groups.

18. Then put the words with the same vowel sound *and* spelling together. Make 4 groups. What do you notice?

EXAMPLE **18.**

You can spell **long i** more than one way.

tie   high

Read on Your Own

FOCUS ON GENRE

Newspaper Article   A news article tells about a recent event. A news article is nonfiction. Quotations show the words a person says about an event. This article tells about a fire.

FOCUS ON WORDS

Words with Long Vowels   When you read and come to a word you don't know, blend the sounds together to read it.

Remember that when two vowels are together, the first is usually long and the second is silent. In words with *igh*, use a long *i* sound. You just learned about words with these spellings:

ie   igh   ui   ue

suit

High Frequency Words   Say these words as whole words when you read.

been	could
four	almost
sound	life
caused	often
between	never

The Times

Friday, June 2, 2008

Hot Crumbs Cause Fire

FULL STORY ON PAGES 8-9

TOKYO, JAPAN—A fire woke Kenji Yamada at 4 A.M. He called the fire station. Soon, he heard the sound of fire trucks.

"I have never seen flames so high and so bright!" Yamada said. "It's true! I almost lost my life!" When he tried to throw water on the fire, he burned four fingers. Paramedics treated him.

Firefighters asked what caused the fire. At first, Yamada didn't have a clue. He went to bed between 10 P.M. and 11 P.M. Then, he smelled smoke. It came from his kitchen. "I think it was something in my trash," he sighed.

Mr. Yamada thinks the fire started in his kitchen.

Trucks came to stop the fire.

When you cook tempura, the oil gets very hot.

Yamada cooked dinner at 8 P.M. He often makes tempura. He put the fried crumbs in his trash can.

Those crumbs could get to be as hot as 100°C. After a while, the crumbs might start a fire. They did last night at Yamada's home. In fact, hot crumbs have been the cause of other fires in Tokyo this year.

Hot crumbs in trash cans can start fires.

Language and Literacy

Think About "Hot Crumbs Cause Fire"

CHECK YOUR UNDERSTANDING

Write sentences that tell what happened in the article. Use a sentence starter from column 1 and a sentence ending from column 2.

EXAMPLE **1.** Yamada made tempura, and the crumbs caused a fire.

Column 1
1. Yamada made tempura,
2. Yamada called the fire station
3. The fire trucks came
4. Yamada burned his hand
5. Hot crumbs caused

Column 2
A. other fires in Tokyo this year.
B. after Yamada called the fire station.
C. and the crumbs caused a fire.
D. because he smelled smoke.
E. when he tried to throw water on the fire.

EXPAND YOUR VOCABULARY

<u>6.</u> Make a concept map like the one below. Work with a group to add community workers. Add words to tell what each worker does.

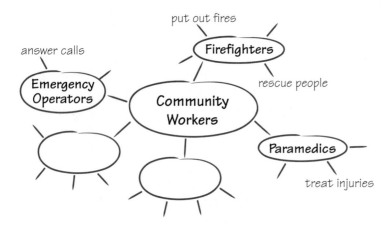

Use the concept map to tell your group about community workers who help in emergencies.

EXAMPLE Firefighters are community workers. They put out fires.

WRITE ABOUT COMMUNITY WORKERS

<u>7.</u> Write 3 clues about a community worker and then ask, "Who is it?" Trade clues with a partner. Try to guess your partner's community worker.

EXAMPLE **7.** He uses a ladder.
He rescues people.
He puts out fires.
Who is it?

Success in Language Arts

▶ **Learn About Paragraphs**

Paragraphs

A **paragraph** is a group of sentences.
All the sentences tell about one main idea.

indent   When you call for help, be ready to answer *who*, *what*, and *where*. Tell the police who needs help. Next explain what happened, or why the person needs emergency help. Then tell where the person is so help can get there quickly.

The **topic sentence** tells the main idea.

The other sentences give **supporting details**. They tell more about the main idea.

Study the lesson. Then do the Exercise.

Practice Your Paragraphs

Think and Discuss

Follow these steps to write a paragraph.

1 Think about your main idea.
What details support it? Make a diagram.

> When you call for help, be ready to answer *who, what,* and *where.*

Tell the police who needs help.	Next explain what happened.	Then tell where the person is so help can get there.

2 Write a topic sentence to tell the main idea. Be sure to indent it.

3 Add the detail sentences.

4 Read your paragraph. Make sure all the sentences tell about one main idea.

In an emergency, call for help.

Exercise

Write a paragraph. Use ideas in this diagram.

> Sue saw a person who needed emergency help. She called for help.

First Sue said who needed help.	Next she explained what happened.	Then Sue explained where the person was so help could get there.

Build Background for "Dog Detectives"

COMMUNITY WORKERS

There are many people who volunteer to help during disasters. Did you know that there are animals that can help, too?

◄ Dogs can help during emergencies.

▲ Rescue workers need all the help they can get during disasters.

Learn Key Vocabulary

Rate and Study the Words Rate how well you know each word. Then:

1. Pronounce the word. Say it aloud several times. Spell it.
2. Study the example.
3. Tell more about the word.
4. Practice it. Make the word your own.

Key Words

earthquake (urth-kwāk) *noun*

An **earthquake** shakes the earth and causes many problems for people. Here you see what an **earthquake** can do to an area.

emergencies (ē-mur-jen-sēz) *noun*

People need help right away during **emergencies**. SAR dogs can help during water rescues and other **emergencies**.

life (lif) *noun*

A person who is alive has **life**. This dog sniffs for clues to help save a **life**.

rescue (res-kyū) *verb*

When you **rescue** people, you save them from harm. These dogs helped **rescue** people after the attacks on September 11, 2001.

police officer (pō-lēs o-fi-sur) *noun*

A **police officer** makes sure laws are followed and helps when there is an emergency. This **police officer** has a dog who also helps.

Practice the Words With a partner, make a Vocabulary Study Card for each Key Word.

Write the word.

front

> rescue

Tell what the word means and use it in a sentence.

back

> to save someone
>
> I rescued a little bird last spring.

Use the cards to quiz your partner. Take turns answering.

Listen and Read Along

FOCUS ON GENRE

Magazine Article   A magazine article is nonfiction. It tells about a topic. Magazine articles usually tell about events that are happening in the world. This article is about dogs that help people during emergencies.

FOCUS ON COMPREHENSION

Cause and Effect   An effect is something that happens. A cause is the reason why an event happens. Look for words like *if*, *then*, and *because* to help you find causes and effects. As you read "Dog Detectives," think about the reasons that dogs do what they do.

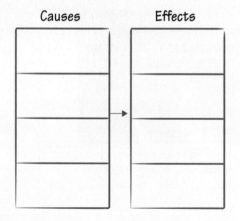

Causes → Effects

DOG DETECTIVES

Dogs make good detectives.

 Selection Recording

SEARCH AND RESCUE

Imagine that you are lost. It is cold and it is dark. Would you believe that a dog could help find you?

Dogs can be trained to help people in **emergencies**. These dogs are called Search-and-**Rescue**, or SAR, dogs. If **police officers** need help, the dogs often find **clues**. If people are lost, the dogs **hunt** for them.

▼ How would you feel if you were lost in a place like this?

Key Vocabulary

emergencies *n.*, sudden and unexpected events that need action

rescue *v.*, to save someone

police officers *n.*, people who enforce laws and help in emergencies

In Other Words

clues things that people leave behind

hunt look

▲ A dog can help police officers look for a person who is missing.

THE NOSE KNOWS

SAR dogs use their noses to find people who are missing. Dogs can smell tiny clues that people leave behind wherever they go. These include **dead skin cells**, pieces of clothing, and hairs. These clues can help a dog to save a missing person's **life**.

▲ This dog helps police officers find clues. The clues help solve crimes.

Key Vocabulary
life *n.*, someone who is alive

In Other Words
dead skin cells very small pieces of skin that fall off

Before You Move On

1. **Main Idea and Details** How do SAR dogs help **rescue** people?
2. **Make Inferences** How do SAR dogs use their sense of smell?

EMERGENCY HELP

SAR dogs have helped during all kinds of emergencies. They have **tracked** missing hikers in Yosemite Park. They've searched through **piles of rubble** after **earthquakes** and other **disasters**. SAR dogs helped rescue workers in New York City after the city was attacked on September 11, 2001. They hunted for survivors buried under fallen buildings.

▲ SAR dogs have hunted for missing hikers in this park.

▲ SAR dogs have helped rescue people after earthquakes.

▼ Dogs helped workers after the September 11, 2001 attacks in New York City.

Key Vocabulary
earthquake *n.*, moving earth

In Other Words
tracked looked for
piles of rubble crumbled houses and buildings
disasters emergencies caused by weather

NOT A GAME

SAR dogs must be strong and they must be smart. Most of all, they must love to play. This is because hard work and active play may seem like the same thing to the dogs. For SAR dogs, looking for missing people may seem like a game of hide-and-seek. But to people, it is not a game. It is a **matter of life and death**. In times like these, dogs make the best detectives.

German shepherds, Labrador retrievers, and Border collies make good SAR dogs.

In Other Words
a matter of life and death very, very important

Before You Move On

1. **Note Details** Name three types of **emergencies** in which SAR dogs have helped people.
2. **Cause and Effect** Why do SAR dogs work hard?

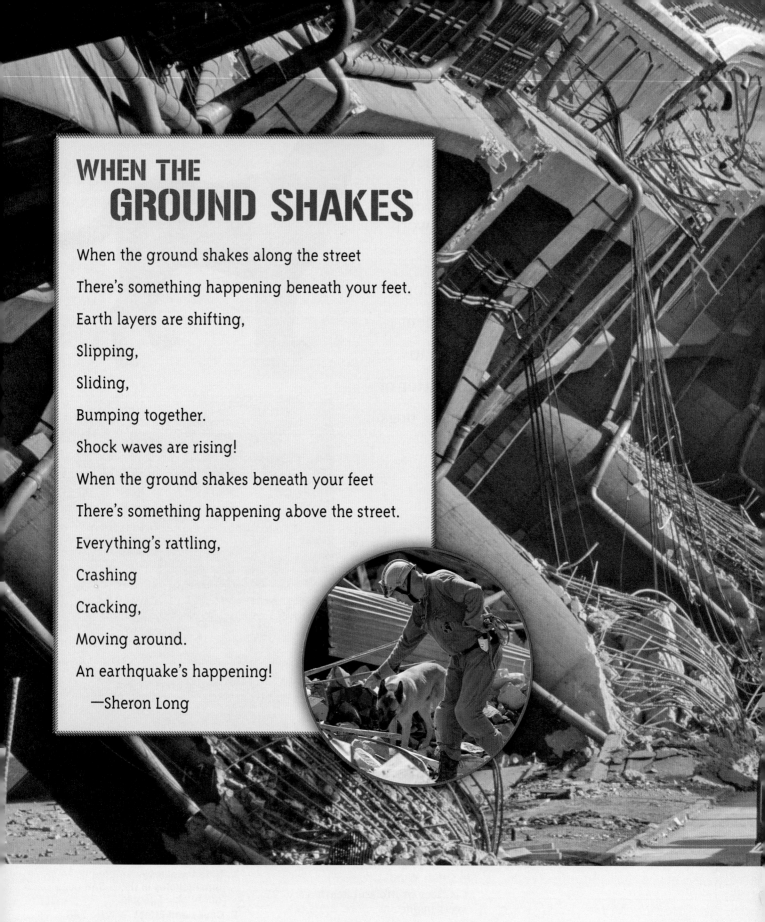

WHEN THE GROUND SHAKES

When the ground shakes along the street

There's something happening beneath your feet.

Earth layers are shifting,

Slipping,

Sliding,

Bumping together.

Shock waves are rising!

When the ground shakes beneath your feet

There's something happening above the street.

Everything's rattling,

Crashing

Cracking,

Moving around.

An earthquake's happening!

—Sheron Long

Before You Move On

1. **Cause and Effect** Why is the ground moving in the poem?
2. **Vocabulary** Name three words that mean *moving*.

Think About "Dog Detectives"

CHECK YOUR UNDERSTANDING

<u>1.–2.</u> **Work with a partner to complete each item.**

1. **Identify Cause and Effect** Make a chart like the one below. Find causes and effects from "Dog Detectives" to complete the chart.

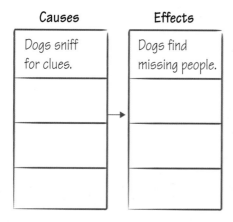

Causes   Effects

| Dogs sniff for clues. | Dogs find missing people. |

2. **Sum It Up** Use your chart to tell about how SAR dogs help and **rescue** people.

REVIEW VOCABULARY

<u>3.–7.</u> **Read the paragraph aloud. Add the vocabulary words.**

> Search-and-_____ dogs help during _____. After disasters like _____, SAR dogs can help _____. SAR dogs can save a person's _____.

Vocabulary
earthquakes
emergencies
life
police officers
rescue

WRITE ABOUT HELPING A FRIEND

<u>8.</u> **Animals can be trained to help people in emergencies. Have you ever helped in an emergency? Write about a time when you were with someone when they needed help.**

Writing Project

Friendly Letter

A friendly letter is a letter you write to tell someone you know about events in your life. A friendly letter has paragraphs with a topic sentence and details. A friendly letter also includes 4 parts: date, greeting, body, and closing.

FRIENDLY LETTER

Write your friend's name in the **greeting** of the letter

Write the date at the top of the letter. This is the **heading** of the letter.

September 28, 2009

Dear Susan,

You will not believe what happened! Today, my neighbor saved my cat, Sam! Sam ran outside when I opened the door. She saw my neighbor's dog, Fred. Fred is a big dog! Sam got scared and quickly climbed up a tree. Then my neighbor, Mr. Adler, came home from work. When I told him what was happening, Mr. Adler got a ladder. He climbed up the ladder and got Sam. I was very grateful that Mr. Adler was there to help me.

I hope that your cat is safe! Please write back to me soon.

Write like you are talking to your friend.

Your Friend,

Amanda

The **closing** includes your signature.

Mr. Adler saved my cat.

Write a Friendly Letter

WRITING PROMPT When were you helped by another person? Who helped you? Write a friendly letter to someone you know telling about the experience.

Prewrite

When you prewrite, you gather ideas and choose your topic. You also make a plan for what you will write. Follow these steps.

1 COLLECT IDEAS

Think of a time when someone did something for you even though that person didn't need to do it. Make a list.

2 CHOOSE A TOPIC

Put your ideas in a web. Think about which idea is best. Remember why you are writing. Remember who will read your friendly letter. Now choose an idea.

Study Sadaf's web. She circled her topic.

3 ORGANIZE YOUR IDEAS

Get your plan down on paper. You don't need to write sentences. Think about the topic sentence. What did you do? How did you help? Then think about the details that tell about what you did.

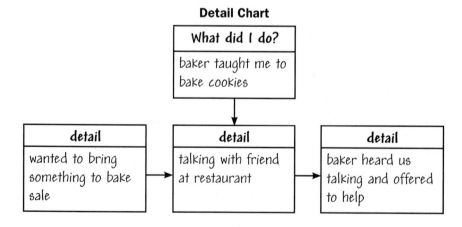

Detail Chart

What did I do?
baker taught me to bake cookies

detail	detail	detail
wanted to bring something to bake sale	talking with friend at restaurant	baker heard us talking and offered to help

Reflect

• Did you pick a good topic?

• Do you have a clear plan?

Draft

When you draft, you begin writing. Use the ideas you gathered in your detail chart to begin your draft. Write a paragraph.

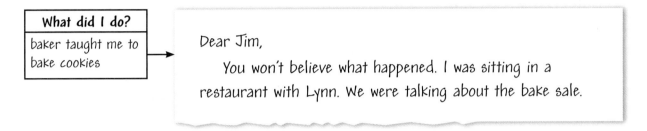

What did I do?
baker taught me to bake cookies

→

Dear Jim,

　　You won't believe what happened. I was sitting in a restaurant with Lynn. We were talking about the bake sale.

Revise

When you revise a draft, you make your writing better. First, you need to know what a reader thinks of your work. Sadaf read her paper to a partner.

Sadaf's Draft

　　Lin wanted to bake something to sell at the bake sale. We couldn't decide if we wanted to make a cake or brownies. The baker offered to help us.

Sadaf's partner says:

" I'm confused. How did the baker know you wanted to bake something? "

Then Sadaf knew she needed to make a change.

Sadaf's Revision

　　Lin wanted to bake something to sell at the bake sale. The baker heard us talking. We couldn't decide if we wanted to make a cake or brownies.‸ The baker offered to help us.

She added a sentence to give more information.

Now follow these steps to revise your letter.

1 DECIDE WHAT TO CHANGE

Read to a partner. Ask your partner to tell what happened in your letter. See if they understood what you wrote. Do you need to add details to tell the whole story?

2 MARK YOUR CHANGES

If you need to add some text, use this mark: ‸.

Reflect

- Did you tell how you helped someone?
- Does the writing sound real?
- Do your words fit the purpose and audience?

Edit and Proofread

After you have revised your draft, check it for mistakes. Follow these steps.

1 **CHECK YOUR POSSESSIVE ADJECTIVES**

When you write and use an adjective that tells who or what owns something, you are using a possessive adjective. Make sure you use the correct adjectives.

2 **CHECK YOUR SPELLING**

Circle each word that may not be spelled right. Look it up in the dictionary or ask for help. Fix the spelling if you need to.

3 **CHECK FOR CAPITAL LETTERS AND COMMAS**

Remember to capitalize proper nouns like people's names, titles, days of the week, and months of the year.

> **EXAMPLE** dan will come with us on saturday.

Friendly letters need a lot of commas, too. Remember to put commas in the heading, the greeting, and the closing of your letter.

> **EXAMPLES** April 17, 2008   Dear Mr. Smith,   Yours truly,

What errors did Sadaf correct in her paper? What errors does she still need to correct?

> We went back to the bakery on saturday *night* (rite.) Chef ben
> showed us how to make he special sugar cookees. We made
> 100 of them for the *may* bake sale. All of us *our* cookies were sold (rite)
> away! We were so proud! I will make some cookies for you soon.
> you friend
> Sadaf

4 **MARK YOUR CHANGES**

Now edit your paper. Use these marks to show your changes.

∧	✄	⌐	◯	≡	/	¶
Add.	Take out.	Replace with this.	Check spelling.	Capitalize.	Make lowercase.	Make new paragraph.

Possessive Adjectives
my
your
his
her
its
our
your
their

Reflect
- What kinds of errors did you find?
- What can you do to keep from making errors?

Publish, Share, and Present

You have finished your friendly letter. Now you are ready to publish your work! When you publish your writing, you put it in final form to share with others. Follow these steps.

❶ FINISH AND DISPLAY

Think about how your writing looks.

- Make sure your handwriting is clear and correct.

- Add drawings to show what happened and how you felt.

- Make a copy to send.

Sadaf Tabrizi
2397 Green Street
Neptune Shores, FL 34744

Jim Finnegan
57821 Sutter Blvd.
New York, NY 10017

❷ READ ALOUD

There are many ways you can share your writing. Read your letter aloud. As you read it, think about your purpose.

- Since you want to tell the events of your story, be sure to organize your ideas in the order they happened.

- If you want your listener to be excited, read a little faster and make your voice sound like you are excited.

Also remember these tips.

Presenting Tips	
If You Are the Speaker:	**If You Are the LIstener:**
• Read loudly and clearly.	• Make a picture of the story in your mind.
• Make your voice sound like what is happening in the letter.	• Pay attention to the reader's voice.

Reflect

- How did using the writing process improve your friendly letter?

- What did you like best about writing a friendly letter?

These kids are working together to make their community look better.

Make a Difference!

How can you make the world a better place?
Draw a picture to show your idea. Get into a
group with students who have ideas like yours.
Make a list of the steps you can take to make
your idea happen.

In This Unit

▶ **Language Development**

▶ **Language and Literacy**

▶ **Language and Content**
Social Science

▶ **Writing Project** ✎

Vocabulary
- Direction Words
- Civil Rights
- Key Vocabulary

Language Functions
- Give Information
- Give Directions
- Express Wants and Feelings

Grammar
- Irregular Past Tense Verbs

Reading
- *R*-Controlled Vowels
- High Frequency Words
- Comprehension: Identify Sequence
- Text Features: Tables and Circle Graphs

Writing
- Personal Narrative

You Made a Difference!

▶ **Language: Give Information**

Listen and sing. CD

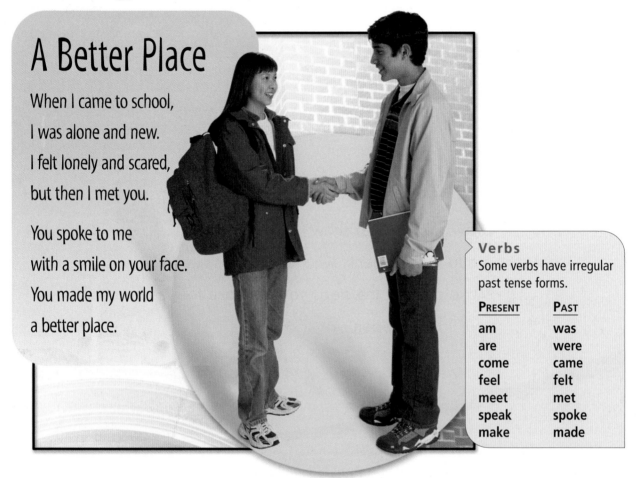

A Better Place

When I came to school,
I was alone and new.
I felt lonely and scared,
but then I met you.

You spoke to me
with a smile on your face.
You made my world
a better place.

Verbs

Some verbs have irregular past tense forms.

PRESENT	PAST
am	was
are	were
come	came
feel	felt
meet	met
speak	spoke
make	made

EXPRESS YOURSELF ▶ GIVE INFORMATION

Imagine you are the boy in the song. Give information about your first day at school. Use these sentences, but make the verb tell about the past.

EXAMPLE **1.** I came to my new school.

1. I <u>come</u> to my new school.
2. I <u>feel</u> worried and nervous.
3. I <u>meet</u> my new teacher.
4. I <u>am</u> curious about my classmates.
5. The students <u>are</u> friendly.
6. I <u>make</u> a new friend.

<u>**7.**</u> **Work with a partner. Talk about someone who made a difference your first day at school. Use some of the past tense verbs that you learned.**

EXAMPLE **7.** I met Sokha. She made me feel happy at my new school.

How Do Kids Help?

▶ **Vocabulary: Direction Words**
▶ **Language: Give Directions**

Luisa pushes Mrs. Adams **around** the pond.

Lee and Mr. Roberts walk **into** the room.

Shabbir goes **up** the ladder.

Jared and his grandfather walk **down** the ramp.

Jim and his grandfather go **across** the bridge.

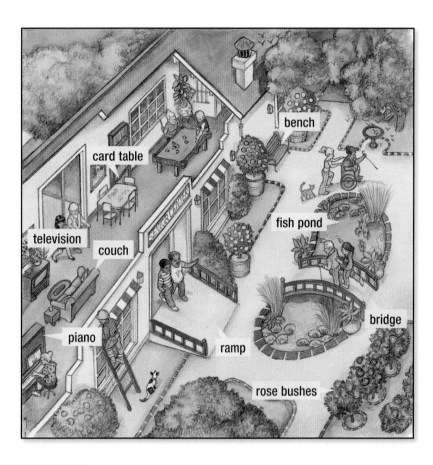

ORAL LANGUAGE PRACTICE ▶ GIVE DIRECTIONS

Work with a partner. Give directions to get:

1. from the rose bushes to the couch
2. from the piano to the bridge
3. from the television to the bench
4. from the fish pond to the card table
5. from the card table to the bench

EXAMPLE **1.** Go around the fish pond. Go up the ramp. Go into the room. There is the couch!

WRITTEN PRACTICE

6. Choose two places in your school. Write directions from one place to the other. Then help your partner follow the directions.

EXAMPLE **6.** Start in our classroom. Go into the hallway. Turn right. Go down the stairs. Walk across the hallway to the first door. Open the door. Go into the room. You are in the band room!

Language Development

Use Your Rights to Change the World

▶ **Vocabulary: Civil Rights**
▶ **Language: Express Wants and Feelings**

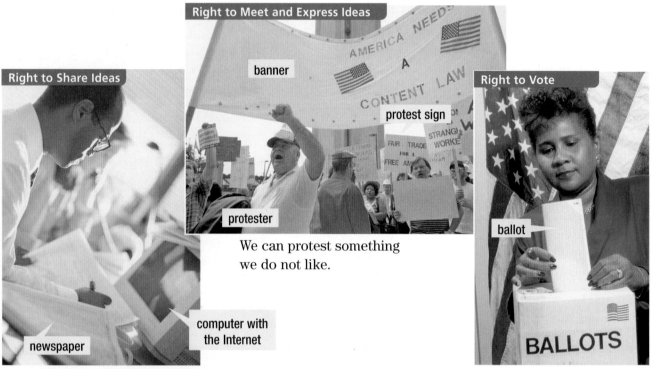

Right to Share Ideas

newspaper

computer with the Internet

We can print our ideas in a newspaper or publish them over the Internet.

Right to Meet and Express Ideas

banner

protest sign

protester

We can protest something we do not like.

Right to Vote

ballot

BALLOTS

When we vote in an election, we choose our leaders.

ORAL LANGUAGE PRACTICE ▶ EXPRESS WANTS AND FEELINGS

1.–3. Who's talking? CD
Listen. Point to the correct picture.
Talk to a partner about what each person wants and feels.

WRITTEN PRACTICE

4. What do you want to change at your school? How can you make those changes?
Work with your class to make a chart like this.

EXAMPLE **4.**

What to Change	Who Makes the Decision	What Strategies to Use
have art class for everyone	school board	go to school board meetings, write letters

Some People Who Led America

▶ **Irregular Past Tense Verbs**

These verbs have irregular past tense forms.

Present	Past	Example
think	thought	Susan B. Anthony and Elizabeth Cady Stanton **thought** women should have the right to vote.
lead	led	Together, they **led** a movement to get more rights for women.
go	went	They **went** to cities around the country.
give	gave	They **gave** speeches to try to change the law.
speak	spoke	They **spoke** at many meetings.
see	saw	Many people **saw** them. In 1920, Congress passed a law that gave women the right to vote.

BUILD SENTENCES

Read each sentence. Change the <u>underlined</u> verb to tell about the past.
Say the new sentence to a partner.

EXAMPLE **1.** In 1965, César Chávez led a protest to get better treatment for farmworkers.

1. In 1965, César Chávez <u>leads</u> a protest to get better treatment for farmworkers.
2. He <u>goes</u> to farms throughout California.
3. He <u>speaks</u> to many farmworkers. By 1970, many growers agreed to fair treatment for the farmworkers.

4. Martin Luther King, Jr., <u>thinks</u> African Americans should have equal rights.
5. He <u>gives</u> many speeches.
6. Thousands of people <u>see</u> him. A new law was passed in 1964 to give all Americans equal rights.

WRITE SENTENCES

<u>7.–10.</u> Write 4 sentences to tell about a person who came to the United States for the first time. How did that person feel?

EXAMPLE **7.** He felt excited to be in a new place.

Listen and Read Along

FOCUS ON GENRE

Biography A biography tells about important events in a person's life. A biography is nonfiction. This biography tells about Martin Luther King, Jr.

FOCUS ON VOCABULARY

Civil Rights Words You have been learning words like the ones below. Use these words as you talk about *Who Was Martin Luther King, Jr.?* Collect more words to put in the web.

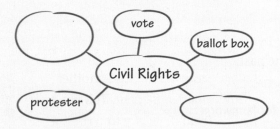

THEME BOOK

Read this biography of Martin Luther King, Jr.

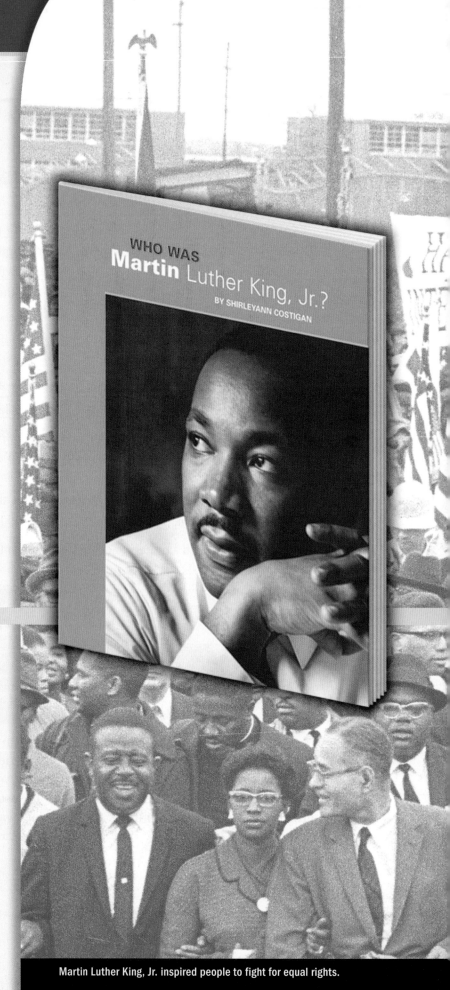

Martin Luther King, Jr. inspired people to fight for equal rights.

Think About *Who Was Martin Luther King, Jr.?*

IDENTIFY SEQUENCE

Work with a group to make a time line for *Who Was Martin Luther King, Jr.?* Follow these steps.

1 What happened first? Draw a dot. Write the year that Martin was born. Then write a sentence that tells what happened in that year.

> ●— **1929**
> Martin was born in Atlanta, Georgia.

2 What happened next? Draw a line. Add another dot for each important date and event. Tell what happened. Use words from the story to write the sentence.

> ●— **1929**
> Martin was born in Atlanta, Georgia.
>
> ●— **1953**
> Martin married Coretta Scott.

3 Use your finished time line to tell the class about the life of Martin Luther King, Jr. Each student in your group can tell about one of the events on the time line.

High Frequency Words

REVIEW HIGH FREQUENCY WORDS

Read the words aloud. Which word goes in the sentence?

play	places
their	to
of	other

1. This woman goes to different _____.

2. She teaches people how _____ read.

3. A lot _____ people thank her.

▲ A reading lesson in a rural school in Nicaragua

LEARN NEW WORDS

Study these words. Say them as whole words when you read.

country	Indra was born in a **country** in Asia.
called	The country is **called** Indonesia.
lived	He **lived** there as a child.
house	He grew up in a **house** built on long posts.
now	Indra came to the U.S. **Now** he lives in California.

PRACTICE

4.–8. Make a map for each new word. Write the word in the center. Complete the other boxes. Then use the word in a sentence of your own.

EXAMPLE   **4.**

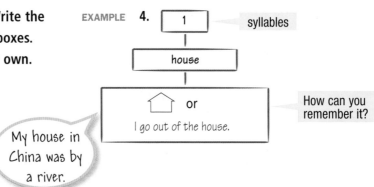

My house in China was by a river.

Take turns saying the words in the box with a partner. After you have both said the words aloud, answer the questions.

9. Which word rhymes with *how*?

10. Which word rhymes with *mouse*?

11. Which words end in the letters *ed*?

More High Frequency Words

> **How to Learn a New Word**
>
> • Look at the word.
> • Listen to the word.
> • Listen to the word in a sentence. Think about its meaning.
> • Say the word.
> • Spell the word.
> • Say the word again.

REVIEW HIGH FREQUENCY WORDS

Read the words aloud. Which word goes in the sentence?

was	again
saw	were
their	began

1. Martin Luther King, Jr. _____ a great leader.
2. People _____ excited to hear him speak.
3. He taught people about _____ rights.

LEARN NEW WORDS

Study these words. Say them as whole words when you read.

American	Last year, Indra became an **American** citizen.
would	He **would** like to help people in Indonesia.
know	He **knows** how they could grow more food.
should	He thinks they **should** plant different crops each year.
also	Indra **also** wants to help the farmers sell their crops.

PRACTICE

<u>4.–8.</u> **Make a map for each new word. Write the word in the center. Complete the other boxes. Then use the word in a sentence of your own.**

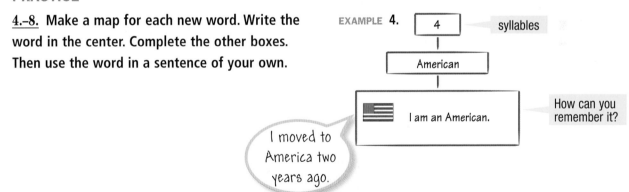

EXAMPLE 4.

4 ← syllables

American

I am an American. ← How can you remember it?

I moved to America two years ago.

Take turns saying the words in the box with a partner. After you have both said the words aloud, answer the questions.

9. Which word has the word *can*?
10. Which word is another way to say *too*?
11. Which words end with the same four letters?

Reading and Spelling

▶ *R-Controlled Vowels*

Listen and sing. CD

Let Hope Burn Bright

Let hope burn bright,
bright as a star,
for everyone.

Let hope sing sweet,
sweet as a song,
for everyone.

Let hope fly high,
high as a bird,
for everyone.

Let hope be strong,
strong as a bear,
for everyone.

CONNECT SOUNDS AND LETTERS

What sound do the underlined letters make?

1.

st<u>ar</u>

2.

h<u>or</u>n

3.

f<u>er</u>n   b<u>ir</u>d

c<u>ur</u>b

4.

ch<u>air</u>   b<u>ear</u>

5.

d<u>eer</u>   t<u>ear</u>

READING STRATEGY

Follow these steps to read a word.

1 Look for a pattern in the word. Do you see a **vowel + r**?

y<u>ar</u>d

b<u>ir</u>d

2 Start at the beginning. Blend the sounds in your head. Then say the word.

yard   y + ar + d = yard   **bird**   b + ir + d = bird

READING PRACTICE

Blend the sounds to read these words.

1. hair   2. skirts   3. forms   4. art   5. wear   6. year

Use what you learned to read the sentences.

7. Carmen is part of a group that helps women in Latin America.
8. The women make shirts and skirts to wear.
9. They also make hair clips and other crafts to sell.
10. Carmen thinks that these crafts are forms of art.
11. Next year, the group would like to sell the crafts in the U.S.

SPELLING PRACTICE

<u>12.–16.</u> **Now write the sentences your teacher reads.**

WORD WORK

<u>17.–24.</u> **Read these words. Then write each word on a card. Match the two words that start with the same sound. What do you notice about the vowel sound?**

cat	porch	jar	bun	deep	car
deer	heat	fat	hear	pond	jam
burn	chirp	chip	far		

EXAMPLE

17.

cat   car

The r changes the vowel sound in a word.

Read on Your Own

FOCUS ON GENRE

Biography   A biography tells about
a person or group of people. This
biography tells about three young
people who help others.

FOCUS ON WORDS

***R*–Controlled Vowels**   When you read
and come to a word you don't know,
blend the sounds together to read it.
Remember an *r* can change the vowel
sound in a word. You just learned about
words with these spellings.

ar	er	air
or	ir	ear
	ur	eer

bird

High Frequency Words   Say these
words as whole words when you read.

country	American
called	would
lived	know
house	should
now	also

Kids Are Helping Kids

▲ Craig Kielburger works to protect kids' rights.

Kids can help other kids in important ways. Nadja, Hafsat, and Craig show us how.

Nadja helped kids in Bosnia. When Nadja was a girl, ethnic groups in Bosnia started a war. Nadja was not safe, even in her house. Kids lived in fear. A lot of them were hurt. Nadja started a radio show. She sang on the air to give children courage. She also published two books. They tell how hard it is to live through a war. She hopes her books will help end fighting in the world.

▲ Nadja Halilbegovich is from Bosnia.

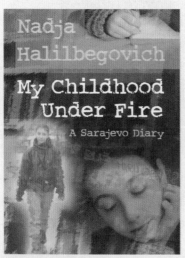

▲ Nadja wrote this book to tell about living in a place with war.

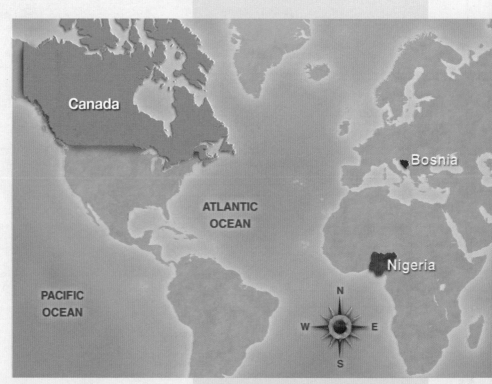

▲ The kids in this selection come from Canada, Bosnia, and Nigeria.

Hafsat helps kids in Nigeria. She formed a group called KIND. The group teaches children their rights. It helps kids know how to be leaders. KIND also helps women and children get fair treatment.

Craig was 12 years old when he read that many kids were made to work in hard jobs for no pay. People treated them very badly. He felt that these kids should not be made to work. He formed a group called Free The Children. Since then, his group has worked in 45 countries.

Think about how American kids can help other kids now. What would you do?

▲ Hafsat Abiola is from Nigeria.

THE KUDIRAT INITIATIVE FOR DEMOCRACY

▲ Craig Kielburger is from Canada.

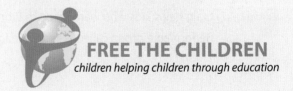

FREE THE CHILDREN
children helping children through education

Think About "Kids Are Helping Kids"

__1.–3.__ Make a chart like the one below. Include information about each kid.

Who Helped Others?	Where?	What Group of People Did He or She Help?	How?
1. Nadja Halilbegovich	Bosnia	children	She published two books. She started a radio show.

__4–6.__ Tell more about each kid. Now tell a partner about each kid and what he or she did. Use information from your chart. Use some of these words and phrases.

brings hope	fair treatment	hard jobs
sang on the air	rights	formed a group
war	published	Free the Children

EXAMPLE **4.** Nadja published two books.
The books tell about the war in Bosnia.

__7.__ Choose one of the kids from pages 50–51 or another person you know. Tell how the person makes a difference.

EXAMPLE **7.** Craig helps kids who were made to work in hard jobs.
He formed a group called Free the Children.

Success in Social Science

▶ **Interpret Data**

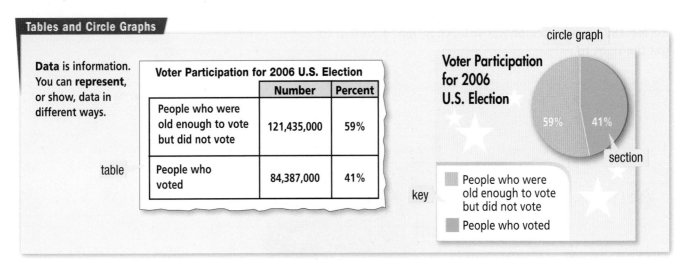

Tables and Circle Graphs

Data is information. You can **represent**, or show, data in different ways.

Voter Participation for 2006 U.S. Election

	Number	Percent
People who were old enough to vote but did not vote	121,435,000	59%
People who voted	84,387,000	41%

table

circle graph

Voter Participation for 2006 U.S. Election

59%   41%

section

key

People who were old enough to vote but did not vote

People who voted

Listen to the article. Study the circle graph below. Then do the Review.

Voting Patterns in U.S. Elections

• **Do Americans make good use of their right to vote?**

In the United States today, you can vote if you are a citizen and if you are 18 years old or older. You also have to register, or sign a paper saying that you want to vote.

It hasn't always been so easy to vote. In the Revolutionary War of 1776, Americans fought the British for the right to vote. For almost a hundred years after the war, only white men could vote. Over the years, several amendments to the United States Constitution have expanded the right to vote:

- In 1870, after the Civil War, the 15th Amendment gave all men of any race the right to vote.
- In 1920, the 19th Amendment gave women the right to vote.
- In 1971, the 26th Amendment lowered the voting age to 18.

Some citizens who are 18 or older do not take the time to register to vote. Others register, but do not vote. Study the circle graph to see data for a typical year.

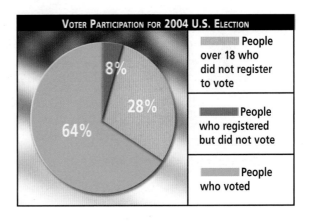

VOTER PARTICIPATION FOR 2004 U.S. ELECTION

8%

28%

64%

People over 18 who did not register to vote

People who registered but did not vote

People who voted

REVIEW

1. **Check Your Understanding** Who can vote in the United States today? Do Americans use their right to vote? Explain your answer.
2. **Vocabulary** How does a circle graph help you to compare data?
3. **Use Circle Graphs** Compare the data for the 2004 election and the 2006 election. In which year did a higher percentage of people vote? How can you tell?

STRIVING FOR CHANGE

Build Background for "Striving for Change"

CIVIL RIGHTS

Before 1920, women could not vote. They had to protest to get the right to vote.

◀ Women protest near the White House in 1917.

SUFFRA[GE] PRISON[ED]

WILL [S]

CARNE[GIE]

MON.

BOXES
NATIONAL WOMAN'S
GENERAL [...]

MR. PRESIDENT HOW LONG MUST WOMEN WAIT FOR LIBERTY?

Official Program WOMAN SUFFRAGE Procession

Washington D.C. March 3, 1913

▲ Program cover for a protest march in 1913

Learn Key Vocabulary

Rate and Study the Words Rate how well you know each word. Then:

1. Pronounce the word. Say it aloud several times. Spell it.
2. Study the example.
3. Tell more about the word.
4. Practice it. Make the word your own.

Key Words

protest (prō-test) *verb*

When people **protest**, they show that they do not like something. These people are **protesting**.

right (rīt) *noun*

A **right** is something that all people have. In the U.S., people have the **right** to say what they think.

sign (sīn) *noun*

A **sign** has a message on it. These women are holding **signs**.

vote (vōt) *verb*

When we **vote**, we make a choice. This woman is **voting** for the next President of the U.S.

women (wi-mun) *noun*

The word **women** is the plural of **woman**. A woman is an adult female. These women lived in 1917.

Practice the Words Make a Category Chart for the Key Words. Compare your chart with a partner's.

Signs	Women	We have the right to...
stop sign	mom	vote
		protest

Category Chart

Language and Content

Listen and Read Along

FOCUS ON GENRE

History Article   A history article tells about real events that happened in the past. A history article is nonfiction. This history article tells about American women who wanted the right to vote.

FOCUS ON COMPREHENSION

Identify Sequence   Writers often tell about events in the order in which they happened. Look for **dates** to help you identify the sequence, or order, of the events.

A New Plan

Alice Paul began fighting for the vote in **1912**. In **1917**, she went to the White House with other women to protest.

STRIVING FOR CHANGE

In the early 1900s, women fought for their right to vote. Some women gave speeches.

 Selection Recording

The Right to Vote

Many **women** worked to get the **right** to **vote**. Some women wrote letters, and others gave speeches. Many walked in parades. One woman did much more. Alice Paul wanted to **make a difference**.

▲ Alice Paul

women ▶

▼ Women marched to the White House in 1917 to demand their rights.

▲ sign

MOTHERS

PREPARE THE CHILDREN FOR THE WORLD
HELP PREPARE THE WORLD FOR THE CHILDREN

uffrage
ED FOR MAR
THE RIGH
EIR CHI

Before You Move On

1. **Details** What did **women** do to get the **right** to **vote**?
2. **Text Feature** Look at the caption. When was the large photo taken?

A New Plan

Alice Paul began **fighting for the vote** in 1912. In 1917, she went to the **White House** with other women to **protest**. They wanted President Wilson to help women get the right to vote. The women carried **signs** that demanded the right to vote.

President Wilson wanted Alice Paul and the other women to stop. The police said the women had to stop. But the women kept protesting. They did not **give up**. The police **arrested some of the women**, including Paul.

▲ President Woodrow Wilson

▼ Women carried signs to protest for their rights.

MR. PRESIDENT HOW LONG MUST WOMEN WAIT FOR LIBERTY?

Key Vocabulary

protest *v.*, to show that you do not like something

sign *n.*, a message printed large enough for many people to read

In Other Words

fighting for the vote working to give women the right to vote

White House place where the President was

give up stop

arrested some of the women took some of the women to jail

Jail Time

The police put Paul in jail for seven months. They did not let her talk to anyone. Paul did not think this was fair. She stopped eating to tell the world that she should not be in jail. The **prison doctors** tried to make Paul eat, but she said no.

▼ Women protested the treatment of Alice Paul in jail.

In Other Words

prison doctors doctors who worked at the jail

Before You Move On

1. **Identify Sequence** What happened when the **women** went to the White House? What happened next?
2. **Cause and Effect** Why did Alice Paul stop eating?

Paul Keeps Fighting

The newspapers wrote about **how Paul was treated** in prison. Many readers got angry and also began to protest. Paul was **set free** after five weeks in jail. She kept fighting for the right to vote.

In 1918, President Wilson supported the women's right to vote. In 1919, **Congress** agreed with the President. In 1920, the states passed the 19th Amendment to the Constitution. Women in the U.S. finally had the right to vote!

▲ The public learned about Alice Paul by reading newspapers.

▼ Women finally won the support of the President.

PRESIDENT WILSON SAYS: "This is the time to support Woman Suffrage."

In Other Words
how Paul was treated what was happening to Paul
set free let out of jail
Congress the part of the government that makes laws

Alice Paul Made a Difference

Paul was happy that women had the right to vote. But she did not stop working for women's rights. Alice Paul continued to make a difference for the rest of her life.

▼ This table shows how more and more American women have voted in elections.

Election Year	Number of Women Voters
1964	39,191,000
1968	40,951,000
1972	44,858,000
1976	45,620,000
1980	49,213,000
1984	54,542,000
1988	54,519,000
1992	60,554,000
1996	56,108,000
2000	59,284,000
2004	67,281,000

▼ Alice Paul celebrates her victory.

Before You Move On

1. **Identify Sequence** What happened when Alice Paul got out of jail?
2. **Text Features** Name the first year when more than 50 million American **women** voted.

Think About "Striving for Change"

CHECK YOUR UNDERSTANDING

<u>1.–2.</u> **Work with a partner to complete each item.**

1. **Identify Sequence** Think about the sequence of events. Make a time line like the one below. Then complete the time line by adding the key events that match the year.

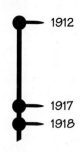

- 1912
- 1917
- 1918

2. **Sum It Up** Use your time line to tell how women got the right to vote.

REVIEW VOCABULARY

<u>3.–7.</u> **Read the paragraph aloud. Add the vocabulary words.**

> Thousands of _____ marched to the White House in 1917. Many of them carried _____ during the march. They came to _____. At that time, they could not _____ in elections. They wanted President Wilson to give them the _____ to vote.

Vocabulary
protest
right
sign
vote
women

WRITE ABOUT CHANGE

<u>8.</u> **Write about something you think should be changed.**

Personal Narrative

A personal narrative is a story you tell about something that has happened in real life. You can tell your story in the order it happened. Showing the sequence helps the reader follow your story.

PERSONAL NARRATIVE

How I Helped My Grandparents

I will never forget how I helped my grandparents when they first came to America. My grandparents wanted to visit their friends who lived near us. My mother drew a map. Then Mom went to her work. I picked up the map and asked my grandparents to follow me. First, we walked downtown. I pointed to each street sign and said the street name in English. Then I pointed to the street's name on the map. My grandparents nodded and looked at the map. Soon we were at their friends' house. When the door opened, my grandmother began to cry. But I knew she was not sad. She was happy. I felt happy, too. I had helped my grandparents.

The **beginning** tells what happened first.

The **middle** gives details about the event.

The **end** tells what happened last.

Write a Personal Narrative

WRITING PROMPT When did you make a difference in the world? When did you help someone? Write a personal narrative to tell your class what you did. Tell how you felt about it, too.

Prewrite

When you prewrite, you gather ideas and choose your topic. You also make a plan for what you will write. Follow these steps.

1 COLLECT IDEAS

Think of ways you have helped. Maybe you helped someone at school, someone younger than you, or even a stranger. Maybe you helped a little. Maybe you helped a lot.

2 CHOOSE A TOPIC

Put your ideas in a chart. Think about which idea is best. Remember why you are writing. Remember who will read your personal narrative. Then choose an idea.

Here is Johanna's chart. She circled her topic.

What I Saw	What I Did and How I Felt
My sister didn't know math.	I taught her subtraction. I felt proud.
Mom wanted to speak to the clerk at the store. She didn't know the English words.	I spoke to the clerk for Mom. I felt happy to help.

3 ORGANIZE YOUR IDEAS

You will tell your story in the order it happened. Get your plan down on paper. You do not need to write sentences. Write the events in a list. Put your list in order. Add numbers.

Story Plan

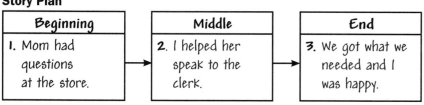

Beginning	Middle	End
1. Mom had questions at the store.	2. I helped her speak to the clerk.	3. We got what we needed and I was happy.

Reflect

- Did you pick a good topic?
- Do you have a clear plan?

Draft

Use your plan to tell your story. For example:

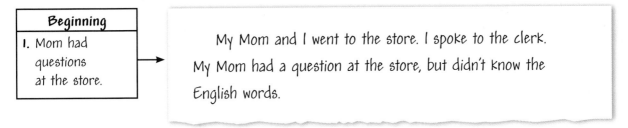

Beginning
I. Mom had questions at the store.

My Mom and I went to the store. I spoke to the clerk. My Mom had a question at the store, but didn't know the English words.

Revise

When you revise a draft, you make your writing better. First, you need to know what a reader thinks of your work. Johanna read her paper to a partner.

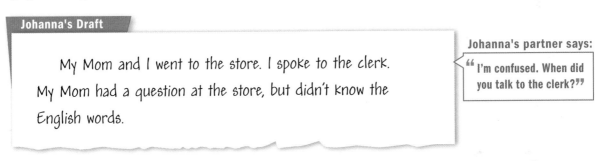

Johanna's Draft

My Mom and I went to the store. I spoke to the clerk. My Mom had a question at the store, but didn't know the English words.

Johanna's partner says:
" I'm confused. When did you talk to the clerk?"

Then Johanna knew she needed to make a change.

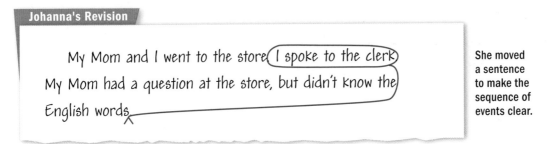

Johanna's Revision

My Mom and I went to the store I spoke to the clerk My Mom had a question at the store, but didn't know the English words.

She moved a sentence to make the sequence of events clear.

Now follow these steps to revise your draft.

❶ DECIDE WHAT TO CHANGE
Read to a partner. Ask your partner to list the events in order. Look to see if the list matches what happened first, next, and last. Do you need to move anything to keep events in order?

❷ MARK YOUR CHANGES
If you need to move some text, use this mark: ◠.

Reflect
- Did you tell how you helped someone?
- Did you describe how you felt?
- Are the events in sequence?

Edit and Proofread

After you have revised your draft, check it for mistakes.

1 CHECK YOUR VERBS

Use what you have learned in this unit. Remember, regular verbs add **-ed** to show that an action happened in the past.

> **EXAMPLE**   Mom want**ed** to speak to the clerk.

An irregular verb has a special form to tell about the past. Study the verbs in the chart.

2 CHECK YOUR SPELLING

Circle each word that may not be spelled right. Look it up in the dictionary or ask for help. Fix the spelling if you need to.

3 CHECK FOR CAPITAL LETTERS

Names of people and days of the week are examples of proper nouns. When you use a proper noun, always capitalize it. Here are a few examples:

> **EXAMPLE**   We went to the store on Tuesday.
>
> I helped Mom and Sal Rojas, our neighbor.

What errors did Johanna correct in her paper? What errors does she still need to correct?

> I spoke
> I ~~speaked~~ to the ⊝clerk⊝ jim johnson. I asked where to find
> the yellow ⊝con.⊝ Then we find it. I feeled happy. I liked helping
> mom. It was not ⊝had⊝ to help, and I made a difference.

4 MARK YOUR CHANGES

Now edit your paper. Use these marks to show your changes:

∧	✗	⌐	◯	≡	╱	¶
Add.	Take out.	Replace with this.	Check spelling.	Capitalize.	Make lowercase.	Make new paragraph.

Verbs

Some verbs have irregular past tense forms.

PRESENT	PAST
am	was
are	were
come	came
feel	felt
go	went
meet	met
speak	spoke
make	made

Reflect

- What kinds of errors did you find?

- How can you keep from making these errors?

Publish, Share, and Reflect

You have finished your personal narrative. Now you are ready to publish your work! When you publish your writing, you put it in final form to share with others. Follow these steps.

1 FINISH AND DISPLAY

Think about how your writing looks.

- Make sure your handwriting is clear.
- Add drawings to show what happened and how you felt.
- Display your work on a class gallery wall.

2 READ ALOUD

There are many ways you can share your writing. For this personal narrative, try reading it aloud. As you read it, think about your purpose.

- Is your narrative funny? Are you reading it to entertain your friend? If so, read it a little faster and use gestures to support the action you are describing.
- Do you want your listener to think seriously about something? If so, read your narrative a little slower and pause at the important points.

Also remember these tips.

Presenting Tips

If You Are the Speaker:	If You Are the Listener:
• Read loudly and clearly.	• Make a picture of the story in your mind.
• Make your voice sound like what is happening in the story.	• Think about how the story connects to your life.

Reflect

- Did writing about this event change the way you think about it?
- What did you like best about writing a personal narrative?

There are many
kinds of animals
on our planet.

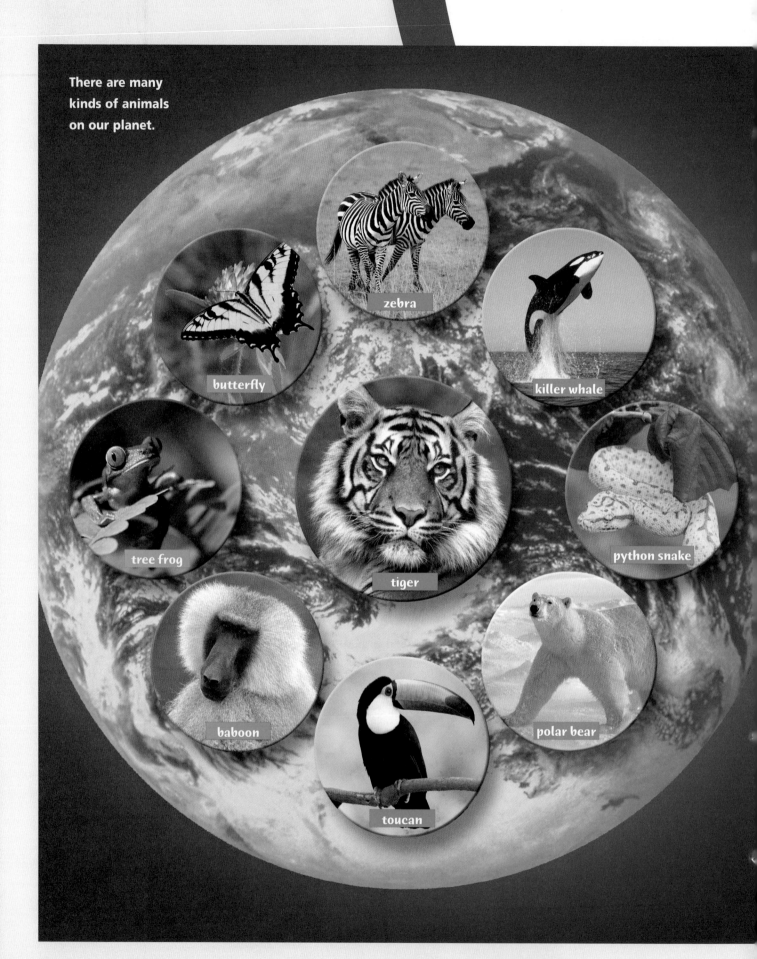

butterfly

zebra

killer whale

tree frog

tiger

python snake

baboon

toucan

polar bear

Our Living Planet

Play this game with a partner. Toss two coins onto the page at left. Make them land on two different animals. Tell one way the animals are the same. Your partner should tell another way the animals are alike. See who can think of the most ways.

In This Unit

▶ **Language Development**

▶ **Language and Literacy**

▶ **Language and Content**
   Science and Mathematics

▶ **Writing Project**

Vocabulary
- Opinion Words
- Animals, Plants, and Habitats
- Key Vocabulary

Language Functions
- Give Your Opinion
- Describe Places
- Make a Suggestion

Grammar
- Sensory Adjectives
- Verbs (*must, should*)

Reading
- Multisyllabic Words
- High Frequency Words
- Comprehension: Identify Details
- Text Features: Line Graphs

Writing
- Fact-and-Opinion Article

Language Development

We Must Care for Our Earth!

▶ **Language: Give Your Opinion**

Listen and sing. CD

Our Earth

We must keep the air clean
for the eagle to fly.
We must clean up our oceans
so the whales can swim by.
I think we should fight
for our water and sky.
We must help our Earth.
I believe we must try!

Opinion Words
People use these words
to give an opinion.

must	**should**
think	**believe**

EXPRESS YOURSELF ▶ GIVE YOUR OPINION

How should we protect plants and animals? Work with your class to think of ideas. Finish each sentence below.

1. We should _____.
2. We must _____.
3. I believe that _____.
4. I think that _____.

EXAMPLE **1.** We should pick up trash.

5.–8. What should we do to help the Earth? Work with a group to think of 4 ideas. Use opinion words.

EXAMPLE **5.** We should keep the rivers clean.

What Lives Around the Water?

▶ **Vocabulary: Animals and Habitats**
▶ **Language: Describe Places**

Seashore: wave, seagull, sand, seal, salt water, crab, seaweed, jellyfish, starfish

Pond: duck, raccoon, frog, fish, dragonfly, fresh water, beaver, turtle

ORAL LANGUAGE PRACTICE ▶ DESCRIBE PLACES

1.–2. **Work with a group. Describe each place. Tell each other what you can see there.**

EXAMPLE **1.** There are big waves at the seashore. There is white sand.

WRITTEN PRACTICE

3.–8. **Write 3 sentences about each picture above. Use adjectives to describe the animals you see.**

EXAMPLE **3.** I see a brown beaver and a very big frog at the pond.

Adjectives

green	large
brown	small
orange	big
white	little

Life in the Forest

▶ **Vocabulary: Plants and Habitats**
▶ **Language: Make a Suggestion**

ORAL LANGUAGE PRACTICE ▶ MAKE A SUGGESTION

<u>**1.**</u> **Who's talking?** CD

Listen. Who is making suggestions? Point to the correct person.
Then act out the scene with a partner.

WRITTEN PRACTICE

<u>**2.–4.**</u> **How can we take good care of nature?**

Write 3 sentences with suggestions.

EXAMPLE **2.** Let's be sure we put out campfires.

> **Suggestions**
> Let's _____.
> Why don't we _____?
> We could _____.
> Can we _____?
> Would you like to _____?

Describe the Earth

▶ **Sensory Adjectives**

Adjectives can tell what something is like.

An adjective can tell how something **looks**.

> The tree is **tall.**

An adjective can tell how something **sounds**.

> A **loud** bird lives in the tree.

An adjective can tell how something **feels**.

> The tree trunk feels **rough.**

BUILD SENTENCES

Look at each picture below. Add an adjective to tell how each thing looks, sounds, or feels. Say each sentence.

EXAMPLE **1.** The desert is hot and dry.

1. The desert is ____.
2. A ____ cactus grows there.
3. The snake makes a ____ sound.

4. The mountain is ____.
5. A ____ deer lives there.
6. The squirrel makes a ____ sound.

WRITE A DESCRIPTION

<u>7.</u> Draw a picture of a scene in nature. Write a description of your drawing. Use adjectives.

EXAMPLE **7.** The brown owl is in the tall tree.
The forest is quiet and cool.

Listen and Read Along

FOCUS ON GENRE

Biography   A biography tells about important events in a person's life. A biography is nonfiction. This biography tells about the life of Rachel Carson.

FOCUS ON VOCABULARY

Habitat Words   You have been learning words like the ones below. Use these words as you talk about *Rachel Carson.* Collect more words to put in the web.

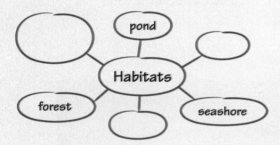

THEME BOOK

Read this biography of Rachel Carson.

Plants, animals, land, water, and air are all part of nature.

Think About *Rachel Carson*

IDENTIFY DETAILS

Make a detail chart and time line for *Rachel Carson*.

❶ Make a chart like the one below. Read the book again. Write what happened on page 9.

Page	Event	Year	Age
9	Rachel was born.	1907	baby
11			
13			
14			
22			

❷ What are some other important events in the book? Complete the chart with more details about Rachel Carson's life. Use words from the book in your chart.

❸ Use your detail chart to tell a group about Rachel Carson's life.

Language and Literacy

High Frequency Words

▲ These people help sick birds.

REVIEW HIGH FREQUENCY WORDS

Read the words aloud. Which word goes in the sentence?

house	head
Another	Answer
New	Now

1. One person holds the bird's _____ .

2. _____ person holds its body.

3. _____ they can help the bird.

LEARN NEW WORDS

Study these words. Say them as whole words when you read.

mountains	Alaska has beautiful beaches and tall **mountains**.
oil	In 1989, a ship spilled **oil** into a bay in Alaska.
found	People **found** sick birds on the beach.
because	The birds got sick **because** they ate the oil when they cleaned their feathers.
few	Many people, not just a **few**, came to help.

PRACTICE

Write the answer to each question. Write the new words on the lines.

4. Which words start with **f**?

_____   _____

5. Which words have 3 letters?

_____   _____

6. Which word rhymes with **two**?

_____

Write each sentence. Add the missing word.   EXAMPLE **7.** Alaska has tall mountains and beautiful beaches.

7. Alaska has tall _ _ _ _ _ _ _ _ _ and beautiful beaches.

8. The oil spill happened _ _ _ _ _ _ _ the ship ran aground.

9. The ship started to leak _ _ _.

10. In just a _ _ _ days, the oil was everywhere.

11. Ten years later, people still _ _ _ _ _ oil on the beaches.

More High Frequency Words

> **How to Learn a New Word**
> - Look at the word.
> - Listen to the word.
> - Listen to the word in a sentence. What does it mean?
> - Say the word.
> - Spell the word.
> - Say the word again.

REVIEW HIGH FREQUENCY WORDS

1.–3. Read the words aloud. Which word goes in the sentence?

very many	1. The planet is _____ important to people.
help need	2. People can _____ keep animals safe.
thank think	3. We need to _____ about ways to save nature.

LEARN NEW WORDS

Study these words. Say them as whole words when you read.

try	The people wanted to **try** to save the birds.
over	When their work was **over**, many birds were saved.
away	The people went **away**, but they did not forget.
why	Everyone asked **why** the spill happened.
story	Newspapers around the world told the **story**.

PRACTICE

Write the answer to each question. Write the new words on the lines.

4. Which words rhyme with **my**?

   _____   _____

5. Which word means **done**?

   _____

6. Which words have 3 letters?

   _____   _____

Write each sentence. Add the missing word.   EXAMPLE **7. Alaska is far away from the other states in the U.S.**

7. Alaska is far _ _ _ _ from the other states in the U.S.
8. _ _ _ did the oil spill happen?
9. Before the spill was _ _ _ _, the oil had coated 1,300 miles of the Alaska shoreline.
10. People worked hard to _ _ _ to save the birds.
11. The _ _ _ _ _ of the Alaska oil spill is a sad one.

Reading and Spelling

▶ **Syllable Types**

Listen and learn. CD

Under the Moon

The silent spider
spins her web.
See the fine silver thread,
under the moon.

The silent turtle
swims in the sea.
Feel the swish of flippers,
under the moon.

The silent owl
hunts his supper.
Hear the whisper of wings,
under the moon.

Listen!

LOOK FOR SYLLABLES IN LONG WORDS

Read the words in each group. Which syllable is the same?

1.  butter

 sister

 letter

2. person

 flipper

 supper

3. ladder

 under

 spider

Follow these steps to read a word.

1 In a long word, look for a syllable you know.

gar den **af ter**

Reading Help

Look for these syllables in long words:

mar	cor	ber	mer
gar	nor	ter	der
par	tor	ner	per

2 Divide the word. Keep the syllable together.

gar den **af ter**

3 Blend the two syllables together to read the word.

gar + den = garden **af + ter = after**

READING PRACTICE

Use what you learned to read the sentences.

1. Garter snakes are small members of the reptile family.
2. In summer, garters can be found in forests, farms, and open lands.
3. A few may make a home in wet corners of a garden.
4. In winter, garters may be hard to find because they stay under the ground.
5. Garters don't bite, so some people keep them as pets!

SPELLING PRACTICE

6.–10. **Now write the sentences that your teacher reads.**

WORD WORK

11.–18. **Make a chart like the one here. Then read these words:**

| hammer | winter | sister | ladder |
| pepper | fruit | perfume | summer |

merchant	person	letter	spider
11.	13.	15.	17.
12.	14.	16.	18.

Write each word in the chart. Put it under the word that has the same syllable.

EXAMPLE **11.**

merchant
11. hammer

Read on Your Own

FOCUS ON GENRE

Science Article   A science article tells us facts and details about something related to science. It is nonfiction. This science article tells us about three different animals in nature.

FOCUS ON WORDS

Syllable Types   When you read and come to a longer word you don't know, look for syllables you know. Then break the word into syllables and blend the syllables together to read the word.

ladder
lad der

High Frequency Words   Say these words as whole words when you read.

mountains	try
oil	over
found	away
because	why
few	story

ANIMALS *in the* WILD

BIGHORN SHEEP

The bighorn sheep is a mountain animal. It is also found in the desert. It can live above the timberline, where few trees grow. Bighorn sheep have large, curled horns and a short tail. They can go up steep trails. Because they have thick fur, they can live through winter storms.

▲ Bighorn sheep live in mountains and in the desert.

▼ White-tailed deer live in the forest.

WHITE-TAILED DEER

You might have heard a story about a white-tailed deer. It is an animal that lives in the forest and has a short tail. It has brown fur in the summer. In the winter, when there is snow, it has gray-white fur. That is why it is so hard to see a white-tailed deer. Many people try.

The male deer has antlers that drop off in the winter and grow again when winter is over. These new antlers soon grow hard and sharp.

COYOTE

The coyote is a desert animal. It is also found in mountains and on flat plains. It has fur and a long tail. The coyote is a member of the dog family. It hunts at night. When the sky looks as dark as oil, you may hear a few coyotes howl. From far away, the howling sounds like a sad song.

▲ Coyotes hunt at night. A coyote howls to communicate with other coyotes.

Think About "Animals in the Wild"

CHECK YOUR UNDERSTANDING

Write the correct answer to each item.

EXAMPLE **1.** The bighorn sheep has large, curled horns.

1. The bighorn sheep has _____.
   A. a long tail
   B. short, sharp antlers
   C. large, curled horns

2. The bighorn sheep can live through winter storms because it has _____.
   D. thick fur
   E. gray-white fur
   F. large, curled horns

3. The deer's antlers grow again in the _____.
   A. spring
   B. winter
   C. summer

4. Why is it hard to see the white-tailed deer in the winter?
   D. It stays in its burrow.
   E. Its fur turns gray-white.
   F. There are a lot of winter storms.

5. The coyote and the _____ are in the same family.
   A. deer
   B. dog
   C. bear

6. What does the coyote do at night?
   D. It howls.
   E. It sleeps.
   F. It turns gray-white.

EXPAND YOUR VOCABULARY

7. **Work with a partner. Make a chart like the one below. Put a ✓ in the correct box. Take turns.**

Animal	Has fur	Howls at night	Has a short tail
Bighorn Sheep	✓		
White-Tailed deer			
Coyote			

Use the chart and the article on pages 84–85 to tell your partner about the animals.

EXAMPLE **7.** All the animals have fur. The bighorn sheep and the white-tailed deer have short tails.

WRITE ABOUT ANIMALS

8. **Choose a wild animal. Write sentences to describe it.**

EXAMPLE **8.** The coyote looks like a dog. It hunts at night.

Success in Science and Mathematics

▶ **Learn About Line Graphs**

Line Graph

A **line graph** shows how something changes over time.

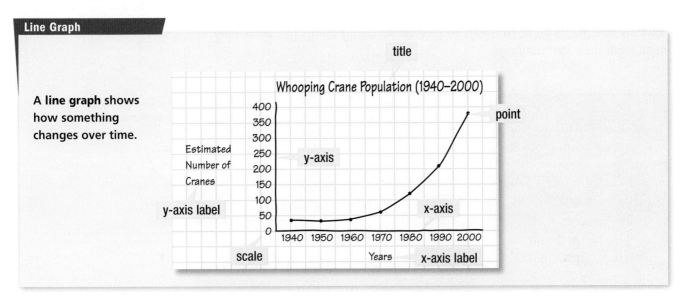

Listen to the article. Study the picture and the graph below. Then do the Review.

The Whooping Crane: An Endangered Bird

• **Can the whooping crane be saved?**

In the 1800s, there were hundreds of whooping cranes in North America. Then the cranes became endangered. Many were hunted. Many of the wetlands where they lived were drained and turned into farms. By the 1940s, only a few whooping cranes were left.

Scientists are working hard to save these cranes. Each spring, whooping cranes lay two eggs and raise only one chick. Some scientists take the extra egg and hatch the chick. Then they release the chick into the wild. This work has helped increase the number of whooping cranes. By 2000, there were about 400 whooping cranes in North America.

The whooping crane is beautiful. It is white with red and black on its head. It has long, thin legs and a long beak.

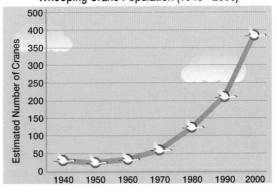

REVIEW

1. **Check Your Understanding** Why did whooping cranes become endangered?
2. **Vocabulary** Name the parts of a line graph.
3. **Use Line Graphs** About how many whooping cranes were counted in 1950? In 1990? In what year were there about 125 whooping cranes?

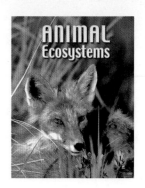

Build Background for "Animal Ecosystems"

ANIMALS, PLANTS, AND HABITATS

Animals and plants all need things to survive. All living things get what they need from their surroundings.

◀ This bear gets what it needs to survive in a forest.

▲ This frog needs to live near water.

Learn Key Vocabulary

Rate and Study the Words Rate how well you know each word. Then:

1. Pronounce the word. Say it aloud several times. Spell it.
2. Study the example.
3. Tell more about the word.
4. Practice it. Make the word your own.

Key Words

ecosystem (ēk-ōh-sis-tum) *noun*

Living things get what they need from the **ecosystem** they live in. Animals and plants live together in **ecosystems**.

forest (for-est) *noun*

A **forest** has many trees and other plants. Many animals live in the trees of this **forest**.

pond (pond) *noun*

A **pond** is a body of water that is smaller than a lake. Frogs and fish live in this **pond**.

soil (soil) *noun*

soil

Plants grow in **soil**. Crops like corn grow in **soil**.

survive (sur-vīv) *verb*

Something that **survives** continues to live. Bears need plants, water, and air to **survive**.

Practice the Words Make an Example Chart for the Key Words and other words from the selection. Compare your chart with a partner.

Ecosystems	Living Things	Non-living Things	Why We Need Ecosystems
pond	trees	air	to survive

Example Chart

Listen and Read Along

FOCUS ON GENRE

Science Article   A science article is a short piece of nonfiction. It tells about a topic that has to do with science. This science article is about ecosystems.

FOCUS ON COMPREHENSION

Details   Authors who write science articles usually give information about a topic. This information includes details about the topic. As you read "Animal Ecosystems," use a detail web to keep track of the information.

> What are the parts of an ecosystem?

This fox finds food, water, and shelter in its ecosystem.

ANIMAL
Ecosystems

Selection Recording

What Is an Ecosystem?

Think of all the things you need to live. You need air to breathe. You need water to drink. You need food to eat.

All living things get what they need from their **ecosystems**. An ecosystem is a group of living and **nonliving things** that work together.

Some ecosystems are small. A **pond** is an ecosystem. It can have fish, frogs, and plants. The water, rocks, and **soil** are part of the ecosystem.

▲ A pond is a small ecosystem.

▲ frog

Key Vocabulary
ecosystem *n.*, all the things that live together in one area
pond *n.*, a body of water that is smaller than a lake
soil *n.*, the ground where things grow

In Other Words
nonliving things things that are not alive

Some ecosystems are large. A **forest** is an ecosystem. The trees, grass, plants, and soil are part of the ecosystem. Birds and animals live there. For example, chipmunks live under the forest's soil. They eat nuts from the trees. Hawks live in forests, too. They build their nests in trees. They eat small animals like chipmunks.

▲ hawk

▼ Trees are homes to many kinds of animals in a forest ecosystem.

▲ chipmunk

Key Vocabulary
forest *n.*, a big area of land covered with trees

Before You Move On

1. **Make Comparisons** How is a **pond ecosystem** the same as a **forest** ecosystem? How is it different?
2. **Details** Name three parts of a forest ecosystem.

Language and Content **93**

Living and Nonliving Things Together

Animals live in ecosystems that have the living and nonliving things they need to **survive**. For example, bears live in ecosystems that have food, water, and places to build homes.

Look at the photograph. The bears and plants are the living things. The water and air are the nonliving things. Bears eat the plants and drink the water. They use the trees and land to build places to sleep.

▼ These bears need the plants, water, and air in their ecosystem.

Key Vocabulary
survive *v.*, to keep on living

Parts of an Ecosystem

Nonliving Things

air

water

sunlight

soil

Living Things

flowers

trees

grass

animal

Before You Move On

1. **Categorize** Name three nonliving things.
2. **Main Idea and Details** Why are trees important to bears?

Changing Ecosystems

Natural forces, like fire and weather, can change an ecosystem. People can change ecosystems, too. When people build roads and buildings, they change the ecosystem. Plants and animals may no longer have what they need. If we want plants and animals to survive, we must help **protect** their ecosystem.

▼ People change animal ecosystems when they build roads and homes.

In Other Words

protect stop bad things from
happening to

This chart shows the number of black bears that are in California.

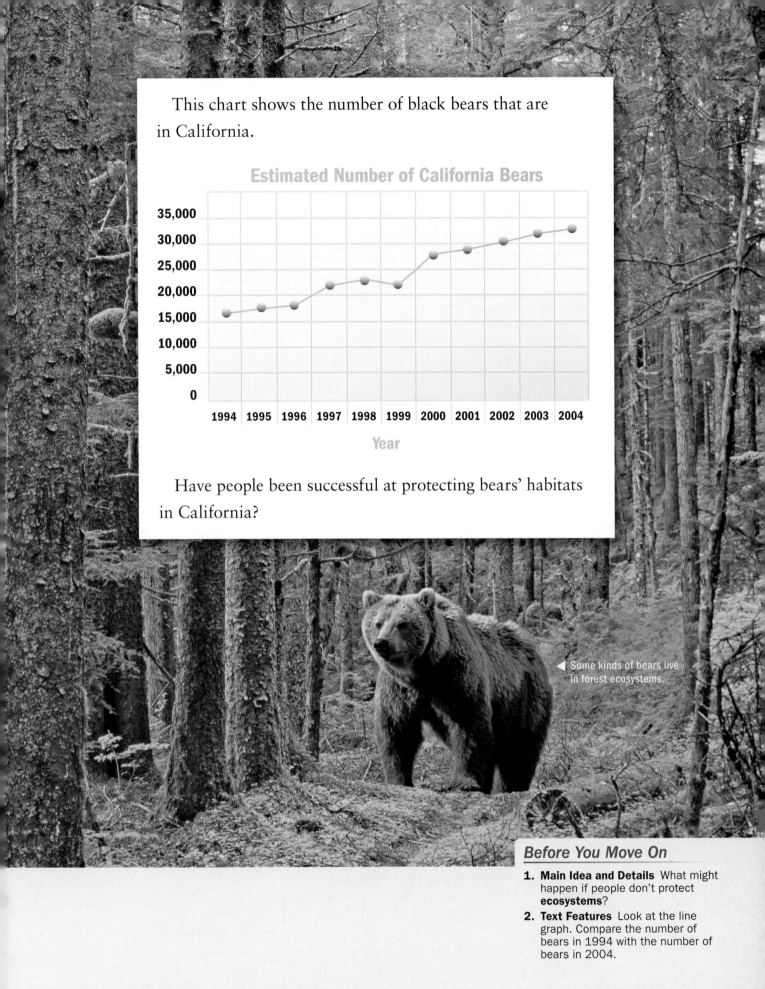

Estimated Number of California Bears

Year	
35,000	
30,000	
25,000	
20,000	
15,000	
10,000	
5,000	
0	

1994 1995 1996 1997 1998 1999 2000 2001 2002 2003 2004

Year

Have people been successful at protecting bears' habitats in California?

◄ Some kinds of bears live in forest ecosystems.

Before You Move On

1. **Main Idea and Details** What might happen if people don't protect **ecosystems**?

2. **Text Features** Look at the line graph. Compare the number of bears in 1994 with the number of bears in 2004.

Think About "Animal Ecosystems"

CHECK YOUR UNDERSTANDING

1.–2. **Work with a partner to complete each item.**

1. Make a detail web like the one below. Use details from "Animal Ecosystems" to complete the web.

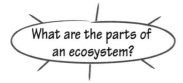

What are the parts of an ecosystem?

2. Sum It Up Use your chart to tell about the parts of an **ecosystem**.

REVIEW VOCABULARY

3.–7. **Read the paragraph aloud. Add the vocabulary words.**

> All living things get what they need to _____ from their
>
> _____. A _____ is an ecosystem with water, rocks, and _____.
>
> A _____ ecosystem has trees, grass, and plants.

Vocabulary

ecosystems

forest

pond

soil

survive

WRITE ABOUT LIFE ON EARTH

8. Write about the plants and animals that you see near your home. How do they **survive**?

Fact-and-Opinion Article

A fact is a piece of information that can be proven as true. An opinion tells what a person thinks or feels about something. Study these opinion words.

Facts and opinions can be combined to write a paragraph.

FACT-AND-OPINION ARTICLE

This is a tree squirrel.

Tree Squirrels

I think that tree squirrels are an important part of our local habitat. Some people believe they are not important. But the fact is that they help in many ways. We have many tree squirrels in our area. Tree squirrels help new trees grow. Most tree squirrels use their strong teeth and powerful jaws to eat nuts and fruits. When they eat, the squirrels move seeds from one place to another. The seeds grow into new trees. Some animals build homes in these trees. Some animals eat parts of the tree. The next time you see a tree squirrel, you should be glad. Think about how it helps our habitat!

> **Opinion Words**
> People use these words to give an opinion.
> **must**   **should**
> **think**   **believe**

You can use opinion words to find the **opinions**.

The **facts** give reasons for the opinion.

Writing Project

> ## Write a Fact-and-Opinion Article
>
> **WRITING PROMPT** Write an article to give facts and opinions about an animal. Then share your article with the class.

Prewrite

When you prewrite, you gather ideas and choose your topic. You also make a plan for what you will write. Follow these steps.

1 CHOOSE AN ANIMAL

Think of animals you want to study. Think of life in the forest, pond, seashore, and farm. Think of animals in the city. Choose an animal.

2 GATHER FACTS

Research your animal. Ask your teacher or librarian for help. Write what you know. Use information sources to check your facts and discover new facts. Make a chart. Write your facts in the first column of the chart.

Gather sensory details about your animal. Think about how it looks, sounds, and feels.

3 WRITE YOUR OPINIONS

What do you think or believe about the animal? Add your opinions to the second column of the chart.

Adjectives	
green	large
brown	small
orange	big
white	little

Fact-Opinion Chart

Facts About Whooping Cranes	My Opinions
1. endangered	1. beautiful birds
2. white with black and red patches	2. save the whooping cranes
3. scientists helping	3. do not hunt whooping cranes
4. about 400 today	
5. have long legs and a long beak	

Reflect
- Did you pick a good topic?
- Do you have a clear plan?

Draft

When you draft, you begin writing. Use the ideas you gathered into your chart to begin your draft.

Facts About Whooping Cranes	My Opinions
I. endangered	I. save the whooping cranes

> Whooping cranes are endangered. We should save the whooping cranes.

Revise

When you revise a draft, you make your writing better. First you need to know what a reader thinks of your work. Carter read his article to a partner.

Carter's Draft

> Whooping cranes have feathers. They have legs and a beak. They are very special.

Carter's partner says:

" I can't picture which bird or tell which sentences are facts and which are opinions. "

Then Carter knew he needed to make a change.

Carter's Revision

> Whooping cranes have white feathers. They have long legs and a long beak. I think they are very special.

He added the opinion words and adjectives.

Now follow these steps to revise your article.

1 DECIDE WHAT TO CHANGE

When you revise a draft, you make your writing better. First you need to know what a reader thinks of your work. Carter read his article to a partner.

2 MARK YOUR CHANGES

If you need to add words, use this mark: ∧.

Reflect
• Did you give facts that support your opinions?
• Did you use opinion words like *think* or *should*?

Edit and Proofread

After you have revised your draft, check it for mistakes.

1 CHECK YOUR ADJECTIVES

When you write, use adjectives to describe things and ideas. Adjectives help readers make a picture in their mind of your writing.

> **EXAMPLE**   The whooping crane is a large, white bird

Adjectives	
green	large
brown	small
orange	big
white	little

2 CHECK YOUR SPELLING

Circle each word that may not be spelled right. Look it up in the dictionary or ask for help. Fix the spelling if you need to.

3 CHECK YOUR COMMAS

Whenever you have a list of more than two things in your writing, separate them with commas. This type of lists is called a series. Be sure you include commas in a series.

> **EXAMPLE**   Whooping cranes, California condors, and wood storks are all endangered.

What errors did Carter correct in his paper? What errors does he still need to correct?

> There are less than 500 whooping cranes in the wild. They live in Canada Florida and Texas. We should write ⟨letturs⟩ to thank each ⟨pirson⟩ in those states for helping the whooping crane. Some flocks migrate. Other flocks live in the same place winter spring ⟨summor⟩ and fall.

4 MARK YOUR CHANGES

Now edit your paper. Use these marks to show your changes:

∧	ℐ	⌐	◯	≡	╱	¶
Add.	Take out.	Replace with this.	Check spelling.	Capitalize.	Make lowercase.	Make new paragraph.

Reflect

• What kinds of errors did you find?

• What can you do to keep from making errors?

Publish, Share, and Present

You have finished your fact-and-opinion article. Now you are ready to publish your work! When you publish your writing, you put it in final form to share with others. Follow these steps.

1 FINISH AND DISPLAY

Think about how your writing looks.

- Make sure your handwriting is clear.

- Turn your paragraph into a poster. Add drawings or pictures.

2 MAKE A PRESENTATION

There are many ways you can share your writing. For this article, try making a presentation. As you make your presentation, think about your purpose.

- To help people picture your animal, use props like posters and pictures to help people understand your presentation.

- Say opinion words clearly to help listeners tell the difference between facts and opinions.

Also remember these tips.

Presenting Tips

If You Are the Speaker:	If You Are the Listener:
• Read loudly and clearly.	• Make a picture of the text in your mind.
• Stop a moment after each fact.	• Pay attention to the reader's voice. Pick out facts and opinions.

Reflect

- How did using the writing process help you understand facts and opinions?

- What did you like best about writing your article?

This photo time line shows important events in this woman's life.

1920　1930　1940　1950　1960　1970　1980　1990　2000　2010　20

1943

1925

1963

2008

PAST AND PRESENT

Look at the time line of this woman's life.
What can you tell about her?
Make a time line of your life.
Draw pictures to show important events.
Label the years. Tell the class about
your past and present.

In This Unit

▶ **Language Development**

▶ **Language and Literacy**

▶ **Language and Content**
Social Science

▶ **Writing Project** ✎

Vocabulary
- History and Historical Records
- Key Vocabulary

Language Functions
- Have a Discussion
- Make Comparisons

Grammar
- Nouns
- Present and Past Tense Verbs
- Object Pronouns

Reading
- Words with *y*
- High Frequency Words
- Comprehension: Make Comparisons
- Text Features: Picture Charts

Writing
- Comparison Paragraph

Language Development

What Is History?

▶ **Language: Have a Discussion**

Listen and sing. CD

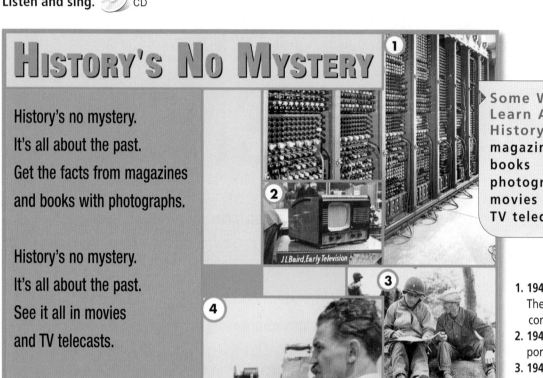

HISTORY'S NO MYSTERY

History's no mystery.
It's all about the past.
Get the facts from magazines
and books with photographs.

History's no mystery.
It's all about the past.
See it all in movies
and TV telecasts.

Find out for yourself
how life used to be.
You will learn a lot of things
when you study history.

Some Ways to Learn About History
magazines
books
photographs
movies
TV telecasts

1. **1946, Pennsylvania** The first electronic computer
2. **1949, England** A portable television
3. **1944, France** A man talks with an American soldier.
4. **1940, Switzerland** A newsreel cameraman
5. **1945, New York** The celebration of the end of World War II

EXPRESS YOURSELF ▶ HAVE A DISCUSSION

Meet with a group. Use the questions below to start a discussion.

EXAMPLE **1.** I like to read books to learn about the past.

1. How do you like to learn about the past?
2. Why is it important to learn about history?
3. Have you seen a movie about the past? Tell about it. What did you learn from the movie?

<u>4.</u> **Say one of the sentences above. Tell one important thing you learned in the discussion.**

EXAMPLE **4.** You can get movies about the past at the library.

How We Learn About the Past

▶ **Vocabulary: Historical Records**
▶ **Language: Make Comparisons**

We call the early 1940s "The War Years" because the U.S. fought in World War II from 1941–1945. Here are some ways you can learn about the 1940s.

diary

newspaper   photograph

history book

Some people wrote about their lives in **diaries** or **journals**. You can read them to see what people's lives were like in the past.

You can read old **newspapers**. They reported the daily events as they happened. **Photographs** made the news come alive.

Look in books written later by **historians**. A historian reads many **sources** and tells the story of the past.

ORAL LANGUAGE PRACTICE ▶ MAKE COMPARISONS

<u>1.–3.</u> **Who's talking?** 🖸 CD

Listen. Three students are talking about their research. Which record of history is each student talking about? Point to the correct picture. Then work with a partner. Compare two of the records shown above. Take turns naming similarities and differences.

WRITTEN PRACTICE ✏️

<u>4.–6.</u> Write 3 comparisons. In each, compare 2 other kinds of records, like movies or magazines. Use words from the box.

EXAMPLE **4.** A magazine and a movie both give us information. A magazine tells about the past with words and pictures, but a movie shows action with pictures that move.

> **Words That Compare**
>
> alike   unalike
> same   different
> and   but
> both

Language Development

The 1940s: Who? What? Where?

▶ **Nouns**

A **noun** names a person, place, or thing.

Margaret Bourke-White

<u>World War II</u> began in 1939.
    thing

<u>Margaret Bourke-White</u> took <u>photographs</u> of the <u>war</u> in <u>Europe</u>.
    person   things   thing   place

<u>Magazines</u> printed her amazing <u>pictures</u>.
   things   things

<u>Americans</u> could see what their <u>soldiers</u> were doing.
  people   people

READ SENTENCES

Say each sentence. Tell if each <u>underlined</u> noun is a person, a place, or a thing.

EXAMPLE **1.** Bill Mauldin is the name of a person.

1. <u>Bill Mauldin</u> also recorded the <u>events</u> of <u>World War II</u>.

2. While he was in the <u>army</u> in <u>Italy</u>, he drew <u>cartoons</u> of American <u>soldiers</u>.

3. His <u>pictures</u> were often published in the <u>newspaper</u> *Stars and Stripes*.

Bill Mauldin

4. Ollie Stewart was a <u>reporter</u>.

5. He was the first <u>journalist</u> from the <u>newspaper</u> *Afro-American* to go to the frontline in <u>North Africa</u>.

6. He was also in <u>France</u> when the <u>war</u> ended there.

Ollie Stewart

WRITE A PARAGRAPH

Write the paragraph. Add the missing words.

award	newspapers	soldiers
Japan	photographs	

The photographer Joe Rosenthal took ___(7)___ during World War II. He was on an island in ___(8)___ when he took a famous picture of six American ___(9)___ lifting a flag. Many magazines and ___(10)___ printed the picture. Joe won an ___(11)___ for the picture.

Joe Rosenthal took this photo in Iwo Jima, Japan, in 1945.

The 1940s: What We Did

▶ **Present and Past Tense Verbs**

A verb changes to show when an action happens.

Use a present tense verb to tell what happens now.

Today, we **listen** to songs on the radio.

Use a past tense verb to tell what happened in the past. To form the past tense, you usually add *-ed*.

In the 1940s, families **listened** to war news on the radio.

Study the verbs in the box. They have a special form to show the past tense.

Present	Past
are	were
build	built
eat	ate
is	was
leave	left
say	said
wear	wore

BUILD SENTENCES

Say each sentence. Add the past tense of the verb in dark type.

EXAMPLE **1.** In the United States, people's lives changed a lot during World War II.

1. **change**   In the United States, people's lives _____ a lot during World War II.
2. **are**   There _____ not many things to buy.
3. **print**   The government _____ special stamps.
4. **use**   Everyone _____ the stamps to get things like sugar and cheese.
5. **plant**   Families _____ gardens to grow food.
6. **wear**   Women _____ simple dresses and shoes.
7. **collect**   Children _____ old rubber, paper, and aluminum.
8. **build**   Factories _____ bombs and airplanes.
9. **eat**   People _____ food like powdered eggs and potatoes.
10. **is**   There _____ not much gasoline either.
11. **say**   Everyone _____ that life was hard.
12. **leave**   The hardest part was when someone _____ to go to war.

People used ration stamps like these.

WRITE SENTENCES

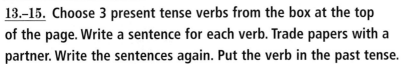

13.–15. Choose 3 present tense verbs from the box at the top of the page. Write a sentence for each verb. Trade papers with a partner. Write the sentences again. Put the verb in the past tense.

EXAMPLE **13.** Factories build airplanes.

Factories built airplanes.

Women worked in airplane factories for the first time during World War II.

World War II: A Tragic Time

▶ **Object Pronouns**

A pronoun can refer to a noun.

Anne Frank was a teenager in the 1940s.

Use these pronouns after an action verb and after words like *to*, *in*, or *with*.

Pronoun	Use for:	Examples
him	a boy or a man	**Adolf Hitler** was Germany's leader in World War II. The Nazi Party was loyal to **him**.
her	a girl or a woman	**Anne Frank** was Jewish. The Nazis made **her** wear a yellow star.
it	a thing	Anne wrote about her life in a **diary**. You can read **it** today.
them	two or more people or things	The **Franks** had to hide during the war. A few friends helped **them**.

BUILD SENTENCES

Look at the noun in the first sentence. Say both sentences. Add the pronoun that refers to, or goes with, the noun.

EXAMPLE **1.** Otto Frank, Anne's father, had an office. The family hid above it.

1. Otto Frank, Anne's father, had an **office**. The family hid above _____.
2. A **boy** named Peter also hid there. Anne became good friends with _____.
3. One horrible morning, the Nazis found the **family**. The soldiers took _____ to prison camps.
4. Anne left her **diary** in the hiding place. A friend found _____.
5. **Anne** died in the prison camps. After the war, Mr. Frank published her diary.
   He wanted people to remember _____.

WRITE A PARAGRAPH

Work with a partner. Write this paragraph. Add the word *him*, *her*, *it*, or *them* in each blank. Take turns reading the paragraph aloud.

EXAMPLE **6.** Many people have read it.

You can read Anne's diary in many languages. Many people have read ___(6)___. Nelson Mandela, a leader in South Africa, said the story encouraged ___(7)___. Several writers have been interested in Anne. They wrote books about ___(8)___. Many people feel Anne's diary helped ___(9)___ to understand what happened in World War II.

Things Changed for Us

▶ Object Pronouns

When you use a pronoun, be sure to tell about the right noun.

Use these pronouns after an action verb and after words like *to*, *in*, or *with*.

Pronoun	Use:	Example
me	for yourself	My sister sent this photo to **me** in 1942.
you	to talk to another person or persons	"I will write to **you** every day," she promised.
us	for yourself and another person	My sister sent letters to **us** from all over the world.
him, her, it, or them	to tell about other people or things	We still read **them** often.

BUILD SENTENCES

Read each sentence. Choose the correct pronoun. Say the complete sentence.

EXAMPLE **1.** During the war, things changed for us.

1. During the war, things changed for ____(us / it)____.
2. Dad planted a garden. I helped ____(him / us)____ take care of it.
3. Mom asked ____(me / you)____ to put up some special curtains.
4. We called ____(it / them)____ "blackout curtains."
5. At night, airplanes couldn't see ____(us / him)____ or our lights through the curtains.
6. I wanted new shoes. Dad said, "We can't buy shoes for ____(them / you)____ now."
7. There wasn't much rubber. Factories used ____(it / us)____ for the war.
8. We missed my sister. We talked about ____(her / him)____ a lot.
9. She wrote some letters just to ____(me / her)____.
10. I still have all of ____(you / them)____.

WRITE A LETTER

<u>11.</u> **Imagine that you are the boy above.**
Write a letter to your sister.
Tell what you are doing.
Use *me*, *you*, *him*, *her*, *it*, *us*, and *them*.

EXAMPLE **11.**

May 1944

Dear Sister,
Dad planted a garden. I help him water it and pull the weeds. We grew tomatoes. I wish you could be with us, but we are so proud of you!

Love,
Jim

Language Development

Listen and Read Along

FOCUS ON GENRE

Historical Account   A historical account gives readers an idea of what life was like in the past. It is nonfiction. This historical account is about World War II.

FOCUS ON VOCABULARY

Words About World War II   You have been learning words like the ones below. Use these words as you talk about *The Children We Remember*. Collect more words to put in the web.

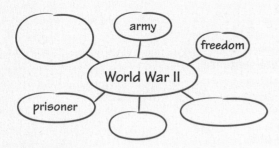

```
            army
                    freedom
        World War II
  prisoner
```

THEME BOOK

Read this historical account about World War II.

The Children We Remember
by Chana Byers Abells

Photographs from the Archives of Yad Vashem, The Holocaust Martyrs' and Heroes' Remembrance Authority, Jerusalem, Israel

Jewish children had to work together to survive during World War II.

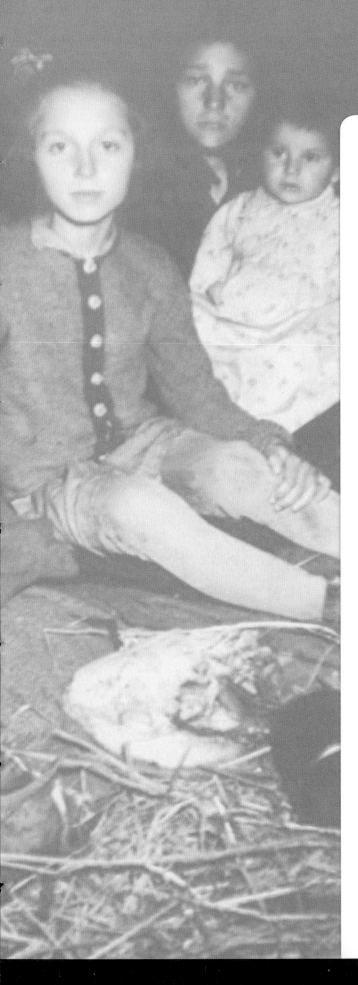

Think About
The Children We Remember

MAKE COMPARISONS

Make a comparison chart to tell about
The Children We Remember. **Follow these steps.**

1 Think about the story. What was life like for
Jewish children before the Nazis took control?
What was life like for them after the Nazis took
control?

2 Show the changes in a chart. In the first column,
write details about what life was like before the
Nazis came. Use pages 4–5 from the book.

Before the Nazis	After the Nazis
Some Jewish children lived in towns.	

3 Read pages 7–18 again. Tell how life changed
after the Nazis came. Write the information in
the second column.

4 Work with a partner. Compare the children's
lives before and after the Nazis. Use your
completed chart.

Before the Nazis	After the Nazis
Some Jewish children lived in towns.	The Nazis took away their homes.

High Frequency Words

REVIEW HIGH FREQUENCY WORDS

Read the words aloud. Which word goes in the sentence?

some	come
celebrate	country
children	American

1. Where did all these people _____ from?
2. They _____ the end of the war.
3. They wave the _____ flag.

1945, New York City People were happy when Germany surrendered.

LEARN NEW WORDS

Study these words. Say them as whole words when you read.

news	People here shout the great **news**: The war is over!
words	I cannot find the **words** to say how happy I am.
much	There is so **much** excitement everywhere.
along	I am an army nurse. I work **along** with 10 other nurses.
question	We all have the same **question**: When can we go home?

PRACTICE

<u>4.–8.</u> **Work with a partner. Read the first new word. Make a sentence with the word. Then have your partner make a sentence with the same word. Take turns. Make as many sentences with each new word as you can.**

<u>9.</u> **Work with a partner. Write each new word on a card. Mix both sets of cards together. Turn them so the words are down. Then:**

- Turn over 2 cards.
- Spell the words. Are they the same?
- If so, use the word in a sentence and keep the cards. If not, turn them over again.
- Take turns. The player with more cards at the end wins.

EXAMPLE **9.**

much

much

m–u–c–h
m–u–c–h
I am learning so much about World War II.

More High Frequency Words

> **How to Learn a New Word**
> • Look at the word.
> • Listen to the word.
> • Listen to the word in a sentence. What does it mean?
> • Say the word.
> • Spell the word.
> • Say the word again.

REVIEW HIGH FREQUENCY WORDS

Read the words aloud. Which word goes in the sentence?

look like	**1.** Nazis did not _____ Jews.
home help	**2.** Jewish children had to _____ each other.
have head	**3.** The children did not _____ much food.

LEARN NEW WORDS

Study these words. Say them as whole words when you read.

before	I hope to be home **before** the end of May.
miss	I will **miss** the nurses in my group.
example	Our group is a good **example** of a successful team.
ever	These nurses are the best friends I **ever** had.
back	Still, it will be so good to get **back** to my family.

PRACTICE

4.–8. **Work with a partner. Read the first new word. Make a sentence with the word. Then have your partner make a sentence with the same word. Take turns. Make as many sentences with each new word as you can.**

9. **Work with a partner. Write each new word on a card. Mix both sets of cards together. Turn them so the words are down. Then:**

- Turn over 2 cards.
- Spell the words. Are they the same?
- If so, use the word in a sentence and keep the cards. If not, turn them over again.
- Take turns. The player with more cards at the end wins.

EXAMPLE **9.**

miss

miss

> m-i-s-s
> m-i-s-s
> I miss my friends
> when I go on a trip.

Reading and Spelling

▶ **Words with y**

Listen and learn. CD

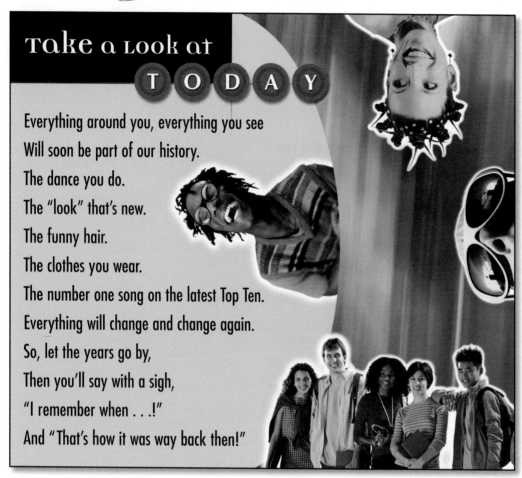

take a look at
TODAY

Everything around you, everything you see
Will soon be part of our history.
The dance you do.
The "look" that's new.
The funny hair.
The clothes you wear.
The number one song on the latest Top Ten.
Everything will change and change again.
So, let the years go by,
Then you'll say with a sigh,
"I remember when . . .!"
And "That's how it was way back then!"

CONNECT SOUNDS AND LETTERS

The letter *y* can have 3 sounds.

Y is a consonant when it comes at the beginning of a word.

2009

JIM'S GUITAR SHOP CALENDAR

<u>y</u>ear

Y is a vowel when it comes at the end of a word.

sk<u>y</u>

Is *y* the only vowel in the word? If so, it sounds like long *i*.

happ<u>y</u>

Does *y* follow a consonant? Is there another vowel? If so, *y* sounds like long *e*.

READING STRATEGY

Follow these steps to read words that end in *y*.

1 Does the word have one vowel or more than one vowel?

try

Y is the only vowel here. So it sounds like long i.

twenty

I see two vowels, e and y. So the y sounds like long e.

2 If there is one vowel, start at the beginning of the word and blend the sounds.

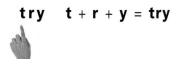

try   t + r + y = try

If there are two vowels, divide the word into syllables. Blend the syllables. Say the long **e** sound for the **y** at the end.

twenty   twen + ty = twenty

READING PRACTICE

Use what you learned to read the sentences.

1. In fifty years, people can look back at your life today.
2. Just make a time capsule that tells your story. Try it!
3. Get a box. On top, write "My Year 2009," for example.
4. Put in your school yearbook, along with things from your hobbies or sports.
5. Include funny things, like an old pair of dirty sneakers.
6. Write words that explain what each thing means to you.

Spelling Help

For words that end in a **consonant + y**, change the y to **i** and add **-es** to form the plural.

sky	skies
penny	pennies

SPELLING PRACTICE

<u>7.–11.</u> **Now write the sentences that your teacher reads.**

WORD WORK

<u>12.</u> **Read these words. Then write each word on a card.**

EXAMPLE **12.**

Sky has 1 syllable.
Puppy has 2 syllables.

puppy	penny	why
sky	candy	funny
twenty	by	sticky
fly	try	my

sky   puppy

Put the words with the long *i* sound in one group.
Put the words with the long *e* sound in another group.
What do you notice?

Read on Your Own

FOCUS ON GENRE

Web Page: Chat Room   In an online chat room, people all over the world can talk to one another. This chat room is about how kids can make history.

FOCUS ON WORDS

Words with *y*   You have just learned about words that end in *y*. Remember that if *y* is the only vowel, it sounds like long *i*. If there are two vowels, then the *y* sounds like long *e*. You also learned about making plurals with words that end in *y*.

puppy   puppies

High Frequency Words   Say these words as whole words when you read.

news	before
words	miss
much	example
along	ever
question	back

PEACE CHAT

SUBJECT OF THE DAY
CAN KIDS MAKE HISTORY?

PEACE PROJECTS

PEACE NEWS

PEACE LINKS

COUNTRY INFO

KIDWORKS FOR PEACE
THE MORE WE KNOW UNDERSTAND EACH OTHER

SUBJECT OF THE DAY:

Can Kids Make History?

SUBJECT OF THE DAY:
Can Kids Make History?

Log In   124 members and 410 guests online   Reply to this Topic   Search   Preferences   Help

Misako Kimura
Japan

Good question! I say YES! More than ever before, kids are making history. In my school, we have a radio show just for kids. We explain news stories in easy words. We help kids understand the news. That way, young people will not miss what's happening in the world.

Mary Boltman
Holland

Hello, Misako. A kid's radio show is a great example of how to make history! I have my own Web site. It tells people where to send food for needy children. My Web site makes me happy. I know I'm helping babies get a good start in life.

Sal Sánchez
USA

Thank you so much, Mary! I'll pass along your Web address to my buddies. I belong to a lucky group of kids. Each year we work at the State House for two weeks. We learn a lot about government before we go back home. I want to get a job in government someday. Then I can really make history.

◀ Misako's school has a radio show that helps kids understand the news.

▲ Mary has a Web site that helps send food to needy children.

◀ Sal goes to the State House every year to learn about government.

Think About "Kidworks for Peace"

CHECK YOUR UNDERSTANDING

Answer each question.

EXAMPLE **1.** Misako tries to help kids understand the news.

1. Misako, Mary, and Sal all have goals. What are they? Finish these sentences:

   Misako tries to _____.

   Mary wants to help _____.

   Sal wants to get _____.

2. How are their goals alike? How are they different? Finish this sentence:

   Both Misako and _____ want to help _____, but Sal wants to find a _____.

3. Do Misako, Mary, and Sal all like what they do? How do you know?

4. Work with your class to complete this chart.

   Then compare ideas. Which ones do you agree with?

Can kids make history?	
Yes	No
My friend Olga sings. She made an album and is famous now.	Kids are too young to make history.

EXPAND YOUR VOCABULARY

<u>5.</u> **Make a word map like the one below. Work with a group to complete it.**

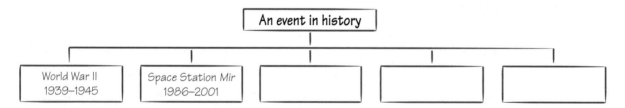

An event in history

| World War II 1939–1945 | Space Station Mir 1986–2001 | | | |

Choose two events from the map. Tell your group about them.
Tell how they are alike or different. Use words from the green box.

alike	and	but
same	both	different

EXAMPLE   WorldWar II was a horrible time when countries fought each other, but countries worked together on Space Station *Mir*.

WRITE ABOUT KIDS AND HISTORY

<u>6.</u> **Pretend you are part of the online chat on page 120.**
Write an e-mail to say what you think: Can kids make history?

EXAMPLE **6.** Yes! My class painted a mural at school. It will be there for a long time!

Language and Content

Success in Social Studies

▶ **Learn About the U.S. Government**

The Three Branches of the U.S. Government

LEGISLATIVE BRANCH: CONGRESS
Senate
House of Representatives

EXECUTIVE BRANCH
President
Vice President
cabinet members
Franklin D. Roosevelt was President during World War II.

JUDICIAL BRANCH
Supreme Court
Chief Justice

KIDWORKS for PEACE created a Web page to explain the kinds of governments in each country. Read their page. Then do the Review.

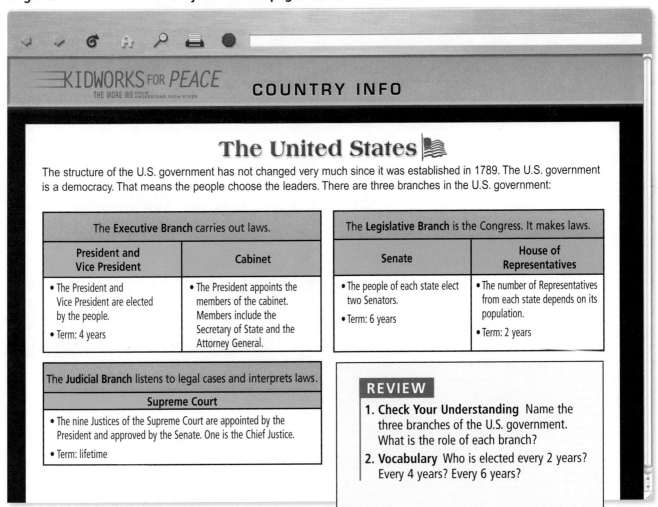

KIDWORKS FOR *PEACE*
THE MORE WE KNOW UNDERSTAND EACH OTHER
COUNTRY INFO

The United States

The structure of the U.S. government has not changed very much since it was established in 1789. The U.S. government is a democracy. That means the people choose the leaders. There are three branches in the U.S. government:

The **Executive Branch** carries out laws.	
President and Vice President	**Cabinet**
• The President and Vice President are elected by the people. • Term: 4 years	• The President appoints the members of the cabinet. Members include the Secretary of State and the Attorney General.

The **Legislative Branch** is the Congress. It makes laws.	
Senate	**House of Representatives**
• The people of each state elect two Senators. • Term: 6 years	• The number of Representatives from each state depends on its population. • Term: 2 years

The **Judicial Branch** listens to legal cases and interprets laws.
Supreme Court
• The nine Justices of the Supreme Court are appointed by the President and approved by the Senate. One is the Chief Justice.   • Term: lifetime

REVIEW

1. **Check Your Understanding** Name the three branches of the U.S. government. What is the role of each branch?
2. **Vocabulary** Who is elected every 2 years? Every 4 years? Every 6 years?

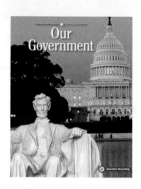

Build Background for "Our Government"

U.S. GOVERNMENT

The leaders of the United States formed a new government in 1787. They wrote the Constitution to tell about the different jobs of the government.

▲ The first leaders of the United States signed the Constitution.

▲ Today, the Capitol Building in Washington, D.C., is a symbol for the U.S. government.

Learn Key Vocabulary

Rate and Study the Words Rate how well you know each word. Then:

1. Pronounce the word. Say it aloud several times. Spell it.
2. Study the example.
3. Tell more about the word.
4. Practice it. Make the word your own.

Key Words

declared (dē-klaird) verb

When something is **declared**, it is spoken clearly and with strength. These people **declared** what they wanted.

freedom (frē-dum) noun

When people want **freedom**, they do not want other people to rule over them. The Washington Monument honors George Washington, who led his people to **freedom**.

government (guv-urn-ment) noun

A **government** directs the way people live in a state or country. The members of Congress are one part of the U.S. **government**.

laws (lawz) noun

Laws are the rules that people in society have to follow. A judge decides if someone is guilty of breaking a **law**.

power (pow-ur) noun

The Three Branches of U.S. Government

Legislative Branch ← Judicial Branch → Executive Branch

When people have **power**, they have strength. The first leaders of the United States wanted to balance the **power** across the three parts, or branches, of government.

Practice the Words Work with a partner. Take turns writing four sentences. Use at least 2 Key Words in each sentence.

> A country's <u>government</u> makes <u>laws</u> for people to follow.

Listen and Read Along

FOCUS ON GENRE

Informational Text   Informational text is used to give facts about a topic. Informational text is nonfiction. This informational text tells about the U.S. government.

FOCUS ON COMPREHENSION

Make Comparisons   When you compare things, you tell how they are alike and different. As you read "Our Government," make notes in a chart about what the parts of our government do. Then you can tell how they are different.

Legislative Branch	Executive Branch	Judicial Branch

The Lincoln Memorial and the Capitol Building in Washington, D.C., are symbols of the U.S. government.

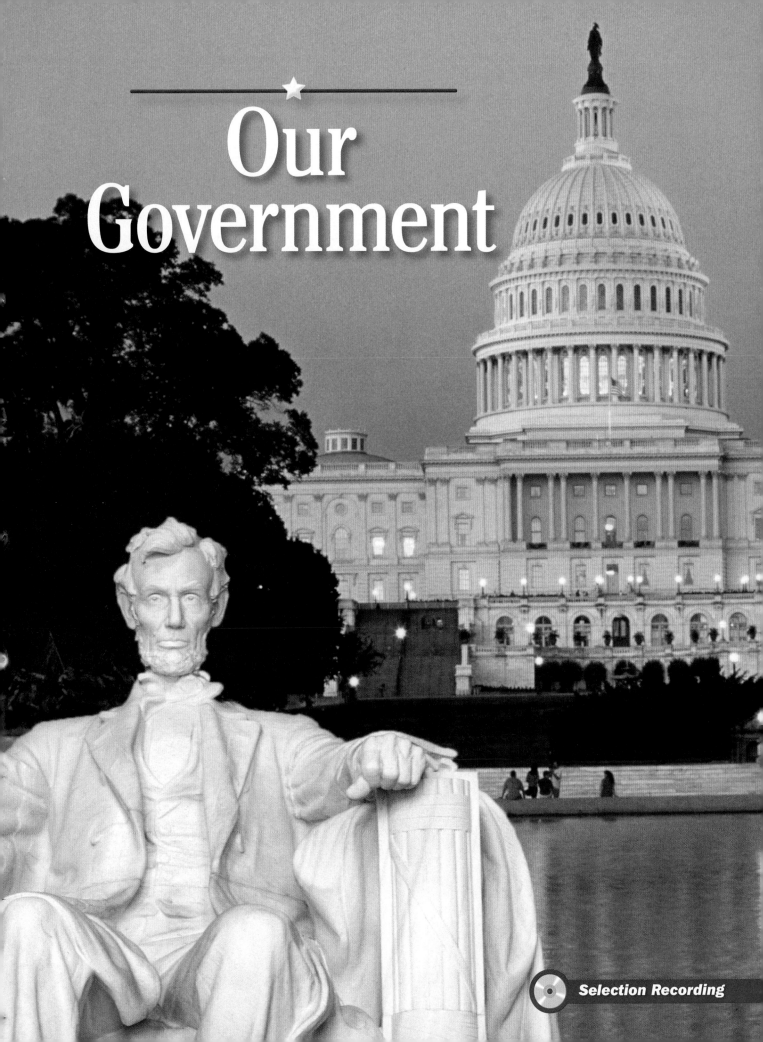

Our Government

Selection Recording

The United States Government

In 1776, American people **declared** their **freedom** and created a new country: the United States of America.

In 1787, leaders of the United States decided to form a new **government**. They wanted to protect people's freedoms.

The leaders wrote the Constitution to name the government's many jobs. Three of those jobs are:

- to make fair **laws**
- to make sure laws are followed
- to protect its people and land

▲ This painting shows George Washington speaking to other U.S. leaders about the Constitution. It was painted in 1856 by Junius Brutus Stearns.

The Washington Monument was built in honor of George Washington, the first U.S. President. ▶

Key Vocabulary

declared *v.*, spoken clearly and with strength

freedom *n.*, having choices and not being ruled by others

government *n.*, group of leaders who direct people

laws *n.*, the rules in society

Three Branches of Government

The Constitution organized the U.S. government into three parts, or branches. The three branches are the legislative branch, the executive branch, and the judicial branch.

The Legislative Branch

This branch of government makes the laws. It is also called Congress. In 1787, Congress had fewer than 100 **members**. In 2007 it had 535! One part of Congress is the Senate. The other part of Congress is the House of Representatives.

◀ Congress works inside the U.S. Capitol.

In Other Words
members people in the group

Before You Move On

1. **Summarize** Why did the United States need a **government**?
2. **Make Comparisons** How much bigger has Congress grown since 1787?

The Two Parts of Congress

 ## The Senate

- The 100 members are called senators.
- Senators are **elected** for six years.
- Senators must be at least 30 years old.

 ## The House of Representatives

- The 435 members are called representatives.
- Representatives are elected for two years.
- Representatives must be at least 25 years old.

▼ Members of Congress meet in this room inside the Capitol Building.

In Other Words
elected chosen by the people

The Executive Branch

The President is the leader of the executive branch and the **head** of the whole government. The President can sign a bill to make it a law or **veto** a bill so it cannot become a law. The President is also in charge of the **military**.

▲ President Bill Clinton signs a bill to make it a law.

In Other Words
head person in charge
veto say no to
military soldiers who protect
the country

Before You Move On

1. **Text Features** How does the chart help you understand the differences between the two parts of Congress?

2. **Compare and Contrast** How is the President's job different from the job of the members of Congress?

The Judicial Branch

This group includes courts where people decide how laws should be followed. The **Supreme Court** is part of this group. The Supreme Court decides whether laws are fair. The Supreme Court has 9 members. It has 1 **Chief Justice** and 8 **Associate Justices**. Once chosen, a Supreme Court Justice can keep the job for the rest of his or her life.

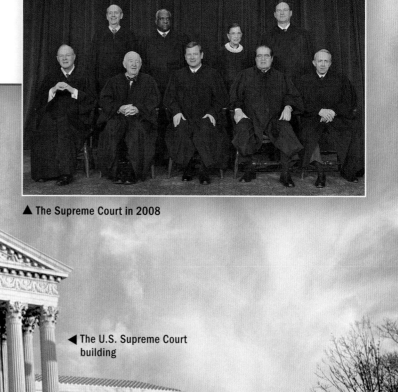

▲ The Supreme Court in 2008

◀ The U.S. Supreme Court building

In Other Words

Supreme Court most important court in our country
Chief Justice leader
Associate Justices other judges

Government Powers

When the government was planned, leaders didn't want any branch of government to have too much **power**. The Constitution says what each branch of government can and can't do. Each branch makes sure the other branches do not get too much power. The three branches work together to run the country.

The U.S. Constitution may look like a piece of paper with words. But it is a very important **document** that protects all of our freedoms.

▼ People can see the U.S. Constitution in Washington, D.C.

Key Vocabulary
power *n.*, strength

In Other Words
document piece of writing

Before You Move On

1. **Inference** Do you think being a Supreme Court Justice is an important job? Why or why not?

2. **Compare and Contrast** How is the Legislative Branch different from the Judicial Branch?

Language and Content

Think About "Our Government"

CHECK YOUR UNDERSTANDING

<u>1.–2.</u> **Work with a partner to complete each item.**

1. **Make Comparisons** Finish the chart about the legislative, the executive, and judicial branches of government.

Legislative Branch	Executive Branch	Judicial Branch
includes senators and congressmen	includes the President	includes Supreme Court justices

2. **Sum It Up** Use your chart to tell how the branches of the U.S. **government** are different. Tell about the different **powers** they have.

REVIEW VOCABULARY

<u>3.–7.</u> **Read the paragraph aloud. Add the vocabulary words.**

> When this country's _____ was planned, people wanted the _____ to make choices. They _____ that no one branch of government should have too much _____. The _____ in the Constitution say what each branch of government can and can't do.

<u>**Vocabulary**</u>

declared

freedom

government

laws

power

WRITE ABOUT JOBS

<u>8.</u> **Write about the jobs of the leaders in your school.**

Comparison Paragraph

In a comparison paragraph, you tell about how two or more things or ideas are alike and different. You use signal words to show how things are alike and different.

COMPARISON PARAGRAPH

An early gas-powered automobile

Signal words show how things are alike and different.

Cars were different in the 1900s than they are today. Today, many people have cars. Things were different in the early 1900s. Only a few people had cars. When we go car shopping today, there are many different kinds to choose from. In the early 1900s, there were very few cars. The first cars started by turning a crank. Cars today start by turning a key or pressing a button. People today are just like people in the 1900s. They both used cars to get where they need to go!

The topic sentence tells what you are comparing.

Support your topic sentence with details.

Words That Compare

alike	unalike
same	different
and	but
both	

Write a Comparison Paragraph

WRITING PROMPT How was life different in the past? Compare your own life to life in a past decade. Then write a paragraph with the information. Share your paragraph with an adult relative or teacher.

Prewrite

When you prewrite, you gather ideas and choose your topic. You also make a plan for what you will write. Follow these steps.

1 COLLECT IDEAS

Pick a time in history to study. Use information sources to learn about the past. Work with your teacher or a librarian to find and use information sources.

2 COLLECT FACTS

Make a chart. Collect facts about the past in the first column of your chart. Collect pictures or make drawings to show life in history.

3 MAKE A PLAN

For each fact about the decade, write how it is the same as or different from today.

> **Some Ways to Learn About History**
> magazines
> books
> photographs
> movies
> TV telecasts

Comparison Chart

1940s	Today
People needed special stamps to buy things.	We can just use money.
Lots of people had gardens for food.	Some people grow gardens for food.
People collected old paper and aluminum.	We recycle paper and aluminum.
People ate powdered eggs and potatoes.	We eat some powdered food, but not eggs.

> **Reflect**
> • Did you pick a good topic?
> • Do you have a clear plan?

Draft

Use the ideas you gathered into your chart to begin
your draft.

> In some ways, life in the 1940s and life today are the same.
> In other ways, life is different.

Revise

When you revise a draft, you make your writing better. First you
need to know what a reader thinks of your work. Robert read his
paragraph to a partner.

Robert's Draft

> In the 1940s, people used special stamps to buy food. They
> grew gardens for food. Now we get food at the store.
> Today, we use money.

Robert's partner says:

" I'm confused. What
are you comparing?"

Then Robert knew he needed to make changes.

Robert's Revision

> In the 1940s, people used special stamps to buy food.
> They grew gardens for food. But Now we get food at the store.
> Today, we use money.

He added a signal
word and moved his
sentences.

Now follow these steps to revise your letter.

1 DECIDE WHAT TO CHANGE

Read to a partner. Ask your partner to list the things you
compared. See if their list matches your planning chart. Do
you need to add any comparison words? Do you need to move
any text to help your writing make sense?

2 MARK YOUR CHANGES

If you need to replace text, use this mark: ‸.

If you need to move text, use this mark: ↶.

Reflect

- Did you use
  signal words?

- Is everything in
  a clear order?

Writing Project

Edit and Proofread

After you have revised your draft, check it for mistakes. Follow these steps.

1 CHECK YOUR NOUNS AND VERBS

When you compare events in the past to current events, you need to make sure you use past and present tense verbs correctly.

> EXAMPLE
>   drove
> We ~~drive~~ to the store yesterday.
>
>   In the 1940s, many people rode horses.

2 SPELLING

Circle each word that may not be spelled right. Look it up in the dictionary or ask for help. Fix the spelling if you need to.

3 CHECK YOUR COMMAS

Whenever you have a list of more than two things in your writing, separate them with commas. This type of list is called a series. Be sure you include commas in a series.

> EXAMPLE
>   I bought a shirt‸ shoes‸ and a sweater.

What errors did Robert correct in his paper? What errors does he still need to correct?

> In the 1940s, people collect^ed old paper‸ aluminum‸ and glass.
> Many
> ~~Manie~~ people still do that today. In the 1940s, some people
> eat powdered eggs, milk and potatoes. We eat some powdered
> food, but not eggs. The ways that people buy things get
> food and recycle today are veree different from the 1940s.

4 MARK YOUR CHANGES

Now edit your paper. Use these marks to show your changes.

∧	℘	⌐	◯	≡	／	⁋
Add.	Take out.	Replace with this.	Check spelling.	Capitalize.	Make lowercase.	Make new paragraph.

Verbs

Some verbs have irregular past tense forms.

PRESENT	PAST
are	were
build	built
eat	ate
is	was
leave	left
say	said
wear	wore
buy	bought

Reflect

- What kinds of errors did you find?

- What can you do to keep from making errors?

Publish, Share, and Present

You have finished your compare and contrast paragraph. Now you are ready to publish your work! When you publish your writing, put it in final form to share with others.

1 FINISH AND DISPLAY

Think about how your writing looks.

- Make sure your handwriting is clear.
- Add drawings or photos to compare life in the past to life today.
- Share your paragraph with an adult. Make a copy and send it with a letter to a relative or family friend.

2 PRESENT

Read your paragraph aloud. Explain how the photos show how life was the same or different. Then listen to other students read.

- Are your facts surprising? Bring history to life! Use your arms and face to show how surprising your facts are. Act out things people do like driving or talking on the phone.
- Do your listeners know about life in history and life today? Invite listeners to ask questions and share ideas about life today or life in history. Compare facts and experiences about different times.

Also remember these tips.

Presenting Tips	
If You Are the Speaker:	**If You Are the Listener:**
• Use your face and body to communicate ideas. • Show the pictures.	• Look at the pictures. • Ask questions. • Make connections to what you know.

Reflect

- What is your opinion about life in the 1940s?
- What did you like best about writing a compare and contrast paragraph?

These people are performing a play.

Tell Me More

What is happening in this play? What are the people saying? What will happen next? Discuss your ideas with your classmates. Then act out the scene together.

In This Unit

▶ **Language Development**

▶ **Language and Literacy**

▶ **Language and Content**
Language Arts

▶ **Writing Project**

Vocabulary
- Story Elements
- Opposites
- Phrases for Times and Places
- Key Vocabulary

Language Functions
- Ask for and Give Advice
- Ask for and Accept a Favor
- Describe Actions

Grammar
- Commands

Reading
- Diphthongs and Variant Vowels
- High Frequency Words
- Comprehension: Story Elements—Characters, Setting, Plot
- Text Features: Literary Elements

Writing
- New Story Ending

Language Development

How to Make a Story

▶ **Language: Ask for and Give Advice**

Listen and chant. CD

Begin with characters,
Some evil, some kind.
Put them in settings
That you have designed.

Throw lots of action
Into the mix.
Stir in a problem
That you can fix.

Cook it for hours
And get to the end.
Share your new story
With all of your friends.

What are the story elements?
A **character** is a person or animal in a story.

The **setting** is the time and place that the story happens.

The **plot** is what happens in the story from the **beginning** to the **middle** to the **end**.

EXPRESS YOURSELF ▶ ASK FOR AND GIVE ADVICE

<u>1.–2.</u> Imagine that you are the superhero in the picture. Ask a partner:
What should I do to get away? Your partner gives you advice. Then change roles.

EXAMPLE **1.** What should I do to get away? You should use your rope and climb the mountain.

<u>3.–6.</u> Talk with a partner. Take turns thinking of advice to give to the monster in the picture. Say 4 sentences.

EXAMPLE **3.** You should drive toward the mountain.

Two Sides of the Story

▶ **Vocabulary: Opposites**
▶ **Language: Ask for and Accept a Favor**

MAKE-BELIEVE CHARACTERS

evil pirate

good fairy

tall giant

strong bear

weak mouse

short elf

young child

brave girl

old woman

frightened dragon

REAL PERSON

ORAL LANGUAGE PRACTICE ▶ ASK FOR AND ACCEPT A FAVOR

<u>1.–4.</u> **Who's talking?** CD

Listen. Which two characters are talking? Point to them.

Act out each scene with a partner. Ask each other for a favor.

WRITTEN PRACTICE

<u>5.</u> **Write a note to one of the characters above.**
Ask for a favor. Read your note to the class.

EXAMPLE **5.**

> Dear Elf,
> I dropped my pencil under the
> steps. I'm too tall to get it.
> You are short. Can you help me?
> Thank you,
> Oscar

A Time and a Place for Everything

▶ **Vocabulary: Phrases for Times and Places**
▶ **Language: Describe Actions**

Read the story. Look for phrases that tell when and where things happen.

In the morning, Paul went up Eagle Mountain. After his walk, he went back home.

During breakfast, Paul sat beside the other men. He ate 275 pancakes.

At 12:00, Paul began to plant trees near his home. He worked from noon to 3:00 and made the North Woods!

Before dinner, Paul walked across Minnesota. He walked until 6:00. His footsteps made 10,000 lakes.

ORAL LANGUAGE PRACTICE ▶ DESCRIBE ACTIONS

<u>1.–4.</u> **Make up settings for 4 new stories about Paul Bunyan.**
Use words from each column to make a sentence that tells the setting.

At 7:00 a.m., During lunch, In the afternoon, Before dinner,	Paul went	around the lake. into the river. up the mountain. through the forest.

EXAMPLE **1.** At 7:00 a.m., Paul went up the mountain.

WRITTEN PRACTICE

<u>5.</u> **Choose a setting you made above. Draw a picture to show it. Then describe the action. Tell the class what happened next.**

EXAMPLE **5.** At 7 a.m., Paul went up the mountain. He walked up the mountain with just three steps.

A Genie at Your Command

▶ **Commands**

> **A command tells someone to do something.**

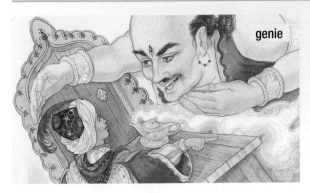

genie

A command can end with a period or an **exclamation mark** .

> Listen to my wish.
> Go to the kitchen.
> Make something for me to eat**!**

BUILD SENTENCES

Aladdin gave the genie a new command every day. Choose the correct word to complete each command. Then say the command.

1. " ___(Get/Paint)___ some slippers for me."

2. " ___(Put/Build)___ a gold ring on my finger."

3. " ___(Swim/Bring)___ gold and jewels to me."

4. " ___(Put/Sing)___ me a song."

5. " ___(Build/Put)___ a new castle for me."

6. " ___(Take/Paint)___ me to the princess."

EXAMPLE **1.** Get some slippers for me.

WRITE COMMANDS

7.–12. Imagine you have your own genie. Work with a partner. Take turns to write 6 commands for the genie. Put a period or an exclamation mark at the end of each command.

EXAMPLE **7.** Do my homework.

Language Development

Listen and Read Along

FOCUS ON GENRE

Fable A fable is a short tale that teaches a lesson. A fable is fiction. This Hmong fable teaches about the dangers of greed.

FOCUS ON VOCABULARY

Opposites You have been learning about words like the ones below. Use these words as you talk about *The Eagle and the Moon Gold*. Collect more words to put in the web.

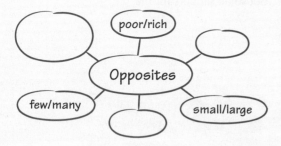

THEME BOOK

Read this Hmong fable about greed.

The
Eagle and the
MOON GOLD

A Fable from the Hmong People
Adapted by Yeemay Chan
Illustrated by Kat Thacker

Making blankets and clothes can be a tradition, just like telling stories.

Think About
The Eagle and the Moon Gold

IDENTIFY CHARACTER TRAITS

Make a character map for the characters in *The Eagle and the Moon Gold*. Follow these steps.

1 Draw a character map like this.

Character	What the Character Does	What the Character Is Like
Yaoh		
the eagle		
Gwa		

2 Read the story again. Think about Yaoh's actions. List them in the second column. What do Yaoh's actions show about his character? Write words to describe Yaoh in the third column.

Character	What the Character Does	What the Character Is Like
Yaoh	He chops wood to stay warm.	hard-working

3 Now think about the eagle and Gwa. Complete the character map for each character.

4 Use your finished map to tell a partner about the three characters in the story.

High Frequency Words

This man is telling a story that is very old.

REVIEW HIGH FREQUENCY WORDS

Read the words aloud. Which word goes in each sentence?

study	story
our	over
before	because

1. He tells a _____.
2. It was first told by _____ grandfathers.
3. They told the story _____ we were born.

LEARN NEW WORDS

Study these words. Say them as whole words when you read.

as	Listen carefully **as** I tell you a story.
sentence	Pay attention to every **sentence** I say.
idea	I got the **idea** for this story from my grandfather.
plants	A frog lived in the garden among the tall **plants**.
into	One day, it jumped and fell **into** a pail of cream.

PRACTICE

<u>4.</u> **Work with a partner. Each partner should have a classroom book or magazine. See which partner can find the most sentences that use one of the new words. Partners should take turns saying the words.**

Write each sentence. Add the missing word.   EXAMPLE **5. The children listen as the man tells a story.**

5. The children listen _ _ the man tells a story.
6. The first _ _ _ _ _ _ _ _ in the story starts with "A frog lived…".
7. The frog came out of the tall _ _ _ _ _ _ where it lived.
8. The frog fell _ _ _ _ a pail of cream.
9. The frog had no _ _ _ _ how to get out of the pail!

More High Frequency Words

> **How to Learn a New Word**
>
> - Look at the word.
> - Listen to the word.
> - Listen to the word in a sentence. What does it mean?
> - Say the word.
> - Spell the word.
> - Say the word again.

REVIEW HIGH FREQUENCY WORDS

Read the words aloud. Which word goes in the sentence?

need	feel		1. Greedy people want much more than they _____.
have	has		2. They are not content with what they _____.
girl	good		3. It is not _____ to be greedy.

LEARN NEW WORDS

Study these words. Say them as whole words when you read.

until	The frog swam and swam **until** its legs got tired.
but	The frog was tired, **but** it did not stop swimming.
seemed	Then the cream **seemed** a little thicker.
each	With **each** kick, the cream got thicker and thicker.
made	In a few minutes, the frog **made** a pail of butter!

PRACTICE

<u>4.</u> **Work with a partner. Take turns telling a story using the new words. One partner can begin the story, and then the other partner finishes it.**

Write each sentence. Add the missing word.   EXAMPLE **5. The frog got tired, but it did not stop swimming.**

5. The frog got tired, _ _ _ it did not stop swimming.
6. _ _ _ _ time it kicked, the frog _ _ _ _ the cream thicker.
7. The frog kicked _ _ _ _ _ the cream turned to butter.
8. The children laughed. They _ _ _ _ _ _ to like the story.

Reading and Spelling

▶ **Diphthongs and Variant Vowels**

Listen and learn. CD

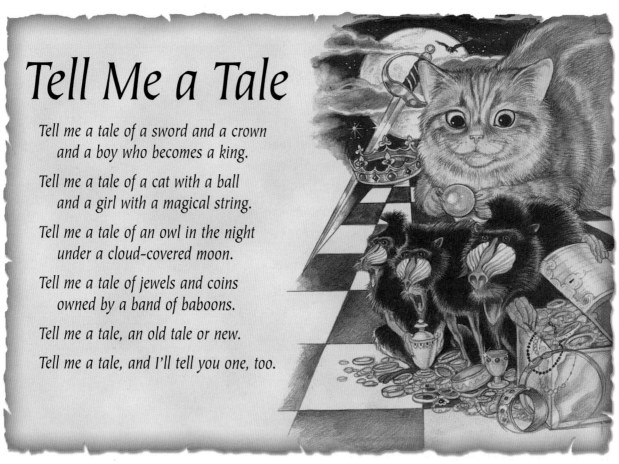

Tell Me a Tale

Tell me a tale of a sword and a crown
and a boy who becomes a king.

Tell me a tale of a cat with a ball
and a girl with a magical string.

Tell me a tale of an owl in the night
under a cloud-covered moon.

Tell me a tale of jewels and coins
owned by a band of baboons.

Tell me a tale, an old tale or new.

Tell me a tale, and I'll tell you one, too.

CONNECT SOUNDS AND LETTERS

Read the words. How do you spell each vowel sound?

1.
   coin   **boy**

2.
   cloud   **crown**

3.
   laundry   **saw**

4.
   salt   **ball**

5.
   moon   **screw**

READING STRATEGY

Follow these steps to read a word.

1 Look for pairs of letters that make a vowel sound.

toy

> When **o** and **y** are next to each other, they combine to make a new sound, like the **oy** in **boy**.

moon

> When **o** and **o** are next to each other, they combine to make a new sound. Here they sound like long **u**.

2 Start at the beginning. Blend the sounds in your head. Then say the word.

toy   t + oy = toy

moon   m + oo + n = moon

READING PRACTICE

Use what you learned to read the sentences.

1. My mother is an author. She writes stories for teens.
2. She also draws pictures to go with each story.
3. I enjoy all of Mom's stories. They are very cool.
4. When she needs a new idea for a story, she goes out.
5. Sometimes I join her. We go to the mall or into town.
6. Mom jots down notes as she watches the crowd.

SPELLING PRACTICE

7.–11. **Now write the sentences that your teacher reads.**

WORD WORK

12. **Write each of these words on a card.**

coin	now	joy	boil	oil
town	toy	moist	count	point
out	loud	owl	clown	boy

Then say each word. Sort the words by vowel sound. Make 2 groups. What do you notice about each group?

> Use **oy** to spell the sound at the end of a word. Use **oi** in the middle.

13. **Now make 4 new groups. Put the words with the same vowel sound *and* spelling together.**

EXAMPLE **13.**

toy   coin

Read on Your Own

FOCUS ON GENRE

Realistic Fiction Realistic fiction tells a story that could actually happen. The characters and events could be real. This realistic fiction tells about a boy who hears a scary story.

FOCUS ON WORDS

Words with Vowel Spellings When you read and come to a word you don't know, blend the sounds together to read it. You have just learned about words with these spellings:

oi	oy
ou	ow
ew	oo
au	aw
al	all

cloud

High Frequency Words Say these words as whole words when you read.

as	until
sentence	but
idea	seemed
plants	each
into	made

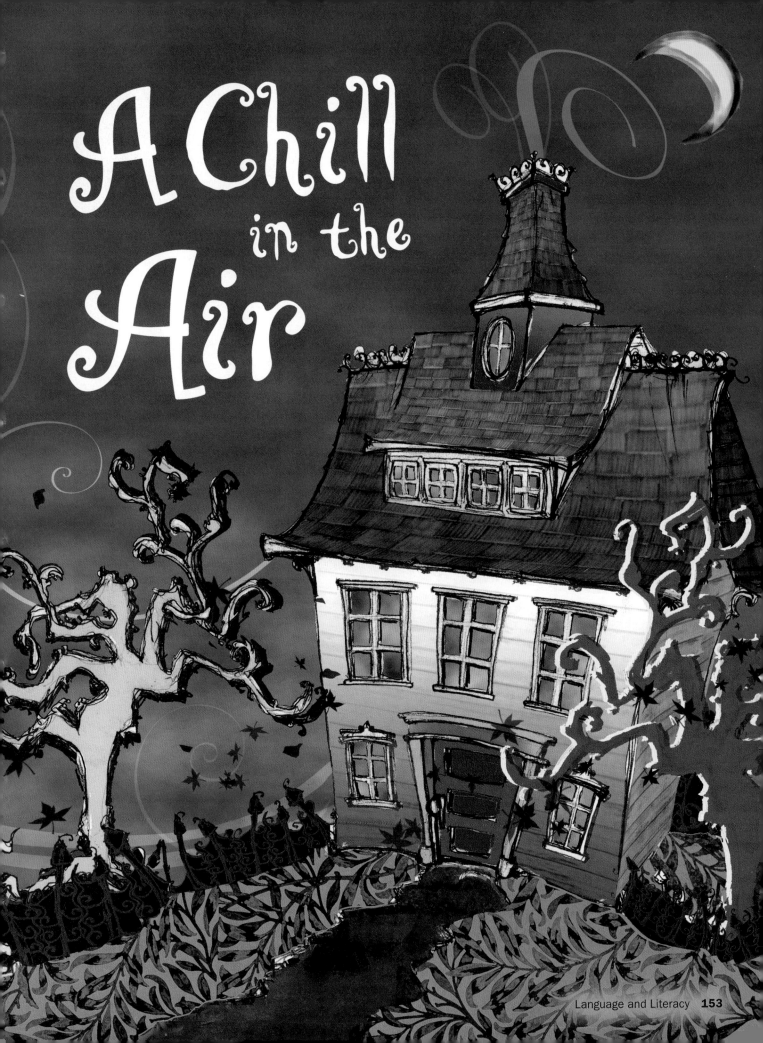

A Chill in the Air

"**W**elcome to your new home, Paul!" Mr. Brown handed Paul a story on tape and a set of keys to his room.

"Thank you! I love stories on tape," said Paul. He liked the room. It had many plants. "I have an idea. Please, come in and join me for tea."

"I can't tonight," said Mr. Brown, "but I hope you enjoy the tape. It's a great story."

Paul nodded. He liked the author very much! He had read every sentence in every one of her stories.

Paul waited until 9:00. He made himself a cup of tea and put the tape into the tape deck. The story was about a small boy who lived in a haunted house. Each time the boy saw an owl, someone died.

As Paul listened, something started to pound on the pipes inside his walls. The sound seemed to grow **louder** and **louder** as the room grew cooler.

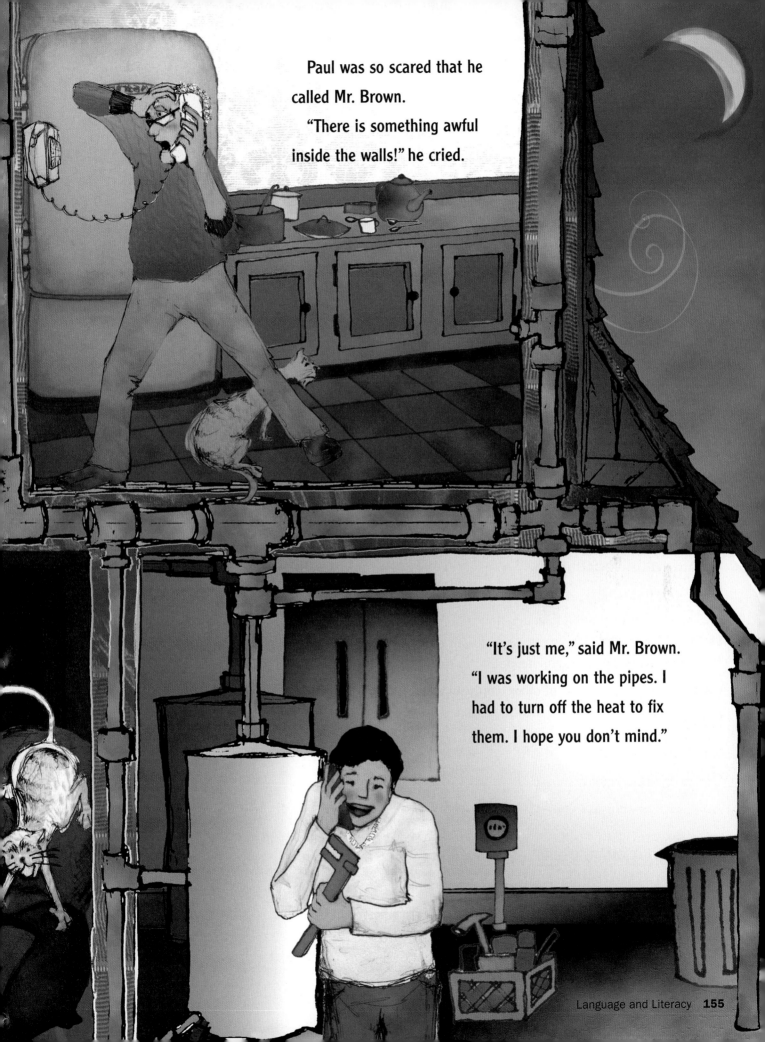

Paul was so scared that he called Mr. Brown.
"There is something awful inside the walls!" he cried.

"It's just me," said Mr. Brown. "I was working on the pipes. I had to turn off the heat to fix them. I hope you don't mind."

Think About "A Chill in the Air"

CHECK YOUR UNDERSTANDING

Make a story map like the one below and complete it.
Tell what happens in the beginning, in the middle,
and at the end of the story on pages 154–155.

Beginning

1. Paul moved into his new _____.
2. Mr. Brown gave Paul _____.
3. Paul asked Mr. Brown _____.

Middle

4. Paul listened to _____.
5. It was about _____.
6. Each time the boy saw an owl, _____.

End

7. Something started to pound on _____.
8. Paul felt _____.
9. The sound was caused by _____.

EXAMPLE **1.**

```
┌─────────────────────────────────────────┐
│              Beginning                    │
│  1. Paul moved into his new home.         │
└─────────────────────────────────────────┘
                    │
                    ▼
┌─────────────────────────────────────────┐
│                                           │
│               Middle                      │
│                                           │
└─────────────────────────────────────────┘
                    │
                    ▼
┌─────────────────────────────────────────┐
│                                           │
│                 End                       │
│                                           │
└─────────────────────────────────────────┘
```

EXPAND YOUR VOCABULARY

Read the sentences.

10. The story was about a man in a <u>new</u> home.
11. Paul was so <u>scared</u>.
12. "There is something <u>awful</u> inside the walls!" he cried.

Work with a group to think of other words that mean *new*,
scared, and *awful*. Make a list. Then say each sentence with a new word.

EXAMPLE

new — different   scared — afraid   awful — terrible

WRITE ABOUT CHARACTERS

<u>13.</u> Choose a character from a story you know.
Write sentences to describe the character.

EXAMPLE **13.** Yaoh was a poor boy. He was wise to listen
to the eagle. He was content with a few coins.

Success in Language Arts

▶ **Learn About Myths**

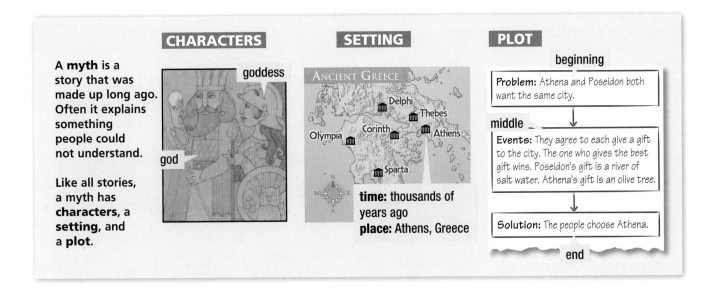

CHARACTERS

goddess

god

SETTING

ANCIENT GREECE

Delphi
Thebes
Corinth
Olympia
Athens

Sparta

time: thousands of years ago
place: Athens, Greece

PLOT

beginning

Problem: Athena and Poseidon both want the same city.

middle

Events: They agree to each give a gift to the city. The one who gives the best gift wins. Poseidon's gift is a river of salt water. Athena's gift is an olive tree.

Solution: The people choose Athena.

end

A **myth** is a story that was made up long ago. Often it explains something people could not understand.

Like all stories, a myth has **characters**, a **setting**, and a **plot**.

Listen to the myth. Then answer the questions.

The Beginning of Athens

Thousands of years ago, the gods were dividing up the land. Poseidon, the god of the sea, found a city that he liked. He wanted it for his own. Athena, the goddess of wisdom, saw the same city. She wanted it, too.

Poseidon and Athena agreed to a contest. They decided to each give a gift to the city and let the people choose the best gift. The winner could have the city.

Poseidon touched the rocky mountainside. A river gushed out. Athena touched the dark earth. An olive tree sprang up.

The people looked at the gifts. They tasted the water. It was salty, like the sea. It was of no use to them.

Then they studied the tree. They saw that they could eat the fat olives or make oil from them.

Poseidon's gift is a river of salt water. Athena's gift is an olive tree.

They knew that they could use the tree's wood to build things. They chose Athena.

Athena named the city Athens. The people built a large building to honor her, but they never forgot Poseidon. For many years, a salty pond and an olive tree remained near the building to remind people of the contest.

CHECK YOUR UNDERSTANDING

1. Who are the two main characters in this myth?
2. What is the setting of this story?
3. Which paragraph tells about the problem in the myth? What happens next? How does the myth end?

Language and Content

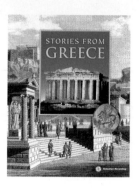

Build Background for "Stories from Greece"

STORYTELLING

In ancient Greece, people told stories called *myths*. These stories have real and imaginary characters.

▲ In ancient times, the Greeks told stories in amphitheaters like this one. The stories from ancient Greece are still told today.

▲ Some myths tell about make-believe animals, like the pegasus shown here.

Learn Key Vocabulary

Rate and Study the Words Rate how well you know each word. Then:

1. Pronounce the word. Say it aloud several times. Spell it.
2. Study the example.
3. Tell more about the word.
4. Practice it. Make the word your own.

Rating Scale

1 = I have never seen this word before.

2 = I am not sure of the word's meaning.

3 = I know this word and can teach the word's meaning to someone else.

Key Words

ancient (ān-shunt) *adjective*

Something that is **ancient** is very old. This **ancient** urn was made in Greece.

characters (ka-rak-turz) *noun*

People who are in stories are **characters**. Many times in Greek myths the **characters** are gods.

▲ Sculpture of some Greek gods

plot (plot) *noun*

The plan or main storyline is called the **plot**. King Midas is a character in one Greek story. As part of the **plot**, everything he touches turns to gold.

▲ King Midas

content (kun-tent) *adjective*

A person who is **content** is happy. King Midas was not **content** even though he lived in a big castle.

greedy (grē-dē) *adjective*

To be **greedy** is to always want more. King Midas was **greedy** for more gold.

Practice the Words With a partner, make an Expanded Meaning Map for each Key Word. Take turns asking questions like "What is a word that is like *greedy*?"

```
        Word and Definition
         /      |       \
Things that are   |    Things that are not
like the word     |    like the word
            Use the word
            in a sentence
```

Expanded Meaning Map

Listen and Read Along

FOCUS ON GENRE

Feature Article   A feature article tells the reader about one topic. A feature article is nonfiction. This article is about stories from Greece and how they are still a part of life today.

FOCUS ON COMPREHENSION

Identify Character Traits   You can learn about characters in a story by thinking about what they say and do. As you read the story of King Midas within this feature article, use the character map below to tell what he is like.

```
              ┌──────────────┐
              │  Character   │
              └──────────────┘
               │            │
      ┌────────────────┐ ┌────────────────┐
      │ What Character │ │ What Character │
      │     Does       │ │     Says       │
      └────────────────┘ └────────────────┘
```

The people of ancient Greece gathered in public places to tell stories. Many stories from Greece are still part of life today.

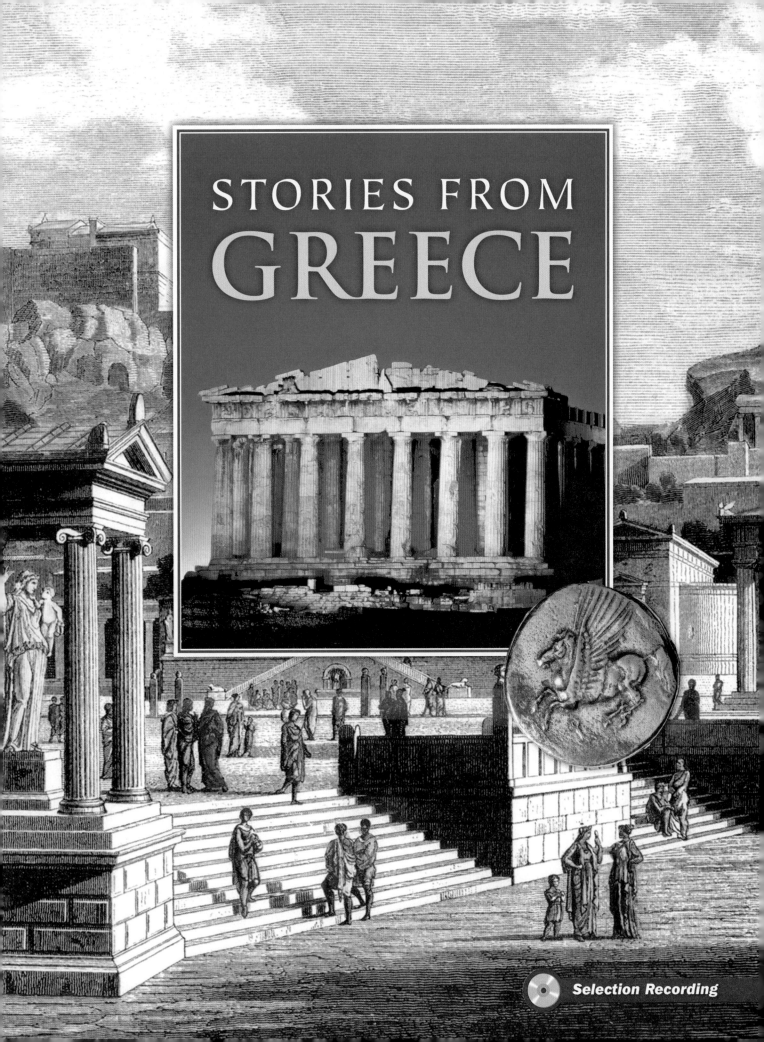

STORIES FROM
GREECE

Selection Recording

The People of Ancient Greece

The **ancient** Greeks lived more than 2,500 years ago. They loved to create stories. They told their stories to each other, and they wrote their stories in books. They also **performed** their stories as plays.

ANCIENT GREECE

▲ Greece is surrounded by water.

▼ Ancient Greeks performed plays in theaters outdoors.

Key Vocabulary
ancient *adj.*, old or from a long time ago

In Other Words
performed acted out

Myths

Many ancient Greek stories were myths. Some myths explain how or why things happened in the world. These myths often used Greek gods as **characters**. The gods had many **powers** and were able to do amazing things.

Other myths had **plots** that taught lessons about how to act. For example, one myth is about a rich king whose greed robs him of what he has.

▼ This art shows three ancient Greek gods.

King Midas

Long ago, King Midas lived in a large, beautiful home. His home was built on land with many trees and flowers. He had a beautiful daughter who loved him very much. King Midas was a rich man. Midas should have been **content** with his riches, but he was a **greedy** man.

One night, a creature named Silenus came to the kingdom. Midas knew that Silenus was friends with one of the gods. Midas gave Silenus food and let him sleep in one of his best rooms.

The god was happy that Midas had **treated Silenus so well**. The god came to Midas and said, "I will **grant you one wish**."

Midas said, "I wish that everything I touch will turn into gold."

Midas touched a bowl. It turned to gold! He smiled at his success.

▲ Midas lived in a beautiful home.

Key Vocabulary

content *adj.*, happy with what you have; not wanting more

greedy *adj.*, not happy with what you have; always wanting more

In Other Words

treated Silenus so well been nice to Silenus

grant you one wish give you one thing that you want

Before long, Midas stopped smiling. *Everything* he touched turned to gold. He could not eat because the food he touched turned to gold. He could not sleep because his bed was hard, solid gold. Midas was hungry and tired.

Midas sat in his garden, looking at the **golden flowers**. He wished he had not been greedy. His daughter sat beside him. She felt sad for him. Before Midas could stop her, she put her arm around

▲ King Midas is a character in a myth. He wanted everything he touched to turn to gold.

him. Midas watched as his beautiful daughter turned to gold.

Midas begged the god to take away his power. The god agreed. Midas was never greedy again.

▲ Midas didn't know his greed would hurt his daughter.

In Other Words
golden flowers flowers he had turned to gold

Before You Move On

1. **Details** What did Midas wish for?
2. **Character Traits** How would you describe King Midas at the beginning of the story?

Greek Stories Today

Think about the plot of the King Midas myth. What does it teach people about being greedy and being content? People can learn from the lesson of the King Midas myth. We can thank the ancient Greeks for giving us stories that are still important today.

▼ Ancient Greeks decorated pottery with pictures from their myths.

◀ Pegasus is a horse with wings.
Pegasus is in many Greek stories.

Statues of the gods showed them
as they appeared in Greek plays
and myths. ▶

▲ This painted dish shows the Greek god,
Dionysus, in a sailing boat.

Before You Move On

1. **Character Traits** How would you describe King Midas at the end of the story?

2. **Comparisons** How is the **plot** of the King Midas myth the same as the story *The Eagle and the Moon Gold*? How is it different?

Language and Content

Think About "Stories from Greece"

CHECK YOUR UNDERSTANDING

1.–2. Work with a partner to complete each item.

1. Identify Character Traits Make a character map like the one below. Complete the chart with what you know about the character King Midas.

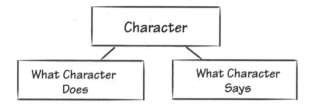

2. Sum It Up Use your character chart to retell the **ancient** story of King Midas to a partner. When was the king **greedy**? When was he **content**?

REVIEW VOCABULARY

3.–7. Read the paragraph aloud. Add the vocabulary words.

There are many old and _____ myths from Greece. The _____ in the stories are people and gods. The stories' _____ taught lessons about how to act. One myth is about King Midas. He was a very _____ king. He was not _____ with what he had. He asked a god to give him the power to turn everything he touched into gold.

Vocabulary

ancient

characters

content

greedy

plots

WRITE ABOUT MYTHS

8. Plan a myth that teaches people a lesson. Make a list that includes the **characters**, the **setting**, and the **plot**.

Writing Project

Short Story

A story has three important parts: character, setting, and plot. When you make up a story, you can invent your own people, places, and events. Some stories are like real life. Other stories are make-believe.

Anything is Possible
by Sarah Jenkins

Alex and Emma walked outside on a sunny, warm Saturday. They were going to the bike store to look for new helmets.

At the store, a woman said, "Hello." She pointed to a red bike in the window. "We're giving this bike away in ten minutes. Write your name on a ticket."

"We won't win," Emma said to Alex.

"Anything is possible," Alex said as he wrote his name on a ticket.

Emma went to look at helmets at the back of the store. Alex waited with the other kids at the front of the store. Alex knew he might not win. But he still felt excited.

Soon the woman walked to a large basket and pulled out a name. She said in a loud voice, "The winner of the new bike is Alex Sanchez!"

Emma ran over to Alex. "I can't believe it! You won!" she said.

He couldn't believe it, either. He felt very excited. That was the day he learned that anything is possible.

Use **quotation marks** to show when someone is talking.

Describe how the **characters** think and feel.

Describe the **setting**: where the story takes place.

The plot tells what happens in the story.

Write a New Story Ending

WRITING PROMPT Write a different ending for *The Eagle and the Moon Gold*. Then share it with the class.

Prewrite

When you prewrite, you gather ideas and choose your topic. You also make a plan for what you will write.

1 DECIDE WHAT TO CHANGE

Make a chart with two columns. In one column, tell what happens in the actual story. Tell what could happen in a new ending in the other column.

Here is Isabel's chart. The second column shows the ideas for her new story ending.

Actual Story Ending	New Story Ending
1. Gwa flies to the moon.	1. Gwa flies to the moon.
2. Gwa tries to get too much gold.	2. Gwa tries to get too much gold.
3. The eagle returns to Earth.	3. Yaoh and the eagle rescue Gwa.
4. Gwa melts into the moon.	4. Gwa becomes a good person.

3 ORGANIZE YOUR IDEAS

You will write your new story ending in the order that events happen. Get your plan down on paper. Draw pictures on a storyboard to plan your ending. Write a sentence under each picture to tell what happens.

Storyboard

Before sunrise, Yaoh rides to the moon.

Gwa and Yaoh ride back to Earth. They get home in the morning.

Gwa gives Yaoh a tiger. He thanks him for his help.

Gwa changes from an evil man to a good man.

Reflect

- Did you make changes to the plot?

- Do you have a clear plan?

Draft

When you draft, you begin writing. Use your ideas to begin
your draft.

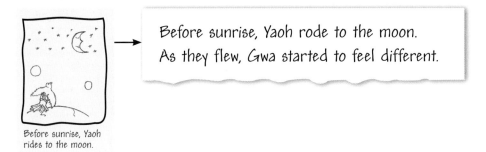

Before sunrise, Yaoh rides to the moon.

Before sunrise, Yaoh rode to the moon.
As they flew, Gwa started to feel different.

Revise

When you revise a draft, you make your writing better. First you
need to know what a reader thinks of your work. Isabel read her
story ending to a partner.

Isabel's Draft

He gave Yaoh a gift. Gwa thanked Yaoh for his help.
They got home early in the morning.

Isabel's partner says:
" I had trouble following
the order of your
sentences. Also, what
was the gift?"

Then Isabel knew she needed to make changes.

Isabel's Revision

a tiger as
He gave Yaoh a gift. Gwa thanked Yaoh for his help.
They got home early in the morning.

She added a detail
and rearranged the
sentences to put the
events in order.

Now follow these steps to revise your story ending.

1 DECIDE WHAT TO CHANGE

Read to a partner. Ask your partner to retell your story. See if
your partner can retell all the events. Do you need to add any
details? Do you need to move any text to help your writing make
sense?

2 MARK YOUR CHANGES

If you need to add text, use this mark: ∧.

If you need to move text, use this mark: ⌒.

Reflect

• Does your new
story have a
clear sequence?

• Did you
give enough
information
about the
characters?

Edit and Proofread

After you have revised your draft, it is time to check it for mistakes.

1 CHECK END MARKS

A command can end with a period or an exclamation mark.

> **EXAMPLE**   I will not steal this great gift.
>
> Come back!

2 CHECK YOUR SPELLING

Circle each word that may not be spelled right. Look it up in the dictionary or ask for help. Fix the spelling if you need to.

> **EXAMPLE**   Yaoh and Gwa were was flying on the eagle's back.

3 CHECK MECHANICS

Remember to use quotation marks to show when a character is speaking. The quotation marks belong only around the words the person says.

> **EXAMPLE**   Yaoh said, "Thank you for helping" me, eagle.

What errors did Isabel correct in her story? What errors does she still need to correct?

> Yaoh said to Gwa, "I will never be greedy again!" Gwa shared
> with his friends. He said "Share my food Share my land
> He was good to everyone in the town. Yaoh and the eagle
> helped Gwa change from an aful person to a good person.

4 MARK YOUR CHANGES

Now edit your paper. Use these marks to show your changes:

∧	℘	⌐	◯	≡	/	¶
Add.	Take out.	Replace with this.	Check spelling.	Capitalize.	Make lowercase.	Make new paragraph.

Reflect

- What kinds of errors did you find?

- What can you do to keep from making errors?

Publish, Share, and Reflect

You have finished your new story ending. Now you are ready to publish your work! When you publish your writing, you share it with others.

1 **FINISH AND DISPLAY**

Think about how your writing looks.

- Make sure your handwriting is clear.

- Add drawings to your story. Turn it into a picture book.

2 **ACT IT OUT**

There are many ways you can share your writing. For this story, try acting it out. As you perform it, think about your purpose.

- Is your story funny? Act it out in a funny way to make your audience laugh.

- Is your story serious? Use a serious tone to make the important messages clear.

Also remember these tips.

Presenting Tips

If You Are the Speaker:	If You Are the Listener:
• Change your voice to bring characters to life.	• Imagine the characters, setting, and plot.
• Move around to show the action.	• Watch and listen to hear and see the story.

Reflect

- How did using the writing process help you understand the characters in a story?

- What did you like best about writing your new ending?

This surfer works hard
to ride the wave.

My Heart Rate

Beats per Minute

200

150

100

50

0   10   20

Seconds of Exercise

PERSONAL BEST

Surfers and other athletes work hard.

Their hearts beat fast. How is your heart?

Sit in a chair and take your pulse.

Hop on one foot for 20 seconds.

Then take your pulse again.

What do you notice?

In This Unit

▶ **Language Development**

▶ **Language and Literacy**

▶ **Language and Content**
   Social Science

▶ **Writing Project**

Vocabulary
- The Body
- Sports
- Key Vocabulary

Language Functions
- Ask for and Give Information
- Express Thanks

Grammar
- Present Tense Verbs
- Pronouns

Reading
- Variant Vowels and Consonants
- High Frequency Words
- Comprehension: Main Idea and Details
- Text Features: Sidebars

Writing
- Procedural Text

Body Basics

▶ **Language: Ask for and Give Information**

Listen and chant. CD

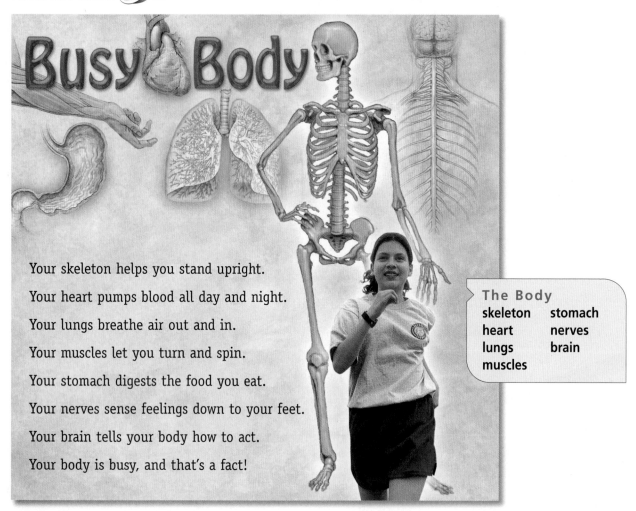

Your skeleton helps you stand upright.

Your heart pumps blood all day and night.

Your lungs breathe air out and in.

Your muscles let you turn and spin.

Your stomach digests the food you eat.

Your nerves sense feelings down to your feet.

Your brain tells your body how to act.

Your body is busy, and that's a fact!

The Body

skeleton   stomach

heart   nerves

lungs   brain

muscles

EXPRESS YOURSELF ▶ ASK FOR AND GIVE INFORMATION

Ask a partner a question about each of these parts of the body. Answer your partner's questions in complete sentences.

1. skeleton   3. lungs   5. stomach
2. heart   4. muscles   6. brain

EXAMPLE **1.** What does the skeleton do?
It supports your body and
protects the heart and lungs.

<u>7.–10.</u> **Tell a partner 4 facts about the body. Then listen as your partner tells you 4 facts about the body.**

EXAMPLE **7.** Muscles help you move.

Our Workout Routine

▶ **Present Tense Verbs**

Use present tense verbs to tell what happens all the time.

We always **exercise** to stay healthy.

Every morning we **run** two miles.

We **stretch** before every run.

Every day we **make** our bodies strong.

BUILD SENTENCES

Say a sentence for each picture below. Choose words from each column.

| Each Every | day morning afternoon Saturday week month | I the boys the girls the people the athletes they | bike. exercise. play. practice. run. swim. |

EXAMPLE **1.** Every afternoon the girls practice.

1.  **2.**  **3.**  **4.**

WRITE SENTENCES

5.–8. With a partner, take turns telling each other about a sport or an exercise you play or do all the time. Then work together to write 4 sentences about the sport or exercise.

EXAMPLE **5.** Every day I play basketball.

Language Development

Meet the Athletes

▶ **Vocabulary: Sports**
▶ **Language: Express Thanks**

She **bowls**.

They play **football**.

They play **tennis**.

She plays **basketball**.

ORAL LANGUAGE PRACTICE ▶ EXPRESS THANKS

<u>1.–3.</u> **Who's talking?** CD

Listen. Point to the correct athlete. Act out the roles you
hear on the CD. Thank your teammate, coach, or another player.

WRITTEN PRACTICE

<u>4.</u> You are a champion athlete and just won an award.
Write a thank-you speech. Tell who helped you play the sport so well.

EXAMPLE **4.** Thank you for the basketball trophy. My coach
helped me a lot. I also want to thank my teammates.
We have the best basketball team in the city!

Watch Them Play

▶ **Pronouns**

Use the correct pronoun when you talk about a person, place, or thing.

goalie

Use these pronouns to tell who does the action.

I	you	he	she	it	we	they

He kicked the ball.

Use these pronouns after an action verb or after a word like _to_, _for_, or _with_.

me	you	him	her	it	us	them

The goalie missed **it**.
The goalie kicks the ball t̲o̲ **her**.

BUILD SENTENCES

Say each sentence. Add the correct pronoun.

EXAMPLE **1.** Our coach talked to us at half time. She gave us a plan.

1. Our coach talked to us at half time. _____**(She/Her)**_____ gave us a plan.
2. Randy got ready. I passed the ball to ___**(he/him)**___ .
3. ___**(He/Him)**___ missed the ball!
4. The other team got the ball. ___**(They/Them)**___ raced away.
5. We chased ___**(they/them)**___ .
6. Our goalie got the ball. She kicked it to ___**(I/me)**___ .
7. I saw Farnez. I shouted to ___**(she/her)**___ .
8. Another player knocked ___**(she/her)**___ down!
9. I had no choice. ___**(I/me)**___ shot at the goal.
10. We scored! The crowd cheered for ___**(we/us)**___ .

WRITE SENTENCES

11.–15. Write 5 sentences. Tell about a sport you like to watch.
Use at least 3 pronouns.

EXAMPLES **11.** I watch hockey with Hari Amrit.

12. She likes the team from San Jose.

Language Development

Listen and Read Along

FOCUS ON GENRE

Science Essay A science essay is a short piece of nonfiction. It tells about one topic that has to do with science. This science essay tells how parts of the body work.

FOCUS ON VOCABULARY

Body Words You have been learning words like the ones below. Use these words as you talk about *Body Works*. Collect more words to put in the web.

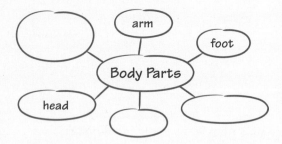

THEME BOOK

Read this science essay about how the body works.

BODY WORKS

by Janine Wheeler

Blood cells are constantly moving through your body.

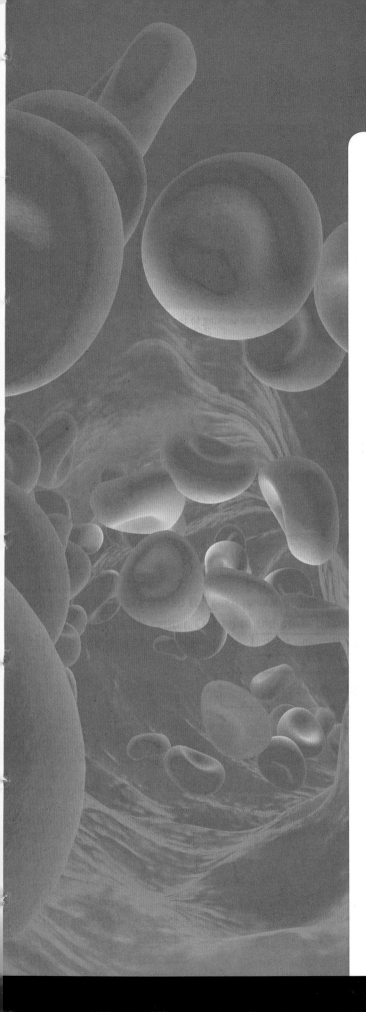

Think About *Body Works*

IDENTIFY MAIN IDEA AND DETAILS

Work in a group. Make diagrams to show the main ideas and details in *Body Works*. Follow these steps.

1 Read pages 6–7 of *Body Works*. What is the most important idea in this section? Write it inside a box, like this:

Main Idea
The skeleton helps your body work.

2 What details in these pages help to support, or explain, the main idea? Write them in boxes connected to your main-idea box, like this:

Main Idea
The skeleton helps your body work.

Detail	Detail	Detail
It is the body's frame.	It is made of bones.	It gives the body shape.

3 Make diagrams for more sections of *Body Works* to show the main idea and details.

    The Muscles   pages 8–9
    The Blood   pages 12–13
    The Lungs   pages 14–15

4 Use your completed diagrams to tell the class what you learned about the body.

Read on Your Own

FOCUS ON GENRE

Newspaper Article A newspaper article tells about a recent event. A news article is nonfiction. Quotations in the article show what a person says. This article tells about the Special Olympics.

FOCUS ON WORDS

Words with Hard and Soft *c* and *g* and Silent Consonants When you read and come to a word you don't know, blend the sounds together to read it. You just learned about words with the letters *c* and *g*. You also learned about words with these silent consonant spellings:

wr	**kn**
gn	**mb**

thumb

High Frequency Words Say these words as whole words when you read.

friends	**talked**
asked	**if**
walked	**even**
trees	**while**
air	**such**

THE TIMES

Monday, August 4, 2008

Summer Games Are a Big Hit

People show their athletic abilities at the Summer Games.

GARDEN CITY— The Special Olympics State Summer Games were such a big hit this weekend at Bridge Park. About 3,000 athletes, coaches, and volunteers came from around the state. Tents were set up in a field by the trees. It became an Olympic village. People walked to other tents and talked with each other.

The rock band Thumbs Up was asked to give a concert at the edge of the park to open the games. A huge crowd came to see the band. Some lucky fans even got to go on stage and sing with the band.

People had fun listening to a rock band.

The next day, the athletes took deep breaths of air. They competed in different sports. They rode bikes, ran, threw a softball, and raced in wheelchairs. Cindy Collins, a 20-year-old from Garden City, won the wheelchair race.

"My next goal is to win at the World Games," Cindy said. "I'm in training now. I move my wrists to make them strong. I also race around traffic cones. If I knock a cone over, I try again."

"I met so many nice people while I was here," Sam Wong, another winner, said. "We're all good friends now!"

Athletes try for gold at the Special Olympics in Bridge Park.

Think About "Summer Games Are a Big Hit"

CHECK YOUR UNDERSTANDING

Write the paragraph. Add the missing words or phrases to tell the main idea and important details in the news article.

EXAMPLE **1–2.** The article is about the Special Olympics State Summer
Games in Garden City.

The article is about the ___(1)___ ___(2)___ State Summer Games in
Garden City. About 3,000 athletes, ___(3)___, and volunteers came for the
games. They stayed in tents in the Olympic ___(4)___. On opening day, a
band gave a ___(5)___ in the park. The next day, the athletes competed.
They rode bikes, ran, threw a softball, and ___(6)___ in wheelchairs. The
winner of the wheelchair race was ___(7)___ ___(8)___.

EXPAND YOUR VOCABULARY

Read the sentences.

9. The runners <u>race</u> around the track.

10. Crowds of people watch them and <u>cheer</u>.

11. Everyone has a <u>good</u> time.

**Work with a group to think of other words that mean *race, cheer,*
and *good*. Make a list. Then say each sentence with a new word.**

EXAMPLE

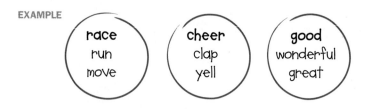

WRITE ABOUT SPORTS

<u>12.</u> **Choose a sport. Give information about it.**

EXAMPLE **12.** You need two teams to play softball.
You use a bat. You use a ball. You use mitts.
One team is at bat.
The other team is in the field.
Players hit the ball and run around the bases.

Success in Social Science

▶ **Learn About Captions**

Captions

A caption is a group of words or sentences. The words or sentences tell about a photograph or an illustration.

caption — Delores "Snooky" Doyle, Shirley Burkovich, and Delores "Pickles" Dries meet Honorary Member Mamie "Peanuts" Johnson at the All-American Girls Professional Baseball League Reunion in 2006.

Read the article. Then do the Exercise.

Women Play Baseball

The sport of baseball stopped when many men went to fight in World War II. In 1943, a new baseball league started: the All-American Girls Professional Baseball League. Over 600 women played for the league from 1943 to 1954.

In 1943, the South Bend Blue Sox won the very first league championship for the All-American Girls Professional Baseball League.

Exercise

Write a caption for the photo below.

Some people did not think girls and women could play baseball as well as men did. But as this photo shows, the women did play well. On April 8, 1948, Chicago player Dorothy Harrell jumped to catch the ball.

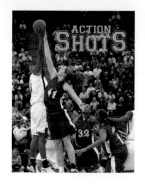

Build Background for "Action Shots"

SPORTS

How do female and male athletes look in photographs? Sports writer
Jane Gottesman asked that question.

◄ These basketball players look
like talented athletes.

▲ These women do not look like talented athletes
in this photograph.

Learn Key Vocabulary

Rate and Study the Words Rate how well you know each word. Then:

1. Pronounce the word. Say it aloud several times. Spell it.
2. Study the example.
3. Tell more about the word.
4. Practice it. Make the word your own.

Key Words

athlete (ath-lēt) *noun*

An **athlete** likes to exercise or play sports. These **athletes** play hockey.

Synonym: player

compete (cum-pēt) *verb*

When athletes **compete**, they try to do better than other athletes. These athletes **compete** against each other in speed skating.

Synonym: contend

female (fē-māl) *adjective*

Female athletes are girls and women. This **female** athlete rides a snowboard.

Synonym: woman

male (māl) *adjective*

Male athletes are boys and men. These soccer players are all **male**.

Synonym: man

photograph (fō-tō-graf) *noun*

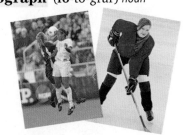

A **photograph** is a picture that is created by a camera and film. Jane Gottesman collected many **photographs** of female athletes.

Synonym: picture

Practice the Words With a partner, make a Vocabulary Study Card for each Key Word.

Write the word.

front

> compete

Tell what the word means and use it in a sentence.

back

> try to win
>
> I can compete in a race.

Use the cards to quiz your partner. Take turns answering.

Language and Content

Listen and Read Along

FOCUS ON GENRE

Article An article tells facts and information about people or an event. It is nonfiction. This article is about photographs of women in sports.

FOCUS ON COMPREHENSION

Main Idea and Details The main idea tells what a selection is about. The details give information about the main idea. As you read "Action Shots," look for the details that tell about the main idea. Use a main idea web like the one below to help you keep track of the details.

Female athletes play basketball and many other sports.

ACTION SHOTS

Selection Recording

A Photo Problem

Jane Gottesman will never forget the day that she read about the 1994 Winter **Olympics**. When she opened her newspaper on that day, she read that both Picabo Street and Alberto Tomba had won silver medals in skiing. There was a **photograph** of Street smiling at the camera and wearing a cowboy hat. In the photograph of Tomba racing, Tomba looked like an **athlete**. Picabo did not. That really **bothered Gottesman**.

Picabo Street and Alberto Tomba at the 1994 Winter Olympics.

Key Vocabulary

photograph *n.*, an image produced by a camera
athlete *n.*, a person who exercises or plays a sport

In Other Words

Olympics skiing competition
bothered Gottesman made Gottesman angry

Sports writer Jane Gottesman noticed that photos often showed male athletes playing sports and female athletes standing still.

Before You Move On

1. **Main Idea and Details** How did Jane feel when she looked at the **photographs** in the newspaper? How do you know?
2. **Make Comparisons** Look at the photos of **athletes**. How are they the same? How are they different?

OLD IDEAS ABOUT WOMEN IN SPORTS

Why are **male** and **female** athletes shown in different ways? Gottesman says it is because of old-fashioned beliefs. For many years, people thought that women should not play sports. People thought sports were for men only. For many years, female athletes were not **taken seriously**.

In 1924, Sonia Henie began to change the way people saw women in sports. Many other women athletes continued to show their strength as athletes. Today, people know that both men and women can **compete**.

◄ Speed skating is a sport at the Winter Olympics.

This table shows when men and women first competed in each Winter Olympic Sport.

Winter Olympics Sport	Men	Women
Alpine Skiing	1936	1936
Biathlon	1924	1992
Bobsleigh	1924	2002
Cross-Country Skiing	1924	1952
Curling	1924	1998
Figure Skating	1924	1924
Freestyle Skiing	1992	1992
Ice Hockey	1924	1998
Luge	1964	1964
Nordic Combined	1924	–
Short Track Speed Skating	1992	1992
Skeleton	1928	2002
Ski Jumping	1924	–
Snowboard	1998	1998
Speed Skating	1924	1960

1. For each sport, calculate the number of years that passed between the first men's competition and the first women's.
2. Make a bar graph that shows your findings.

Key Vocabulary

male *adj.*, having to do with a boy or man
female *adj.*, having to do with a girl or woman
compete *v.*, to try to do better than another person

In Other Words

taken seriously respected

SONIA HENIE BREAKS THROUGH

Sonia Henie was 11 years old when she competed in the 1924 Olympics. Before then, figure skaters did one move at a time. During the **competition**, Henie put the different skating moves together and performed them to music. She did jumps and spins. She was athletic. Henie impressed the judges and shocked **the public**.

Although she didn't win a medal in 1924, Henie won gold medals in figure skating in 1928, 1932, and 1936. She also won ten world championships. Her athletic style changed the sport of figure skating. In the process, she helped change people's minds about what female athletes could do.

▲ Figure skater Sonia Henie showed that women could be great athletes.

In Other Words
competition event
the public people watching her

Before You Move On

1. **Main Idea and Details** What is a reason why photos of **male** and **female athletes** are different?
2. **Personal Opinion** How would you like to look in a sports photo?

JANE'S PROJECT

Gottesman started to study sports photos in **the media.** She counted the photos of men. She counted the photos of women. There were many more photos of men. Also, there were not many photos of women as they played sports.

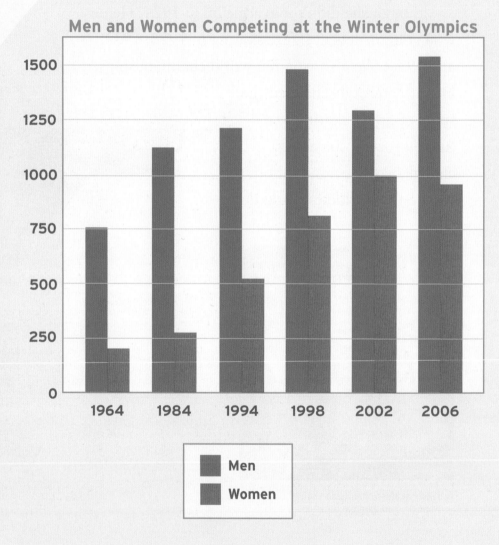

Men and Women Competing at the Winter Olympics

In Other Words

the media newspapers, magazines, radio, and TV

LOOKS IN A BOOK

Gottesman began to **collect** photos of women in sports. She looked for photos that showed women athletes while they competed. After a few years, Gottesman put the photos together into a book. She published the book to show others what she saw—women are strong athletes.

Next time you see a photo of an athlete in a newspaper or magazine or on television or the Internet, think of Jane Gottesman. She worked to change the way that we look at women in sports. Did she succeed?

▲ Picabo Street is a famous skier.

▲ Michelle Kwan is a figure skater who has competed in many events.

▲ U.S. hockey player Sarah Tueting (left) helped her team win a gold medal at the Olympics.

▲ Tricia Byrnes jumps in the air as she competes in a snowboarding event.

In Other Words
collect gather

Before You Move On

1. **Personal Opinion** Are you interested in reading Jane Gottesman's book? Tell why or why not.
2. **Cause and Effect** What does Jane hope her book will do?

Think About "Action Shots"

CHECK YOUR UNDERSTANDING

1.–2. Work with a partner to complete each item.

1. **Main Idea and Details** Make a web like the one below. Then complete the web using information from the selection.

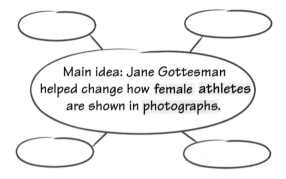

Main idea: Jane Gottesman helped change how female athletes are shown in photographs.

2. **Sum It Up** Use your web to tell about what Jane Gottesman did.

REVIEW VOCABULARY

3.–7. Read the paragraph aloud. Add the vocabulary words.

> Both men and women _____ in sports. Jane Gottesman saw a _____ of a female _____ named Picabo Street. Gottesman wondered why _____ athletes looked different in photographs than _____ athletes.

Vocabulary
athlete
compete
female
male
photograph

WRITE ABOUT SPORTS

8. Write about a sport that you like or one that you would like to try.

Procedure

A procedure tells the steps you use to do something. When you write a procedure, write the steps in the order they should be done.

PROCEDURE

How to Do a Sit-Up

Write a procedure in **steps** to make it easy to read.

Step 1: First, lie on your back on the floor. Bend your knees and keep your feet on the floor. Make sure your back is flat on the floor.

Step 2: Put your hands behind your head to give your head and neck support.

Step 3: Next, slowly lift your body up towards your knees. Let your middle do the work, not your arms.

Step 4: Finally, lower your body back to the ground slowly.

Use **order words** like *first*, *next*, and *finally*.

Doing sit-ups is good exercise.

Writing Project

Write a Procedure

WRITING PROMPT What are some of your healthy habits? Write a procedure telling a friend how to do an exercise that you enjoy.

Prewrite

When you prewrite, you gather ideas and choose your topic. You also make a plan for what you will write. Follow these steps.

1 CHOOSE A TOPIC

Think about all of the exercises you do. Which exercises could you explain how to do in writing? Which exercises do you think other people might like to do also?

2 ORGANIZE YOUR IDEAS

To write a procedure, you need to give instructions step-by-step. Write each step in the exercise in order. Use a sequence chain. Practice the exercise to test your sequence chain. Make sure you do not leave any steps out of the procedure.

Hiro made this Sequence Chain to show how to do push-ups. Did he forget any steps?

Sequence Chain

Push-Ups

1. lie on stomach on floor, put toes on ground
↓
2. put hands flat on ground, bend elbows
↓
3. push body up with arms
↓
4. lower body almost back to the ground

Reflect
- Did you pick a good topic?
- Did you include every step?

Draft

When you draft, you begin writing. Use the ideas you gathered in your sequence chain to begin your draft.

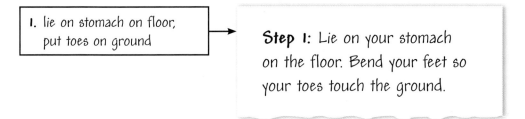

| 1. lie on stomach on floor, put toes on ground |

Step 1: Lie on your stomach on the floor. Bend your feet so your toes touch the ground.

Revise

When you revise a draft, you make your writing better. Stay focused. Procedures only include important details. Take out details that are not important.

Test your focus. Have a partner follow the procedure.

Hiro's Draft

Step 2: Next, put your hands flat on the ground. Sometimes the floor is cold. Bend your elbows.

Hiro's partner says:

"Is the temperature of the floor important?"

Then Hiro knew he needed to make changes.

Hiro's Revision

Step 2: Next, put your hands flat on the ground. ~~Sometimes the floor is cold.~~ Bend your elbows.

He took out a sentence that didn't give instructions.

Now follow these steps to revise your procedure.

① DECIDE WHAT TO CHANGE

Read to a partner. Ask your partner to follow your procedure. See if your partner can demonstrate all the steps. Do you need to take out any text that is not important?

② MARK YOUR CHANGES

If you need to take out text, use this mark: ⌿.

Reflect

- Did you stay focused?
- Can the reader follow the steps?

Edit and Proofread

After you have revised your draft, it is time to check it for mistakes.

1 CHECK YOUR PRONOUNS

Some pronouns are used only after verbs and words like *to, for,* or *with*. Remember to use pronouns correctly in your writing.

> **EXAMPLE** Stand across from your partner. Pass the ball to her.

2 CHECK YOUR SPELLING

Circle each word that may be misspelled. Look it up in the dictionary or ask for help. Fix the spelling if you need to.

3 CHECK FOR CAPITAL LETTERS

Procedures usually include commands. Like any other sentence, commands begin with a capital letter. Remember to capitalize the first word in each sentence.

> **EXAMPLE** Stand up straight.
>
> Hold your arms out to your sides.

What errors did Hiro correct in his procedure? What errors does he still need to correct?

Pronouns	
I	me
you	you
he	him
she	her
it	it
we	us
they	them

Step 3: <u>t</u>hen start to straighten your arms. Push your body up with they. Hold ~~they~~ them in ~~plase~~ place.

Step 4: Finally, lower your body back to the ground. keep each fut bent.

---

4 MARK YOUR CHANGES

Now edit your paper. Use these marks to show your changes:

∧	ℒ	⌐	◯	≡	/	¶
Add.	Take out.	Replace with this.	Check spelling.	Capitalize.	Make lowercase.	Make new paragraph.

Reflect
- What kinds of errors did you find?
- What can you do to keep from making errors?

Publish, Share, and Reflect

You have finished your procedure. Now you are ready to publish your work! When you publish your writing, you put it in final form to share with others. Follow these steps.

1 FINISH AND DISPLAY

Think about how your writing looks.

- Make sure your handwriting is clear.
- Add drawings to show steps in your procedure.
- Make a class exercise book. Create a table of contents for your exercise book.

2 DEMONSTRATE

There are many ways you can share your writing. For this procedure, try demonstrating it. As you follow the steps, think about your audience.

Ask your listeners if they have seen or done your exercise. As you listen, choose a focus.

- If you have seen or done the exercise, focus on how to do it better.
- If you have not seen or done the exercise, go slowly and focus on each step. Ask questions.

Also remember these tips.

Presenting Tips

If You Are the Speaker:	If You Are the Listener:
• Read loudly and clearly.	• Follow each step.
• Stop for a moment after each step.	• Ask questions.

Reflect

- What have you learned about writing steps in a process?
- Which exercise do you enjoy doing the most? Why?

The pictures show music from the 5 different parts of the United States.

MIDWEST/Wisconsin

MIDWEST/Illinois

NORTHEAST/New York

WEST/California

WEST
MIDWEST
NORTHEAST
SOUTHWEST
SOUTHEAST

SOUTHEAST/Kentucky

SOUTHWEST/Arizona

WEST/Hawaii

SOUTHEAST/Georgia

This Land Is Our Land

There are many kinds of music played in the United States. Listen to some. Which music do you like the most? On a map, find the place where it is played. CD

In This Unit

▶ **Language Development**

▶ **Language and Literacy**

▶ **Language and Content**
Social Science

▶ **Writing Project**

Vocabulary
- American History
- Landforms and Bodies of Water
- Geography
- Key Vocabulary

Language Functions
- Ask and Answer Questions
- Give Directions

Grammar
- Questions with *How?* and *Why?*
- Capitalization: Proper Nouns (geographical names)

Reading
- Multisyllabic Words
- High Frequency Words
- Comprehension: Classify
- Text Features: Product Maps

Writing
- Biography

Language Development

Who Built America?

▶ **Language: Ask and Answer Questions**

Listen and chant. CD

The Builders of Our Nation

The Pilgrims sailed across the sea
To practice their religion in Plymouth Colony.

Colonists built new American towns.
They won their liberty from the British crown.

Explorers traveled across the land
So our growing nation could expand.

To reach the Pacific, in long wagon trains,
The pioneers traveled from the golden plains.

Immigrants escaped from hunger and strife
To seek work, education, and a better life.

All of us here in our nation today
Are the many faces of the U.S. of A.

People in History
Pilgrims
colonists
explorers
pioneers
immigrants

EXPRESS YOURSELF ▶ ASK AND ANSWER QUESTIONS

<u>1.–6.</u> **Work with a partner. Ask each other 6 questions about the chant. Then answer your partner's questions.**

EXAMPLE **1.** Who sailed across the sea? The Pilgrims sailed across the sea.

Question Words	
who	when
what	where

<u>7.–12.</u> **Imagine you are a Pilgrim and have just arrived at Plymouth Colony. Ask a partner 3 questions about the new American towns. Then switch roles.**

EXAMPLE **7.** Where did the Pilgrims practice their religion?

People of America

▶ Questions With *How?* and *Why?*

You can use the word *how* or *why* to ask a question.

Use *how* to ask about the way people do something.

How did the pioneers travel?
They traveled in wagons.

Use *why* to ask for a reason.

Why did the pioneers travel west?

They traveled west **because** they wanted land to farm.

You can use *because* to answer a question with *why*.

BUILD QUESTIONS

Read each answer. Then ask 2 questions to go with the answer: *How* _____? *Why* _____?

EXAMPLE 1. How do scientists do experiments?
Why do they do experiments carefully?

1.

Scientists do experiments carefully because they want to get correct results.

2.

Soldiers fight bravely because they want to protect their country.

3.

Most cowboys ride horses very well because they spend a lot of time on horseback.

4.

Farmers use machines to harvest their crops because machines work quickly.

WRITE ANSWERS

Work with a partner. Use the chant on page 210 to find the answer to each question below. Take turns writing an answer as a complete sentence. Use the word *because*.

EXAMPLE 5. The Pilgrims left home because they wanted to practice their religion.

5. Why did the Pilgrims leave home?
6. Why did explorers travel across the land?
7. Why did immigrants come to the United States?
8. Why did pioneers leave the plains?

Our Natural Treasures

▶ **Vocabulary: Landforms and Bodies of Water**
▶ **Language: Give Directions**

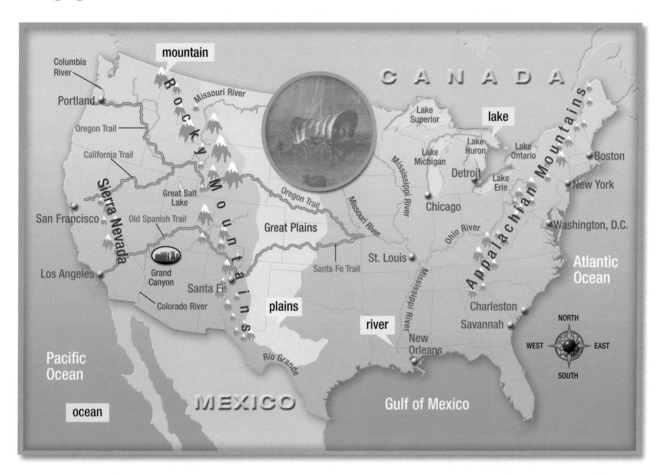

ORAL LANGUAGE PRACTICE ▶ GIVE DIRECTIONS

<u>1.–2.</u> **Who's talking?** CD

Listen. Two students are giving directions to the pioneers.
What route is each student describing? Trace it on the map.

WRITTEN PRACTICE

<u>3.</u> Work with a partner. Draw the outline of the United States. Mark where you
are now. Where do you want to go? Label the landforms along the way. Have your
partner label the cities. Then take turns writing directions to get there.

EXAMPLE **3.** How to go to Washington, D.C., in the northeastern part of the country:

- Start in New Orleans. Go north along the Mississippi River.
- Follow the Ohio River east. Keep going east until you get to Washington, D.C.

Americans from Other Lands

▶ **Capitalization: Proper Nouns**

A **proper noun** names a particular person, place, or thing.

Capitalize the proper names of:	Examples
countries, cities, and states	John Muir was born in **Scotland** in 1838. He moved to **Portage, Wisconsin**, when he was 11 years old.
bodies of water	Muir walked 1,000 miles to the **Gulf of Mexico**.
landforms	Muir studied the plants and animals of the **Yosemite Valley**.

STUDY SENTENCES

Say the sentences. Look at the <u>underlined</u> words. Do they need capital letters? If so, tell why.

EXAMPLE **1.** *Guangzhou* needs a capital letter. It is the name of a city.

1. I. M. Pei was born in <u>guangzhou</u>, China.
2. In 1935, he came to <u>massachusetts</u> to study <u>architecture</u>.
3. One of the buildings he designed is at the foot of the <u>rocky mountains</u>.
4. Another is next to <u>boston harbor</u>.
5. He designed other buildings across the <u>country</u>.

6. Alexandra Nechita was born in <u>romania</u>.
7. Now the young artist lives in Los Angeles, California, near the <u>pacific ocean</u>.
8. She designed a giant angel sculpture in the <u>city</u>.
9. Her other artwork is in galleries from <u>hawaii</u> to <u>new york</u>.
10. When she was 12 years old, she met the Emperor of <u>japan</u>.

WRITE SENTENCES

<u>11.–20.</u> Write the sentences above with the correct capitalization.

EXAMPLE **11.** I. M. Pei was born in Guangzhou, China.

Listen and Read Along

FOCUS ON GENRE

Song A song can be a fun way to tell a story. The words are called lyrics. This song tells about different groups of people throughout American history.

FOCUS ON VOCABULARY

Words About People in American History You have been learning words like the ones below. Use these words as you talk about *All Across America*. Collect more words to put in the web.

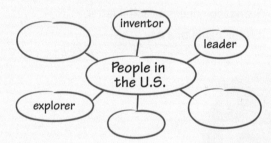

People in the U.S.
- inventor
- leader
- explorer

THEME BOOK

Read or sing this song about the many different people who built the U.S.A.

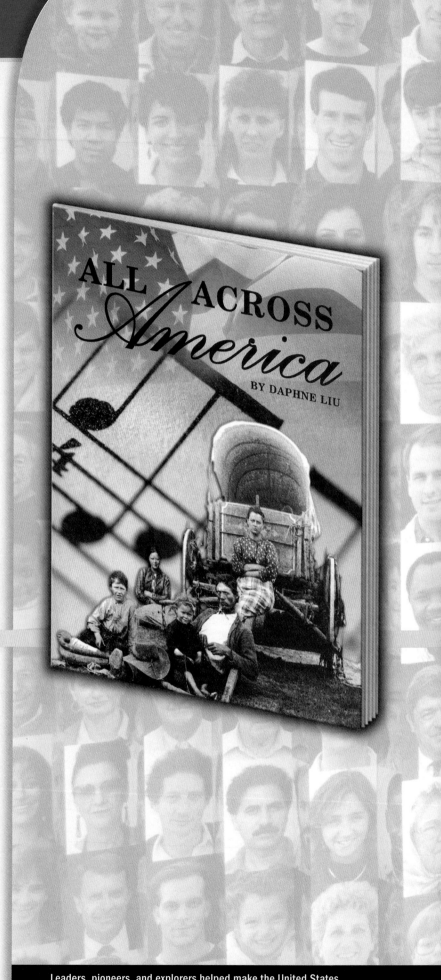

Leaders, pioneers, and explorers helped make the United States what it is today.

Think About
All Across America

CLASSIFY

Make a category chart about the people in *All Across America*. Follow these steps.

1 Draw a chart with two columns, like the one below. In column 1, write the categories of people from pages 2–3 of *All Across America*.

Category	Examples
explorers	
pioneers	
cowboys	
inventors	

2 Read the book again. As you read, put the name of each person you read about in the correct category. (Some people may belong in more than one category.)

Category	Examples
explorers	Meriwether Lewis, William Clark, Sacagawea, York, John Wesley Powell, Sally Ride

3 Compare your finished category chart with a classmate's chart. Did you list the same people? Talk about the people you included in the chart.

High Frequency Words

REVIEW HIGH FREQUENCY WORDS

Read the words aloud. Which word goes in each sentence?

lives	life
my	by
no	knows

1. This girl _____ in Alaska.
2. Her home is _____ a frozen lake.
3. She _____ how to keep warm.

A thick coat keeps this Alaskan girl warm.

LEARN NEW WORDS

Study these words. Say them as whole words when you read.

state	Alaska is the largest **state** in the United States.
than	It is much bigger **than** Texas.
high	Alaska has very **high** mountains.
million	It has about 51 **million** acres of parks.
form	The Aleutian Islands **form** a long chain of islands.

PRACTICE

Answer the question.

4. Which words end in **n**? _____ _____
5. Which words have 4 letters? _____ _____ _____
6. Which word has the most letters? _____
7. Which word has 2 **t**'s? _____

8. **Work with a partner. Write each new word on a card. Mix both sets of cards together. Turn them so the words are down. Then:**

• Turn over 2 cards.
• Spell the words. Are they the same?
• If so, use the word in a sentence and keep the cards. If not, turn them over again.
• Take turns. The player with more cards at the end wins.

EXAMPLE 8.

state

state

s-t-a-t-e
s-t-a-t-e
I live in the state
of Texas.

More High Frequency Words

How to Learn a New Word

- Look at the word.
- Listen to the word.
- Listen to the word in a sentence. What does it mean?
- Say the word.
- Spell the word.
- Say the word again.

REVIEW HIGH FREQUENCY WORDS

Read the words aloud. Which word goes in the sentence?

groups	words
see	says
move	read

1. There are many _____ of people in the U.S.
2. People come to the U.S. to ____ the sights.
3. You can ____ about the history of the U.S.

LEARN NEW WORDS

Study these words. Say them as whole words when you read.

sea	The Aleutian Islands stretch far out into the **sea**.
near	Little Diomede Island in Alaska is **near** Russia.
miles	It is only 2.5 **miles** away!
explore	To **explore** Juneau, the capital city, go in summer.
earth	Alaska is one of the coldest places on **Earth**.

PRACTICE

Answer the question.

4. Which word has an **x**? _____
5. Which words have 5 letters? _____ _____
6. Which words start with an **e**? _____ _____
7. Which words have the letters **ea** in them? _____ _____ _____

<u>8.</u> **Work with a partner. Write each new word on a card. Mix both sets of cards together. Turn them so the words are down. Then:**

- Turn over 2 cards.
- Spell the words. Are they the same?
- If so, use the word in a sentence and keep the cards. If not, turn them over again.
- Take turns. The player with more cards at the end wins.

EXAMPLE 8.

sea

sea

s-e-a
s-e-a
There are islands
in the sea.

Reading and Spelling

▶ **Multisyllabic Words**

Listen and learn. CD

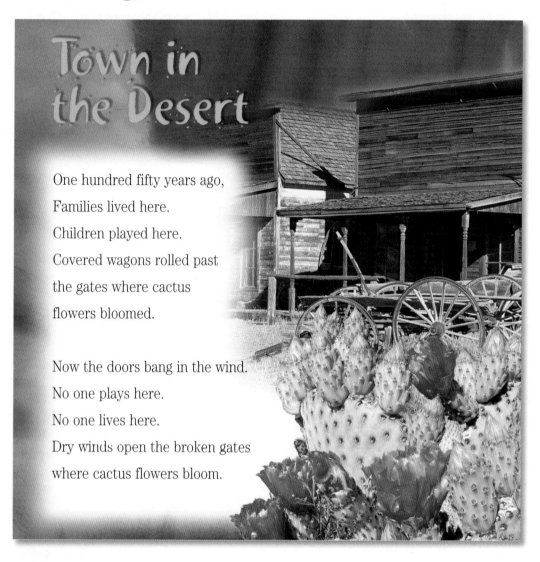

Town in the Desert

One hundred fifty years ago,
Families lived here.
Children played here.
Covered wagons rolled past
the gates where cactus
flowers bloomed.

Now the doors bang in the wind.
No one plays here.
No one lives here.
Dry winds open the broken gates
where cactus flowers bloom.

STUDY LONG WORDS

How should you divide each word into syllables? Look for the pattern.

1.	2.	3.	4.	5.
c̲a̲ctu̲s̲	h̲u̲ndr̲e̲d	o̲p̲en gate	w̲a̲g̲o̲n	a̲sl̲e̲ep

READING STRATEGY

Follow these steps to read long words.

1 Look for the pattern of vowels and consonants in the middle of the word.

canyon *There are 2 consonants between 2 vowels.*

music *There is one consonant between 2 vowels.*

2 Blend the syllables together to read the word.

You can break words like music either way. See which way sounds right

canyon
▲
can + yon = canyon

music   or   music
      ▲   ▲
mu + sic = music

*This one sounds right. The **u** is **long**.*

READING PRACTICE

Use what you learned to read the sentences.

1. About one hundred fifty years ago, California became the thirty-first state.
2. Adults and children traveled over 2,000 miles to build homes there.
3. They built cabins in the high mountains and in the low deserts.
4. They built farms all across the open lands.
5. They built cities near the lakes, the rivers, and along the coast.
6. Today, millions of people enjoy living in this sunny state.

SPELLING PRACTICE

7.–11. Now write the sentences that your teacher reads.

WORD WORK

12.–20. Read the newspaper article. Find all the words with two syllables. Make a chart. Write the words under the words with the same pattern.

Boy Wins Essay Contest

Chen Lu is on his way to Boston! He won first place in an essay contest called "This Land Is Our Land." The contest was open to all students in grades 5 through 8. Chen won a medal and a visit to Boston. Chen's essay, "The Broken Wagon," was based on a book he read.

canyon ▲	event ▲	cabin ▲
12.	15.	18.
13.	16.	19.
14.	17.	20.

EXAMPLE **12.** essay

Read on Your Own

FOCUS ON GENRE

Travel Article   A travel article tells facts and details about a place to visit. A travel article is nonfiction. This travel article tells about the Grand Canyon.

FOCUS ON WORDS

Multisyllabic Words   When you read and come to a longer word you don't know, look for the patterns of consonants and vowels in the word. Break the word into syllables and then blend the syllables to read the word.

wagon

High Frequency Words   Say these words as whole words when you read.

state	sea
than	near
high	miles
million	explore
form	earth

DEEP
CANYON

What could be more exciting than to go back a million years in time? A visit to the Grand Canyon in the state of Arizona will take you there. It took the Colorado River millions of years to cut through the land and form the Grand Canyon.

The river cut so deep into the earth that you can see nine thick layers of rock. These layers sit one on top of the other, like pancakes. The bottom layer is the oldest. At this level, you may see some of the oldest rocks on Earth.

The Grand Canyon is located in the northwestern corner of Arizona.

◄ The last layer of rock in the Grand Canyon is the oldest rock on Earth.

There are high waterfalls in the Grand Canyon.

"Relaxing in the Grand Canyon is easy!"

There is a lot to do in the Grand Canyon. Take a raft across rapids where the river runs fast. Enjoy a picnic near a high waterfall. Go to the North Rim that is 8,000 feet above sea level. Explore 400 miles of trails. Look for tiny birds.

Hike

Raft

Camp

At the end of the day, relax in a cabin or a tent. There is no limit to what you can see and do in the Grand Canyon!

Language and Literacy

Think About "Deep Canyon"

<u>1.</u> **Make a concept map like the one below. Work with a partner to add other details. Use the finished map to discuss what you learned about the Grand Canyon.**

The Grand Canyon

What can you see there?

layers of rock

What can you do there?

ride a boat

EXPAND YOUR VOCABULARY

Work with a partner. Read the first sentence aloud. Have your partner add different words. Take turns. Make as many new sentences as you can.

2. The Grand Canyon _____.

3. The Colorado River _____.

4. There is a lot to do at the Grand Canyon.
   You can _____.

5. It is fun to be outdoors, where you can see _____.

EXAMPLE **2.** The Grand Canyon is very old.
The Grand Canyon has a river
and waterfalls.

WRITE ABOUT A VISIT TO THE GRAND CANYON

<u>6.</u> **Imagine you are at the Grand Canyon. Write a postcard to a friend. Tell what you see and do there.**

EXAMPLE **6.**

Dear Kashmir,

I am in the Grand Canyon! The rocks are beautiful. Yesterday, I hiked on a trail. I took a lot of photos. Some day, I want to take a raft down the river.

Your friend,
Alex

Kashmir Komanapali
300 S. Orange Street
Miami, FL 33109

THE GRAND CANYON

Ride the Rapids!

Success in Social Science

▶ **Learn About Regions of the U.S.**

Product Maps

A **region** is a part of a country.

The **geography** of a region includes its physical features, like mountains, rivers, forests, or deserts.

A **product map** shows what is produced in a region.

state

product map

ARIZONA

NEW MEXICO

OKLAHOMA

TEXAS

product

🐂 Cattle
🟤 Copper
☁ Cotton
🔥 Natural Gas
⬤ Oil

The **climate** of a region is what the weather is usually like there. In the Southwest the weather is usually hot and dry in the summer.

Listen to the article. Then do the Review.

The Southwest: A Region of Richness

• **What is the southwestern region of the United States like?**

The southwestern region of the United States is made up of Arizona, New Mexico, Texas, and Oklahoma. It covers over 572,300 square miles.

Most of the region has a warm and dry climate in the summer. For example, it is about 83°F in Houston, Texas, in July. Only 3 to 4 inches of rain fall there at that time.

You can see interesting landforms in the region. One of the most famous is the Grand Canyon. Flat-topped hills called **mesas** are in Arizona and New Mexico. Texas has many dry plains.

The Southwest produces useful products. There is a lot of oil and natural gas throughout the region. Many people raise cattle, too. Cotton and copper are two other important products from the region.

Mesa

Oil Well

The Southwest was once part of Mexico. Cities, rivers, and other places still have Spanish names. Mexican celebrations are important in the culture of the region. Many Mexican Americans live in the Southwest.

Most people who live in the Southwest live near the major cities. For example, more than 2,144,491 people live in the Houston, Texas, area.

The Southwest is a region of richness from its geography to its products.

Midwest   Northeast

West

Southwest   Southeast

REVIEW

1. **Check Your Understanding** What is the Southwest like?
2. **Use Product Maps** What does Arizona produce? What does Texas produce?
3. **Vocabulary** Name the other regions in the United States. In which region do you live?

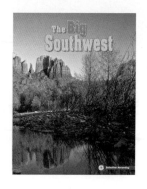

Build Background for "The Big Southwest"

GEOGRAPHY

The United States has many different regions. The Southwest is a big region of the United States with fun things to see.

▲ People see giant cactus plants when they visit the Southwest.

▲ Tortoises are one of the animals that live in the deserts of the Southwest.

Learn Key Vocabulary

Rate and Study the Words Rate how well you know each word. Then:

1. Pronounce the word. Say it aloud several times. Spell it.
2. Study the example.
3. Tell more about the word.
4. Practice it. Make the word your own.

Key Words

states (stāts) *noun*

The U.S.A. is divided into 50 **states**. Four big **states** make up the Southwest.

explore (ek-**splor**) *verb*

When you **explore** a place, you look around and find out about it. People come to the Southwest to **explore** the land and rivers.

miles (mīlz) *noun*

A **mile** is a far distance. The desert in the Southwest stretches for many **miles**.

culture (**kul**-chur) *noun*

A **culture** is a way of life. People with different **cultures** live together in the Southwest.

cowboy (**kow**-boi) *noun*

A **cowboy** takes care of animals that live on a ranch. Here you see a **cowboy** riding a bull.

Practice the Words With a partner, make a Vocabulary Study Card for each Key Word.

Write the word.

front
> explore

Tell what the word means and use it in a sentence.

back
> look around
> I like to explore caves.

Use the cards to quiz your partner. Take turns answering.

Language and Content

Listen and Read Along

FOCUS ON GENRE

Travel Article   A travel article tells about a place that people might like to visit. It is nonfiction. This travel article tells about a region of the United States called the Southwest.

FOCUS ON COMPREHENSION

Classify   When you classify ideas or objects, you put them into groups. Classifying can help you remember important information. As you read "The Big Southwest," use a chart to help you put information into groups.

Plants in the Southwest	Animals in the Southwest	People in the Southwest

The Southwest is a big and interesting place to visit.

The Big Southwest

 Selection Recording

Welcome to the Southwest

The Southwest is made up of four large **states**. Yet the Southwest has fewer people than any of the other **regions**. The Southwest is known for sagebrush, cactus, and dry, dusty land. The Southwest is home to many different people. Come **explore** the big Southwest!

Key Vocabulary

states *n.*, parts of a political union, like the United States of America

explore *v.*, to look around and find out things about a place

In Other Words

regions areas

THE SOUTHWEST

Colorado River

Grand Canyon

ARIZONA

NEW MEXICO

OKLAHOMA

Rio Grande River

TEXAS

MEXICO

Gulf of Mexico

▼ In the Southwest, even the plants are big!

▲ Texas is the biggest state in the Southwest.

▼ Deserts, canyons, and rivers are some of the amazing places in the Southwest.

Before You Move On

1. **Main Idea and Details** How would you describe the Southwest?
2. **Classify** What states are part of the Southwest?

Cactus

The Dry Deserts

The Southwest has **miles** and miles of desert land to explore. The deserts are hot and dry. In some places, you can see nothing but sand. Sometimes deserts go without rain for months.

Even though the Southwest is dry, it still has cactuses and many other plants. These plants are able to live without a lot of water. A cactus plant is a tall plant. You will see amazing plants on your tour of the big Southwest.

◀ The desert can be a colorful place.

▼ In the desert, sand dunes look like waves.

Key Vocabulary
miles *n.*, great distances

Desert Animals

Life in the Southwest desert is hard. The weather is often hot. The desert also has very little water. Yet animals have found ways to **survive**. Some animals never drink. They get water by eating seeds and plants. Many animals hunt and eat at night. This keeps them out of the hot sun.

▼ This bat hunts at night, when the desert is cool.

A desert bird eats a cactus flower. ▶

▼ A tortoise bites into a cactus.

In Other Words
survive stay alive

In Other Words
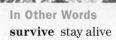

Before You Move On

1. **Classify** What kinds of plants and animals live in the desert?
2. **Details** How do animals survive in the desert?

People and Cultures in the Southwest

Cowboy culture is a big part of the Southwest. Rodeo is a Southwest tradition. You might meet a cowboy or a rodeo clown on your trip to this region.

Rodeo clowns help ▶
keep riders safe.

▲ A cowboy holds on tight as a bull tries to shake him off.

Key Vocabulary

cowboy *n.*, a person who takes care of cattle

culture *n.*, a way of life, including food, music, and language

There are many different people with different cultures in the Southwest. Imagine who you might meet on a trip around the Southwest.

Native Americans have lived in the Southwest for thousands of years. ▶

▼ More recently, people have moved to big cities like Dallas, Texas.

Before You Move On

1. **Inference** How might a rodeo clown help keep the **cowboys** safe?
2. **Classify** Which **cultures** have lived in the Southwest for thousands of years?

Think About "The Big Southwest"

CHECK YOUR UNDERSTANDING

1.–2. Work with a partner to complete each item.

1. **Classify** Make a chart like the one below. Complete the chart with what you know about life in the Southwest.

Plants in the Southwest	Animals in the Southwest	People in the Southwest

2. **Sum It Up** Use your chart to tell a partner about life in the Southwest.

REVIEW VOCABULARY

3.–7. Read the paragraph aloud. Add the vocabulary words.

> Many people come to _____ the Southwest. The four big _____ that make up the Southwest are filled with interesting places, such as the Grand Canyon. It is many _____ wide. You are sure to see a _____ and many other interesting people. There are people with different _____ who come to the Southwest from other countries.

Vocabulary

states

explore

miles

cultures

cowboy

WRITE ABOUT A U.S. REGION

8. Write about a state in the U.S. that you would most like to explore. Explain why.

Biography

A biography tells about a person's life. Biographies include facts and information to help the reader understand the person and why they are special. A short biography is called a biographical sketch.

Always begin with a topic sentence.

Use details to support the topic.

BIOGRAPHICAL SKETCH

Thomas Jefferson

Thomas Jefferson is an important man in U.S. history. He was born in 1743 in Virginia. He was a good student, and became a lawyer. In 1775, he became a very important person in America. He was a member of the Second Continental Congress. Then in 1776, Jefferson wrote the first draft of the Declaration of Independence. He served as vice president from 1797 until 1801. He became president in 1801, and was reelected in 1804. One of his biggest accomplishments was the Louisiana Purchase in 1803. This purchase of land from France made the United States twice as big. Thomas Jefferson died in 1826.

A biography should answer *who, what, where, how,* and *why* questions.

In 1803, Thomas Jefferson completed the Louisiana Purchase. This map shows the size of the Louisiana Purchase.

You can use images to support ideas.

Writing Project

Write a Biographical Sketch

WRITING PROMPT A biography tells about a person's life. Write a biographical sketch to tell your class about a famous American. What makes the person special?

Prewrite

When you prewrite, you gather ideas and choose your topic. You also make a plan for what you will write.

1 COLLECT IDEAS

Think about some people you would like to learn more about. Look through books, on the Internet, or ask a teacher or librarian for help.

> Stephanie Kwolek
> Jonas Salk
> Dr. Sally Ride
> Duke Ellington

2 GATHER FACTS

Brainstorm research questions. Put each question on a card. Then find answers. Go to pages 354–357 for help on how to use information sources. Draw or gather images, too.

Mario's Research Cards

Organize your information. Show the main idea. Then give the details:

- when and where the person lived
- why the person is famous
- what the person did

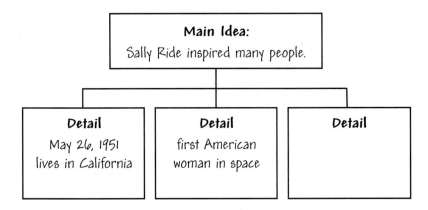

Reflect

- Did you choose a special person?
- Did you answer all of your questions about that person?

Draft

Use your organizer to write the **topic sentence**. Tell the person's name and what he or she did.

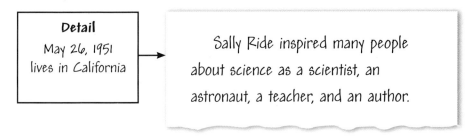

Detail
May 26, 1951
lives in California

→ Sally Ride inspired many people about science as a scientist, an astronaut, a teacher, and an author.

Then write the rest of the paragraph using **details**.

Revise

When you revise a draft, you make your writing better. First, you need to know what a reader thinks of your work. Mario read his paper to a partner.

Mario's Draft

Dr. Sally Ride was born on May 26, 1951, and lives in California. She was an astronaut.

Mario's partner says:

" **Where in California does she live?** "

Then Mario knew he had to make changes. What additional changes can he make?

Mario's Draft

Dr. Sally Ride was born on May 26, 1951, and lives in ^San Diego, California. She was an astronaut.

Now follow these steps to revise your paper.

1 DECIDE WHAT TO CHANGE

Read to a partner. Your partner will ask you questions with *who, what, when, where, how,* and *why.* Do you need to add text to develop your ideas?

2 MARK YOUR CHANGES

If you need to add text, use this mark: ∧.

Reflect

- Do you have a clear topic sentence and details?

- Did you develop your ideas?

Edit and Proofread

Check your paragraph for mistakes. Follow these steps.

1 CHECK PROPER NOUNS

Remember to capitalize proper nouns, titles, and initials of people when you write.

2 CHECK YOUR SPELLING

Circle each word that may be misspelled. Look it up in the dictionary or ask for help. Fix the spelling if you need to.

3 CHECK YOUR DATES

When you write dates, always capitalize the name of the day of the month. Always place commas after the day of the week and the date. If you list only the month and year, place a comma after the month.

Proper Noun	Example
cities, states, countries	Tampa, Florida United States
bodies of water	Gulf of Mexico
landforms	Appalachian Mountains
people's names, titles, and initials	Dr. Sally Ride P. T. Barnum Dwight D. Eisenhower

EXAMPLE   Franklin D. Roosevelt became president on Wednesday, January 20, 1937.

Ben Nighthorse Campbell was born in April, 1933.

What errors did Mario correct in his paper? What errors does he still need to correct?

> She was born in los angeles, near the pacific ocean. Sally Ride joined NASA in january 1978. She trained for many years to become an astranaut. On june 18 1983, Sally Ride rode the spase shuttle Challenger into space. The astranauts who went with her into spase were named captain robert l. crippen, Frederick h. Hauck, Colonel John M. Fabian, and dr. Norman E. Thagard.

4 MARK YOUR CHANGES

Now edit your paper. Use these marks to show your changes:

∧	℘	⌐	◯	≡	/	⌐
Add.	Take out.	Replace with this.	Check spelling.	Capitalize.	Make lowercase.	Make new paragraph.

Reflect

- What kinds of errors did you find?

- What can you do to keep from making errors?

Publish, Share, and Reflect

You have finished your biographical sketch. Now you are ready to publish your work! When you publish your writing, you share it with others. Follow these steps.

1 FINISH AND DISPLAY

Think about how your writing looks. Get it ready to share.

- Make sure your handwriting is clear.
- Add drawings or photographs to show the person and support ideas.
- Display it on a bulletin board.

2 READ ALOUD

There are many ways you can share your writing. Try reading your biographical sketch aloud. As you read, think about your purpose.

- If you are sharing your biographical sketch to give information, pause after each sentence to give your listeners time to think. Show pictures to help them understand.
- If you are sharing your biographical sketch to inspire, change your voice so listeners focus on important parts.

Also remember these tips.

Dr. Sally Ride

Dr. Sally Ride is a scientist and astronaut. She was born on May 26, 1951, and lives in California. She was the first American woman in outer space. She was a mission specialist in space. Later she wrote three books about space. Now she is a physics teacher at a university in San Diego.

Presenting Tips

If You Are the Speaker:	If You Are the Listener:
• Pause after giving important information.	• Make notes to remember the information.
• Show pictures.	• Use the real picture to make more pictures in your mind.
• Change your voice.	• Pay attention to the speaker's voice.

Reflect

- How did answering questions help you complete your research?
- What did you like best about writing a biography?

These pictures show the many steps it takes to get food from the farm to your table.

WATER

SELL AND BUY

PLANT

HARVEST

TRANSPORT

PLOW

HARVEST TIME

Work with a partner.
What is the correct order for the pictures?
Use the pictures to tell how broccoli comes
from the farm to your table.

In This Unit

▶ **Language Development**

▶ **Language and Literacy**

▶ **Language and Content**
  Science

▶ **Writing Project**

Vocabulary
- Farming
- Key Vocabulary

Language Functions
- Buy or Sell an Item
- Give Information

Grammar
- Subjects and Word Order
- Predicates and Word Order

Reading
- Suffixes: *-ly, -y, -less, -ful*
- Prefixes: *-un, -re*
- High Frequency Words
- Comprehension: Make Comparisons
- Text Features: Flow Charts

Writing
- Report

The Market Price

▶ **Language: Buy or Sell an Item**

Listen and sing. CD

At the Farmers' Market

Every day, my customers say,
"How many apples are in a bag?"
Every day my customers say,
"How much does one bag cost?"

"How many? How much?" is all I hear.
I answer a hundred times,
"Three dollars, please, for a bag of twelve.
In bills or quarters or dimes."

Every day my customers say,
"How much does one bag cost?"
I put a tag on every bag,
But the tags keep getting lost!

Questions

Use *how many* to ask about things you can count.

> **How many** apples are in a bag?
> **How many** bags can I buy for $6.00?

Use *how much* to ask about a price.

> **How much** do the apples cost?
> **How much** are the apples?

EXPRESS YOURSELF ▶ BUY OR SELL AN ITEM

Work with a partner. Act out a scene at a farmers' market.
One partner buys and one partner sells the food shown below.

EXAMPLE **1. Buyer:** How much are the apples?
Seller: They are $3.00 a bag.

1.

apples
$3.00 for a bag

2.

green peppers
3 for $1.00

3.

carrots
50¢ per pound

4.

lettuce
$1.00 each

5.–8. With a partner, imagine you are setting up a farmers' market.
Use questions with *how many* and *how much* to decide which foods
you will sell and how much foods cost.

EXAMPLE **5.** How much are the apples?
They are $3.00 a bag.

Down on the Farm

▶ **Vocabulary: Farming**
▶ **Language: Give Information**

The farmer plows the field and plants the lettuce.

The farmer waters the field.

The farmer gets help to harvest the crop.

ORAL LANGUAGE PRACTICE ▶ GIVE INFORMATION

<u>1.–3.</u> Work with a partner. Use farming words to tell each other about the pictures above.

EXAMPLE **1.** The farmer drives a tractor. The tractor makes rows in the field.

WRITTEN PRACTICE

<u>4.–6.</u> Write 3 questions about farmers' work. Trade papers with a partner. Write answers to your partner's questions.

EXAMPLE **4.** What does a farmer do first?
The farmer plows the field.

Place Your Order

▶ **Subjects and Word Order**

Sentences usually follow this pattern: subject → verb. In a sentence, a subject tells about someone or something. The subject usually comes first in a sentence. A subject is a noun or noun phrase.

| To find the subject in a sentence, ask yourself: Whom or what is the sentence about?

This family likes to eat at this restaurant. The girl is placing her order. The server is taking the order. The woman and boy are looking at the menu.

BUILD SENTENCES

Look at the pictures below. Add a subject with a noun to make a complete sentence.

EXAMPLE **1.** The woman is reading the menu.

1. _____ is reading the menu.

2. _____ is placing an order.

3. _____ is taking an order.

4. _____ is thinking about what to eat.

WRITE ABOUT PEOPLE AT A RESTAURANT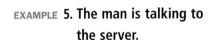

5. Work with a partner. Pretend you are both at a restaurant. Take turns writing sentences about what the people at the restaurant are doing. Remember to use this order: subject → verb.

EXAMPLE **5.** The man is talking to the server.

What Are They Doing?

▶ **Predicates and Word Order**

In a sentence, a predicate tells what is happening or what someone is doing. The predicate usually comes second in a sentence. A predicate has a verb.

> **To find a predicate in a sentence, ask yourself: What is the subject doing?**

This girl is eating nachos. She takes a big bite. She likes the soft and warm cheese. She thinks the peppers are too hot!

BUILD SENTENCES

Look at the pictures below. Add a predicate with a verb to make a complete sentence.

EXAMPLE **1.** The boy is eating ice cream.

1. The boy _____ .

2. These friends _____ .

3. This teacher _____ .

4. This woman _____ .

WRITE COMPLETE SENTENCES

5. Work with a partner. Write sentences about a family having dinner together. Remember to use this order: subject → verb.

EXAMPLE **5.** Matt's family goes to a restaurant. Matt sits down at the table first. He reads the menu.

Language Development

Listen and Read Along

FOCUS ON GENRE

Informational Text   An informational text gives facts and details about a topic. It is nonfiction. This informational text tells about six crops that are grown in the United States.

FOCUS ON VOCABULARY

Farming Words   You have been learning words like the ones below. Use these words as you talk about *Crops*. Collect more words to put in the web.

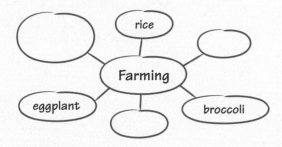

THEME BOOK

Read this informational text about crops.

Farmers in the United States use land to grow crops such as wheat and corn.

Think About *Crops*

MAKE COMPARISONS

Work with a partner. Make a comparison chart for *Crops*. Follow these steps.

1 Set up a chart like the one below.

Crop	Planting	Harvesting	Products
cranberries			
wheat			
cotton			
potatoes			
oranges			
sugar cane			

2 Read the book again. As you read, fill in the rest of the chart. Tell how farmers plant and harvest each crop. Tell what products are made from the crops.

Crop	Planting	Harvesting	Products
cranberries	in bogs	by machine	juice, sauce
wheat			

3 Use your completed chart to compare the crops. Talk to a partner. Discuss how some of the crops are alike. Discuss how they are different. Use words like these:

alike	same	but
and	both	different

High Frequency Words

This woman is working in her garden.

REVIEW HIGH FREQUENCY WORDS

Read the words aloud. Which word goes in each sentence?

too	good
watch	why
each	earth

1. She takes _____ care of the garden.
2. This is _____ she does it.
3. She gives _____ plant what it needs.

LEARN NEW WORDS

Study these words. Say them as whole words when you read.

weigh	Ana buys tomatoes that **weigh** over 2 pounds.
beautiful	The **beautiful** tomatoes are firm and bright red.
special	They come from a **special** market across town.
own	"I want to grow my **own** tomatoes," Ana thought.
any	She did not have **any** seeds, so she bought some.

PRACTICE

<u>4.</u> Make flash cards. Write each new word on one side of a card. On the other side, write a sentence with the word. Leave the new word blank. Above the sentence, draw a picture of the sentence. Work with a partner. Guess the word for the sentences on each other's cards.

EXAMPLE **4.**

weigh

I _____ more than a baby.

Write each sentence. Add the missing word.

5. You can grow your _ _ _ flowers at home.
6. Sunflowers are big. The flowers can _ _ _ _ _ more than a pound!
7. Plant many colorful flowers. They will make your garden look _ _ _ _ _ _ _ _ _!

EXAMPLE **5.** You can grow your own flowers at home.

<u>8.–9.</u> **Find the 2 words you didn't use.** Write sentences with those words.

EXAMPLE **8.** I can grow any plant in my garden.

More High Frequency Words

> **How to Learn a New Word**
> - Look at the word.
> - Listen to the word.
> - Listen to the word in a sentence. What does it mean?
> - Say the word.
> - Spell the word.
> - Say the word again.

REVIEW HIGH FREQUENCY WORDS

Read the words aloud. Which word goes in the sentence?

time	try	1. Plants take ____ to grow.
year	young	2. Some plants grow well all ____ long.
been	need	3. All plants ____ sun and water.

LEARN NEW WORDS

Study these words. Say them as whole words when you read.

indoors	Ana planted the seeds **indoors**, by her kitchen window.
warm	It was winter, but her kitchen was **warm** and sunny.
healthy	Soon, she had strong and **healthy** seedlings.
cold	By the end of April, the **cold** weather was over.
outdoors	It was time to put her plants **outdoors** in the yard.

PRACTICE

4. Make flash cards. Write each new word on one side of a card. On the other side, write a sentence with the word. Leave the new word blank. Above the sentence draw a picture of the sentence. Work with a partner. Guess the word for the sentences on each other's cards.

EXAMPLE **4.**

indoors

We stayed _____ during the storm.

Write each sentence. Add the missing word.

5. Sunflower seeds can be planted
   _ _ _ _ _ _ _ _ in the garden at the start of spring.

6. Other seeds must be planted inside the house. The pots stay _ _ _ _ _ _ _ for a few weeks.

7. In the summer when it gets _ _ _ _ outside, you can put the young plants in your garden.

EXAMPLE **5.** Sunflower seeds can be planted outdoors in the garden at the start of spring.

8.–9. Find the 2 words you didn't use. Write sentences with those words.

EXAMPLE **8.** It is too cold to grow vegetables in the winter!

Reading and Spelling

▶ **Prefixes and Suffixes**

Listen and learn. CD

Young Corn

We replant, and then we wait
for corn to sprout from healthy seeds.
The unseen roots push silently
deep into the earth.

We replant, and then we wait
for corn to grow from healthy seeds.
The graceful plants reach proudly
toward the endless sky.

STUDY WORD PARTS

You can add a **prefix** to the beginning of a word.

Prefix	Meaning	Example
un-	not	unseen
	the opposite of	unlock
re-	again	replant
	back	repay

You can add a **suffix** to the end of a word.

Suffix	Meaning	Example
-ly	in a certain way	proudly
-y	full of	healthy
-less	without	endless
-ful	full of	graceful

READING STRATEGY

Follow these steps to read a word with a prefix or suffix.

1 Look for a prefix or a suffix. Cover it. Then read the root word.

untie   **tie**

> When I cover the prefix **un–**, I see a word I know: **tie**.

2 Uncover the prefix or the suffix. Blend the syllables to read the entire word.

un + **tie** = **untie**

> **Untie** means "the opposite of tie."

Reading Help

Sometimes the letters **re** and **ly** are not prefixes or suffixes. To find out, cover **re** or **ly** and see if you are left with a word. For example:

real   silly

al   sil

READING PRACTICE

Use what you learned to read the sentences.

1. Insects are killing the healthy plants in Matt's garden.
2. He will not use insect sprays. They are messy and unsafe.
3. So he buys ladybugs that eat the harmful insects.
4. When he replants each spring, he fills his garden with these wonderful red bugs.
5. In a few months, Matt will proudly show you his garden.
6. It will be full of vegetables and harmless red bugs!

SPELLING PRACTICE

7.–11. **Now write the sentences that your teacher reads.**

WORD WORK

12.–16. **Read the newspaper article. Find words with the prefix _un-_.**
Make a chart like the one shown here. Write each word next to its meaning.

The Top Tomato

Tomato lovers from all over the county unpacked crates of big, juicy tomatoes for the Tomato Festival on Sunday.

Fernando Robles, of Oak Park, grew a tomato unlike any other. It weighed 6.4 pounds! Pat Tanaka, also of Oak Park, was unhappy. Her 5.1 pound tomato won second place. Fernando remains unbeaten three years in a row.

"My secret is to find the best tomato on the vine, and then take off the unwanted ones," says Fernando.

Words with _un-_	Meaning
12.	emptied
13.	not beaten
14.	not wanted
15.	sad
16.	different from

EXAMPLE **12.** unpacked

Read on Your Own

FOCUS ON GENRE

Informational Text   Informational text tells facts and details about a topic. It is nonfiction. This informational text tells about where plants grow.

FOCUS ON WORDS

Words With Prefixes and Suffixes
When you read and come to a word with a prefix or suffix, cover the prefix or suffix and read the root word. Then uncover the whole word and read it. You just learned about words with these prefixes and suffixes:

<u>Prefixes</u>	<u>Suffixes</u>	
un	less	ly
re	ful	y

happy   <u>un</u>happy

High Frequency Words   Say these words as whole words when you read.

weigh	indoors
beautiful	warm
special	healthy
own	cold
any	outdoors

Plants in greenhouses can grow all year round.

Many Places to Plant a Plant

Farmers plant on a big scale! They fill huge fields with millions of seeds. Plants grow well in these open fields, but not all plants are grown there. Many plants are first grown indoors, in greenhouses and in nurseries. Unlike open fields, these shelters protect plants from too much heat or cold. They also protect young plants from harmful diseases, insects, and weeds.

▲ Plants are grown outside and inside. Plants grown inside are protected.

Greenhouses have glass walls that let the sunshine in. Plants that like heat grow well inside the warm, sunny space. On really cold days, steam pipes heat and reheat the greenhouse to keep the plants healthy. Any summer crops, such as peppers and eggplant, can be grown year-round in greenhouses. Did you know that an eggplant can weigh as much as 8 pounds?

A nursery is another place where plants grow in a sheltered place. Some nurseries grow special plants and collect their seeds. They sell some of the seeds and use others to grow more beautiful plants.

▲ Expensive plants like orchids are grown in nurseries.

Some nurseries are huge, with a shop that sells plants and gardening tools. After people buy plants from the nursery, they replant them outdoors in gardens at home. Visit a nursery! Get a daisy plant and some roses. Buy a rake. You'll be ready to start a garden of your own.

▲ Plant your own garden at home!

Think About "Many Places to Plant a Plant"

CHECK YOUR UNDERSTANDING

<u>1.</u> Make a concept map like the one below. Work with a partner to add details to it. Use your finished map to compare places to grow plants.

EXAMPLE **1.** A greenhouse has glass walls, but an open field is unprotected. Both places are often sunny and warm.

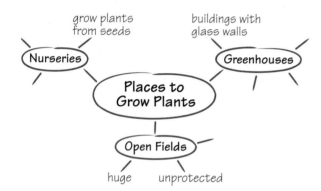

EXPAND YOUR VOCABULARY

<u>2.</u> Work with a group to collect compound words. Look for compound words in the selection on pages 256–257. Find the 2 words in each compound word and write them on cards. Then put the words together to show the compound word.

EXAMPLE **2.**

WRITE MORE COMPARISONS

<u>3.–8.</u> Collect words and phrases related to plants. Find things to compare. Write 6 comparisons. Use the words in the box to tell how the things are alike or different.

both	alike	different
and	same	but

EXAMPLE **3.** Peppers and carrots are both vegetable crops. Carrots taste sweet, but peppers are hot and spicy.

Success in Science

▶ **Learn About Plants**

Flow Chart: Life Cycle of a Plant

soil — sprout

The **seed** sprouts. It grows into a **plant**.

bud — stem

The **plant** forms a **bud**.

flower — leaf

The **bud** blooms into a **flower**.

seeds — flower

The **flower** has the **seeds** that start the cycle over again.

Listen to the article. Then do the Review.

Oranges: From Tree to Market

• **How are oranges grown?**

Although farmers start some crops with seeds, farmers grow orange crops in a different way. Growers start by planting young **grafted** trees.

A grafted tree is made of two trees. The farmer takes a part of one young tree and attaches it to the roots of another young tree. The trees grow together to make a stronger tree. A grafted tree also produces fruit that is better than the fruit of an ungrafted tree. The grafted trees start producing oranges after about 2 years.

When the oranges are ripe, farmers harvest the fruit. Most farmers pick oranges by hand. Then they take the oranges to a storage area.

Farmers sell almost half of the harvested oranges to people who make orange juice. They also sell oranges to people who make perfumes, oils, jams, and candies. Some oranges go directly to a market where you can buy them.

Development of an Orange Tree

grafting scar

A grafted tree ready to be planted

bud

A young orange tree

fruit

A mature orange tree

REVIEW

1. **Check Your Understanding** Why do farmers graft orange trees?
2. **Check Your Understanding** What are some of the ways that people use oranges?
3. **Vocabulary** Follow these 3 steps to draw and label a sunflower:
   Step 1 Draw the stem and leaves.
   Step 2 Draw the flower head.
   Step 3 Add these labels: *stem, leaf, flower*.

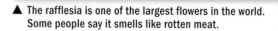

Build Background for "Plant Power"

PLANTS

Plants make our world a more beautiful place. Plants also help to keep us healthy.

◀ Trees are plants. Giant redwoods like these are some of the tallest trees in the world.

▲ The rafflesia is one of the largest flowers in the world. Some people say it smells like rotten meat.

Learn Key Vocabulary

Rate and Study the Words Rate how well you know each word. Then:

1. Pronounce the word. Say it aloud several times. Spell it.
2. Study the example.
3. Tell more about the word.
4. Practice it. Make the word your own.

Key Words

beautiful (byū-ti-ful) *adjective*

Something that is **beautiful** is nice to look at. These wildflowers are **beautiful**.

energy (en-ur-jē) *noun*

When you have **energy**, you feel strong. This squirrel gets **energy** from eating plants.

healthy (hel-thē) *adjective*

When you are **healthy**, you are not sick. Vegetables like broccoli can help people stay **healthy**.

oxygen (ok-si-jen) *noun*

People breathe in a gas called **oxygen**. Plants give off the **oxygen** that is in the air.

vitamins (vī-tuh-minz) *noun*

The body needs **vitamins** to stay healthy. Fruits like blueberries have many **vitamins** that people need.

Practice the Words Make an Example Chart for the Key Words and other words from the selection. Compare your chart with a partner's chart.

What do plants make?	Who eats plants?	What do we get when we eat plants?
oxygen	people, animals	vitamins

Example Chart

Listen and Read Along

FOCUS ON GENRE

Informational Text   Informational text is nonfiction. People read informational text to learn facts about a topic. This informational text tells about different kinds of plants and how they grow.

FOCUS ON COMPREHENSION

Comparisons   When you compare different objects, you tell how they are alike and how they are different. As you read "Plant Power," think about comparisons you can make. Use a chart to help you.

Type of Plant	Lives	Grows	Examples

PLANT POWER

Hikers stand among giant redwood trees.

Plants with a Purpose

Plants come in many sizes and shapes. The tallest plants are trees. Some stand higher than tall buildings. Other plants are very small. Some are smaller than your hand.

All plants are important. Why? Without them, we could not survive. Plants make food. Plants also make **oxygen**. Oxygen helps animals and humans breathe. Plants are important to all living things.

▼ These sunflowers have large, yellow flower heads.

Key Vocabulary
oxygen *n.*, a kind of gas that is in the air

▲ This crocus is a small plant with purple flowers.

◄ The redwood tree is one of Earth's largest plants.

Before You Move On

1. **Note Details** What gas do plants make?
2. **Compare and Contrast** Name 2 large plants and 2 small plants.

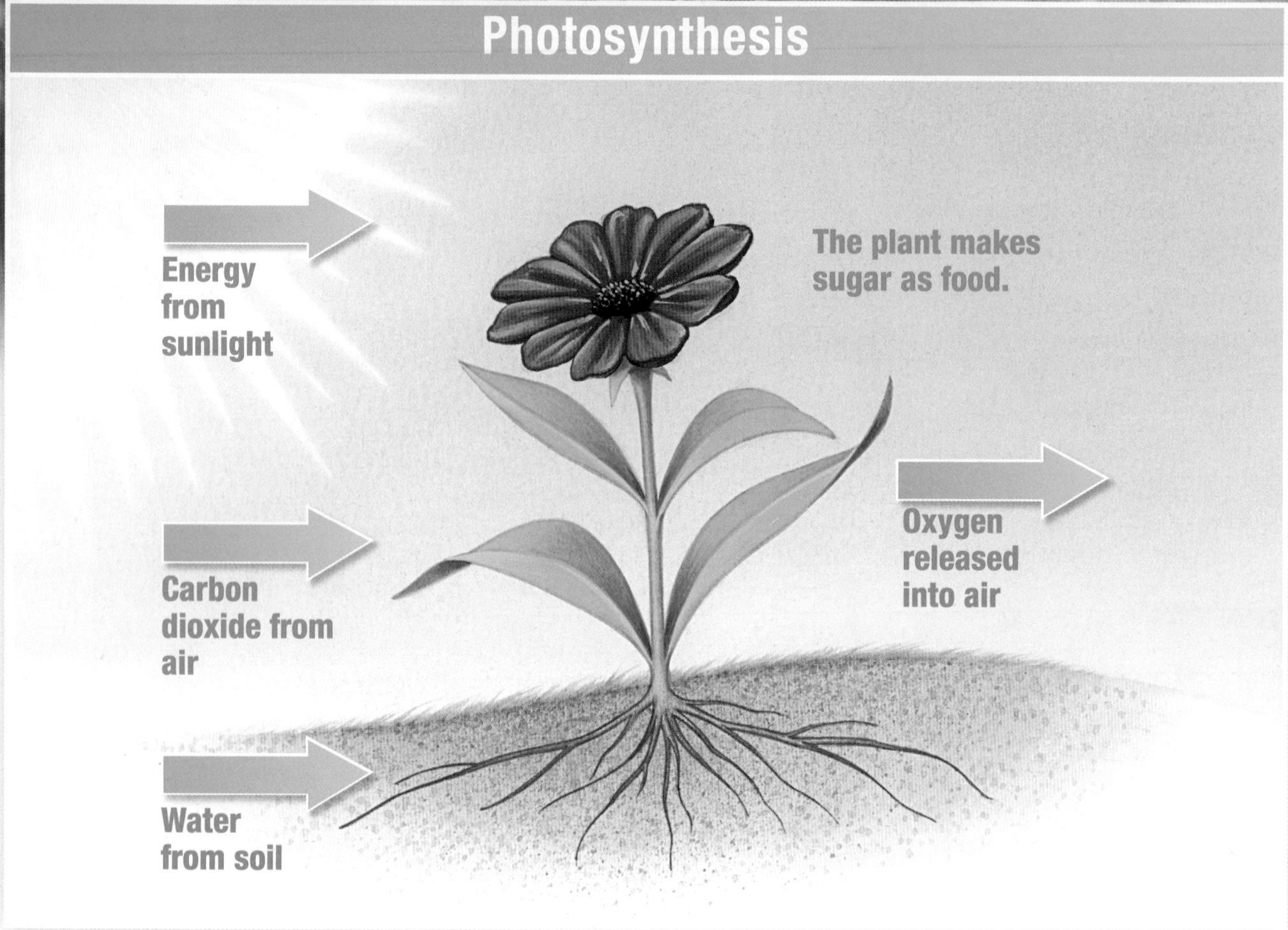

Photosynthesis

Energy
from
sunlight

The plant makes
sugar as food.

Carbon
dioxide from
air

Oxygen
released
into air

Water
from soil

▲ Plants use sunlight, carbon dioxide, and water to make sugar and oxygen.

Food for Plants

Plants also make their own food. This process is called photosynthesis. In photosynthesis, plants use water, **carbon dioxide**, and sunlight to make a kind of sugar and oxygen. This sugar is the food that gives plants **energy** to live and grow.

Key Vocabulary
energy *n.*, the power to move and do things

In Other Words
carbon dioxide a colorless and invisible gas

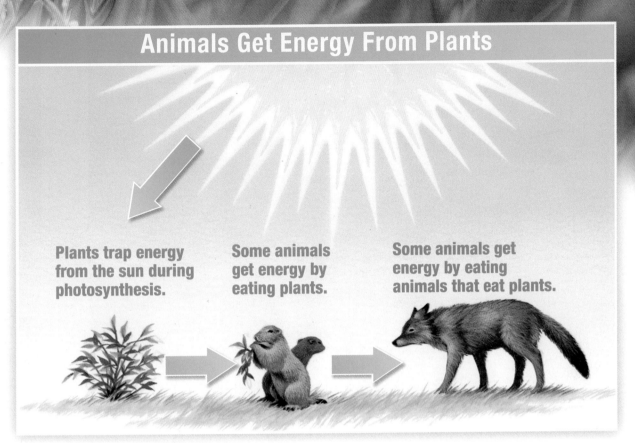

Animals Get Energy From Plants

Plants trap energy from the sun during photosynthesis.

Some animals get energy by eating plants.

Some animals get energy by eating animals that eat plants.

▲ Animals get energy by eating plants or animals that eat plants.

Food from Plants

Plants get energy from the food they make. Animals also get energy from plants. How? Animals get energy by eating plants. Or animals eat other animals that have eaten plants. The sugar that plants make is used by both plants and animals!

Before You Move On

1. **Text Features** How do plants make their own food?
2. **Inference** What do you think would happen if there were fewer plants on the earth?

▲ Broccoli

Please Pass the Plants!

The fruits and vegetables you eat are plants or plant parts. These plants help you stay **healthy**. They give you **vitamins** and minerals that your body needs. Eating fruits and vegetables, such as blueberries and broccoli, can protect you against disease.

▲ Blueberries

Key Vocabulary

healthy *adj.*, being well and not sick

vitamins *n.*, substances that make you grow and be healthy

▲ Plants are an important part of life on Earth.

So the next time you look at a plant, don't just think about how **beautiful** it is. Think about how plants help living things, like humans, stay alive.

Key Vocabulary
beautiful *adj.*, pretty

Before You Move On

1. **Comparisons** Look at the photos. How are the plants the same? How are they different?
2. **Inference** Is it important for people to eat plants? Why or why not?

Think About "Plant Power"

CHECK YOUR UNDERSTANDING

<u>1.–2.</u> **Work with a partner to complete each item.**

1. **Make Comparisons** Make a comparison chart like the one below. Then complete the comparison chart using information from the selection and what you know about plants.

Type of Plant	Description	Examples
trees	tall; can be taller than buildings	apple tree, orange tree

2. **Sum It Up** Use your comparison chart to tell about different kinds of plants.

REVIEW VOCABULARY

<u>3.–7.</u> **Read the paragraph aloud. Add the vocabulary words.**

> Plants are _____ to look at, but they also help to keep people _____. They give you _____ and minerals that your body needs. People get _____ by eating plants. Plants also make the gas _____ that is in the air we breathe.

Vocabulary

beautiful

healthy

energy

oxygen

vitamins

WRITE ABOUT PLANTS

<u>8.</u> **Write about your favorite food that comes from a plant.**

Report

A report is used to give facts about a topic. You need to research information to write a report.

REPORT

Many fruits, including grapes, are grown in California.

Crop Report: Grapes and Corn

Grapes and corn are very different crops. Grapes grow on woody vines. Because grapes grow on vines, grape farms are called vineyards. Some grape vines are hundreds of years old! In winter, when the grapes are not growing, the bare vines are still in the field. Corn is grown on farms. Corn grows on tall stalks. Every year the corn stalks are cut down. Farmers plant new corn every year. Grapes and corn are also harvested in different ways. Some grape growers use machines, but many grape growers still get help to pick grapes by hand. Most corn is harvested with big combines that pick and separate the crop. There are so many differences between grapes and corn that most farmers do not grow both grapes and corn on the same farm.

Always begin with a **topic sentence.**

Use **details** to support the topic. Organize details to compare the crops.

Write a Report

WRITING PROMPT Research and compare two crops. Then write a report and share information with the class.

Prewrite

When you prewrite, you gather ideas and choose your topic. You also make a plan for what you will write. Follow these steps.

1 CHOOSE A TOPIC

Think about different kinds of crops that you like to eat. Choose two crops to compare.

2 COLLECT FACTS

Research information about the two crops. Look through books, on the Internet, or ask a teacher or librarian for help. Write your facts on cards.

This card shows Nancy's topic.

Potatoes
A potato is a vegetable.
Farmers plant seed potatoes with machines.
Many potatoes are grown in Washington and Idaho.
Farmers use a potato combine to harvest potatoes.
Potatoes can be brown, gold, purple, or red.

3 ORGANIZE YOUR IDEAS

Organize your facts. Make a Venn diagram to compare the two crops.

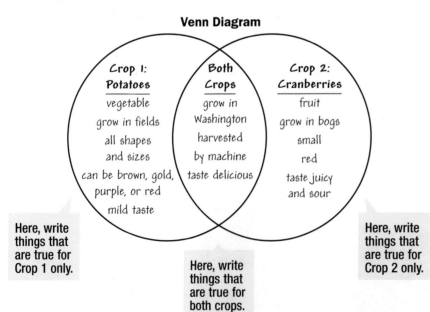

Venn Diagram

Crop 1: Potatoes
- vegetable
- grow in fields
- all shapes and sizes
- can be brown, gold, purple, or red
- mild taste

Both Crops
- grow in Washington
- harvested by machine
- taste delicious

Crop 2: Cranberries
- fruit
- grow in bogs
- small
- red
- taste juicy and sour

Here, write things that are true for Crop 1 only.

Here, write things that are true for both crops.

Here, write things that are true for Crop 2 only.

Reflect

• Did you pick a good topic?

• Do you have a clear plan?

Draft

Use your Venn diagram to begin your draft.

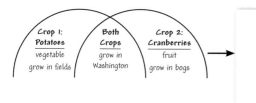

Potatoes are vegetables that grow in fields. Cranberries are fruits that grow in bogs.

Revise

When you revise a draft, you make your writing better. First you need to know what a reader thinks of your work. Nancy read her draft to a partner.

Nancy's Draft

Cranberries and potatoes are grown in the same place. Carrots are grown in fields, too. Most cranberries are red. Potatoes are colorful. They are both grown in Washington.

Nancy's partner says:

" You tell about where they're grown in different places. "

" What colors are potatoes? "

" Why did you talk about carrots? "

Then Nancy knew she needed to make changes.

Nancy's Revision

Cranberries and potatoes are grown in the same place.
~~Carrots are grown in fields, too.~~ Most cranberries are red.
brown, gold, purple, or red
Potatoes are ~~colorful~~ They are both grown in Washington.

She took out a sentence that wasn't about her topic. She also moved a sentence and added details.

Now follow these steps to revise your crop report.

1 DECIDE WHAT TO CHANGE

Read your report to a partner. Ask your partner to restate information from your report. Do you need to make any changes to make your report more detailed or clearer?

2 MARK YOUR CHANGES

If you need to take out text, use this mark: ℘.

If you need to move text, use this mark: ↶◠.

If you need to replace text, use this mark: ⋀.

Writing Project

Edit and Proofread

Check your crop report for mistakes. Follow these steps.

1 CHECK YOUR SENTENCES

The subject is the part of a sentence that tells about someone or something. The predicate tells what is happening. Be sure each of your sentences includes a subject and a predicate.

> EXAMPLES Peaches grow on trees.
>
> Many farmers plow their fields with tractors.

2 CHECK YOUR SPELLING

Circle each word that may be misspelled. Look it up in the dictionary or ask for help. Fix the spelling if you need to.

3 CHECK YOUR PROPER NOUNS

Proper nouns always begin with a capital letter. Names of places, like cities and states, are proper nouns.

> EXAMPLE Wheat is grown in Kansas.

What errors did Nancy correct in her report? What errors does she still need to correct?

Potatoes are also grown in idaho. Cranberries are also grown in wisconsin. Potatoes and cranberries are both *healthfur* (healthfull.) Potatoes contain a lot of potassium. Cranberries a lot of vitamin C (have) Potatoes come in many different sizes. as large as a shoe. Others are as small as a golf ball. Most cranberries are very small. They both grow quicklee. They both are harvested by machines. They both are delicious!

4 MARK YOUR CHANGES

Now edit your paper. Use these marks to show your changes.

∧	✗	⌐	◯	≡	╱	¶
Add.	Take out.	Replace with this.	Check spelling.	Capitalize.	Make lowercase.	Make new paragraph.

Reflect

- What kinds of errors did you find?

- What can you do to keep from making errors?

274 Unit 8 Harvest Time

Publish, Share, and Reflect

You have finished your report. Now you are ready to publish your work! When you publish your writing, you put it in final form to share with others. Follow these steps.

1 FINISH AND DISPLAY

Think about how your writing looks.

- Make sure your handwriting is clear.
- Add photographs, graphs, and drawings to your report.

2 PRESENT

There are many ways you can share your writing. For this report, try giving a presentation. As you read aloud, think about your purpose.

- Support your presentation with graphs, pictures, and diagrams. Point to each crop as you talk aout it.
- Invite listeners to ask questions and share knowledge.

Also remember these tips.

Presenting Tips

If You Are the Speaker:	If You Are the Listener:
• Show the pictures. Point to them as you speak.	• Look at the pictures. Watch the speaker.
• Respond to questions and information.	• Ask questions and share what you know about the crops and foods.

Reflect
- How did using the writing process help you organize your information?
- What did you like best about writing your report?

Who is your favorite
music star?

LIVE in CONCERT!

SHERIFF

8

Superstars

There are all kinds of stars! Work with a group. Draw a star you like. Describe your star to the class.

In This Unit

▶ **Language Development**

▶ **Language and Literacy**

▶ **Language and Content**
Science

▶ **Writing Project**

Vocabulary
- Idioms
- Space
- Key Vocabulary

Language Functions
- Agree and Disagree
- Give Information

Grammar
- Future Tense Verbs
- Verb Tense Review (present, past, future)
- Contractions

Reading
- Multisyllabic Words
- High Frequency Words
- Comprehension: Relate Goal and Outcome
- Text Features: Photos, Captions, and Callouts

Writing
- Poem

Music Stars

▶ **Language: Agree and Disagree**

Listen and chant. CD

What Do You Think?

This band is great! They sound alright!

Yes, I agree! I think you're right!

No way, I don't enjoy this band!

It's just no good. In fact, it's bad!

But listen to their great new song!

It is the best!

You are so wrong!

Their music is one of a kind.

They leave all other bands behind.

I disagree! That isn't true!

OK. Let's find something else to do.

Idioms
No way!
no good
one of a kind
leave all other
  bands behind

EXPRESS YOURSELF ▶ AGREE AND DISAGREE

Read each opinion. Say if you agree or disagree.

EXAMPLE **1.** I agree. Jazz music is great. I disagree. I don't like jazz music.

1. Jazz music is great.
2. CDs are better than tapes.
3. All kids like the same music.
4. Music videos are beautiful.

5.–7. Work with 2 partners. Each of you gives an opinion about music stars. Then one partner says a statement that agrees with your opinion. The other partner says a statement that disagrees with it.

EXAMPLE **5.** Rock stars have a hard life.
I agree because they are never alone.
I disagree. They have a lot of money.

You Will Be a Star Some Day!

▶ **Future Tense Verbs and Contractions**

A verb in the future tense tells what will happen later, or in the future.

Here are some ways to show the future tense.

will + verb	Our band **will play** at the park next week.
am **are** + **going to** + verb **is**	I **am going to play** the guitar. You **are going to sing**. The concert **is going to be** great!
we'll + verb	We will practice tonight. **We'll practice** tonight. The contraction for *we will* is *we'll*.
won't + verb	We will not stop until we know every song! We **won't stop** until we know every song! The contraction for *will not* is *won't*.

BUILD SENTENCES

Change each sentence to tell about the future.
Say each sentence 2 different ways.

EXAMPLE **1.** We will practice at Ana's house.
We are going to practice at Ana's house.

1. We practice at Ana's house.
2. You and Ana learn a new song.
3. It sounds great.
4. Many people hear our music at the park.
5. We become superstars!

Use the contraction *won't* to make each sentence
negative. Say the new sentence.

EXAMPLE **6.** I won't sing.

6. I will sing.
7. You will play the guitar.
8. Ana will get worried.
9. We will forget the songs.
10. The audience will want to leave.

WRITE ABOUT YOUR FUTURE

11. **You, too, can become a superstar! Maybe**
you'll be a star in music, maybe in math.
Write what you will do to become a superstar.

EXAMPLE **11.** I am going to learn to write computer games.
I'll write every day.
I will make a popular game.

Stars in the Sky

▶ **Vocabulary: Space**
▶ **Language: Give Information**

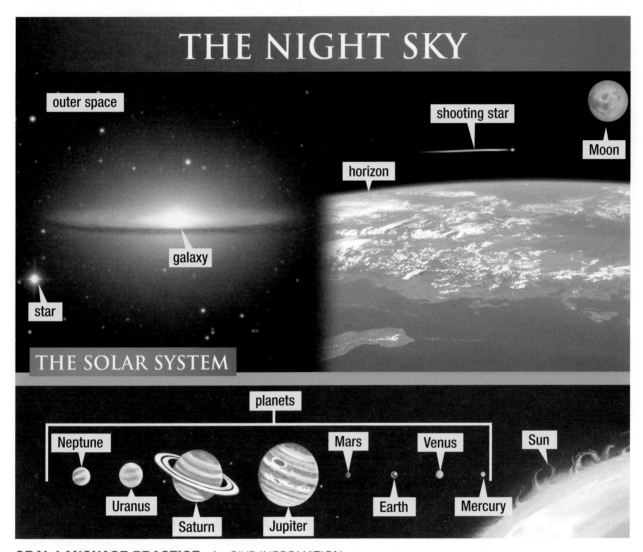

THE NIGHT SKY

outer space

shooting star

Moon

horizon

galaxy

star

THE SOLAR SYSTEM

planets

Neptune

Mars

Venus

Sun

Uranus

Earth

Mercury

Saturn

Jupiter

ORAL LANGUAGE PRACTICE ▶ GIVE INFORMATION

<u>1.–6.</u> Study the pictures. Tell a partner 3 facts about the night sky. Have your partner tell you 3 facts about the solar system.

EXAMPLE **1.** Earth is the third planet from the Sun.

WRITTEN PRACTICE

<u>7.</u> Work with a partner. Take turns writing sentences about a trip to outer space. Use future tense. Describe what you will see on your trip.

EXAMPLE **7.** I will go to outer space.
I'll see many stars.
I will fly by Venus and Mars.

Star Power

▶ **Verb Tenses**

The tense of a verb shows when the action happens.

Tense	Tells	Example
Past	what happened earlier	The star Antares **formed** millions of years ago.
Present	what is happening now	It now **shines** with a bright orange light.
Future	what will happen later	Some day Antares **is going to explode**. It **will turn** into a supernova, or exploding star.

BUILD SENTENCES

1.–9. Read the words below. Choose words from each column to make a sentence. Use each verb correctly.

| Mars | traveled
revolved
moved

travels
revolves
moves

will travel
is going to revolve
will move | in outer space

around the Sun | in the past.

today.

in the future. |

EXAMPLE **1.** Mars moved around
the Sun in the past.

WRITE A DESCRIPTION

10.–15. Work with a partner. Write a sentence each to describe the Moon in the picture. Then write a sentence each to describe the Moon last night. What will the Moon look like tomorrow night? Write a sentence each to describe it.

EXAMPLE **10.** The Moon is big and bright.

Language Development

Listen and Read Along

FOCUS ON GENRE

Fantasy   A fantasy is a fictional story with unusual settings and characters. A fantasy tells us about things that could not happen in real life. This fantasy tells a love story about the Sun and the Moon.

FOCUS ON VOCABULARY

Solar System Words   You have been learning words like the ones below. Use these words as you talk about *Sunny and Moonshine*. Collect more words to put in the web.

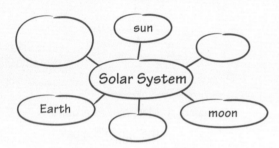

THEME BOOK

Read this fantasy about the Sun and the Moon.

People create stories to explain how things might happen in outer space.

Think About
Sunny and Moonshine

IDENTIFY GOAL AND OUTCOME

What does Moonshine want? Make a goal-and-outcome map for *Sunny and Moonshine*. Follow these steps.

1 Draw a map like the one below.

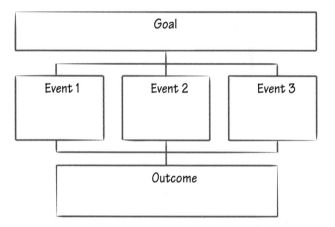

2 Read pages 4–8 of *Sunny and Moonshine* again. Write Moonshine's goal in the top box.

3 Read the rest of the book again. What happens when Moonshine tries to reach her goal? Write an event in each of the small boxes. Write what happens at the end of the story in the last box.

4 Use your completed goal-and-outcome map to retell the story to a partner.

High Frequency Words

A band plays a song at night.

REVIEW HIGH FREQUENCY WORDS

Read the words aloud. Which word goes in each sentence?

great	large
Do	Does
most	may

1. I think this band plays _____ music.
2. _____ you like it, too?
3. They _____ play a song for you!

LEARN NEW WORDS

Some words have more than one meaning. Read each sentence.
Think about the meaning of the word in dark type.

show	*verb*	Let me **show** you my new guitar.
show	*noun*	I am going to play it in the **show** tonight.
right	*adverb*	I need to practice to play the songs **right**.
right	*adjective*	I strum the strings with my **right** hand.
close	*adverb*	I keep the music book **close** to me while I play.
close	*verb*	**Close** it now and see if I can play the song.
watch	*verb*	Many people will come to **watch** us perform.
watch	*noun*	I have to check my **watch** so I won't be late.
kind	*adverb*	I wonder what **kind** of music people will like.
kind	*adjective*	I hope the audience will be **kind** and won't shout "Boo!"

PRACTICE

Write each sentence. Add the missing word.   EXAMPLE **4.** The show will start at 7:30.

4. The _ _ _ _ will start at 7:30.
5. Come at 7:00 so you can sit _ _ _ _ _ to the stage.
6. My _ _ _ _ _ broke. I don't know what time it is.
7. I can't wait to _ _ _ _ you how well we play.
8. Sometimes I _ _ _ _ _ my eyes while I play.
9. I hope I sing all the _ _ _ _ words to the songs.
10. Look for me on the _ _ _ _ _ side of the stage.

More High Frequency Words

Read the words aloud. Which word goes in the sentence?

Yes	You
plants	picture
tomorrow	until

1. ___, I can go to the show!

2. I will take a ____ of the singer.

3. I will tell you about the show _____.

This music star plays a song.

Some words sound the same as others, but they are spelled differently and have different meanings. These words are called <u>homophones</u>. Read each sentence. Think about the meaning of the word in dark type.

by	I have to stop **by** the music store.
buy	I want to **buy** tickets for the show tonight.
for	They are **for** my friends Jeff, Luz, and Peter.
four	**Four** tickets cost $60!
write	Jeff says, "I'll **write** you a check for $10."
right	"That's not **right**," I tell him. "You owe me $15."
no	"**No** I don't," he says. "You borrowed $5 from me last week."
know	"Yes. I **know** what you're talking about," I answer.
here	"I have your tickets **here**," I tell my friends.
hear	They say, "We can't wait to **hear** some great music!"

Write each sentence. Add the missing word.   EXAMPLE **4.** We have four seats up in the front.

4. We have _ _ _ _ seats up in the front.

5. _ _ _ _ are our seats!

6. Are you sure those are the _ _ _ _ _ ones?

7. I cannot wait _ _ _ the show to start!

8. I think I will _ _ _ a t-shirt on the way out.

9. I will _ _ _ _ _ the band a fan letter when I get home.

10. We all _ _ _ _ this will be a great show!

Reading and Spelling

▶ **Multisyllabic Words**

Listen and learn. CD

Starship Earth

Safely,
And silently,
Earth goes around the Sun.
And each time our Earth circles that Sun
Another year is done.

Gracefully,
Silently,
Earth spins while she rings the Sun.
And each time our Earth has completely spun
Another day is done.

STUDY LONG WORDS

How many syllables are in each word? Look for letter patterns and word parts.

eagle
▲

fifteen
▲

telescope
▲▲

hold carefully
▲ ▲

READING STRATEGIES

There are several ways to read a long word.

1 Look for familiar parts—prefixes, suffixes, or endings like *-ed* or *-ing*. Cover them.

completely   **complete**

2 Figure out how to divide the root word.

complete

com   plete

I can look for a letter pattern. I see a vowel, three consonants, and another vowel.

complete

com   plete

Or, I can look for a vowel pattern. I need to keep the vowel, consonant, and final e together.

3 Blend the syllables to say the root word. Then uncover the suffix and read the entire word.

com + plete   **com + plete + ly = completely**

READING PRACTICE

Use what you learned to read the sentences.

1. Chan waited on the rooftop beneath the night sky.
2. He carefully checked his watch. It was close to midnight.
3. The North Star twinkled in the middle of the night sky.
4. Chan was able to see Venus. Then he saw a flash of light!
5. Was it a rocket launch? No! It was just lightning.

SPELLING PRACTICE

<u>6.–10.</u> Now write the sentences that your teacher reads.

WORD WORK

<u>11.–16.</u> **Read the newspaper article. Find the words with 3 syllables. List them. Divide them into syllables.**

EXAMPLE **11.** important   im por tant

A Star in Space

Here is some news for fans of Kim Mills. The film star will go to Houston to train for an important space flight with NASA. She will hopefully blast off sometime in June.

"I have to prepare for the flight," Ms. Mills said with excitement.

The star plans to act in two different films this fall: *A Terrible Surprise* and a remake of *The Forbidden Planet*.

Read on Your Own

FOCUS ON GENRE

Legend   A legend is a story that is told by older people to younger people. No one knows if a legend is true or make-believe. This legend is about Native American calendars.

FOCUS ON WORDS

Multisyllabic Words   When you read and come to a longer word you don't know, look for familiar parts. Then divide the root word into syllables. Blend the syllables to read the entire word.

telescope

Multiple-Meaning Words and Homophones   Look for these words as you read.

Multiple-Meaning Words	Homophones
show	by/buy
right	no/know
close	here/hear
watch	for/four
kind	right/write

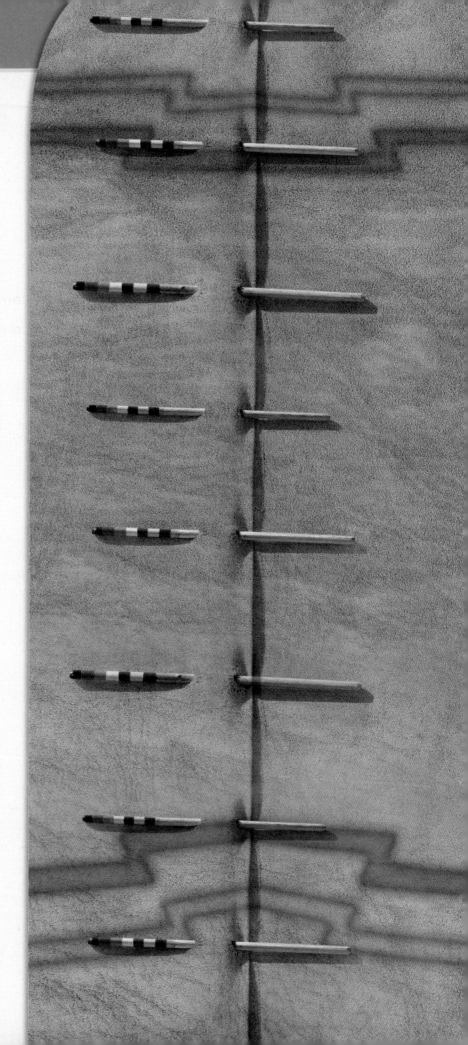

FIFTH MOON'S STORY

In the Old Time, Winter stayed on Earth forever. Rain and snow fell on the land. It was quite a show. Fields and rivers were covered by snow. The Earth Children looked at their calendars. When would the cold end? They asked Sun to show kindness, "Please tell Winter to go away!"

The kind Sun went by Winter's house. Winter sat all alone. He was huddled close to a cold fire. Sun came and sat on Winter's right side. Winter recognized Sun. "Go away!" Winter shouted. He tried to push Sun out and close the door.

"No!" Sun exclaimed. "It is you who must go. Leave the Land of the Earth Children. Leave here now!" Winter frowned. He blasted Sun with icy rain, but he was not able to make Sun leave.

Sun kept shining and shining. At last, Winter began to melt away. He grew smaller and smaller until he became the size of a snowflake. Sun then called for Owl. Owl flew into the room. Sun said, "Take Winter to the snows in the far north. It is the right place for him. He will remain there a long time." Owl did as Sun asked.

Suddenly, the Land of the Earth Children began to grow warm. Green leaves reappeared on the trees of every kind.

The people came together to celebrate. They danced joyfully, for gentle Spring came back into their land.

Think About "Fifth Moon's Story"

CHECK YOUR UNDERSTANDING

<u>1.</u> Make a goal-and-outcome map like the one below and complete it.
Use the completed map to retell "Fifth Moon's Story" to a partner.

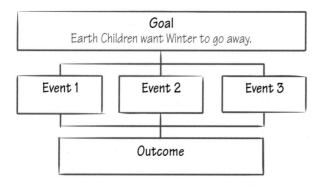

EXPAND YOUR VOCABULARY

<u>2.</u> Make a chart like the one below. Work with a group to add words.
Tell about the weather and what you do in each season.

Season	Weather	Activities
winter	cold, snowy, icy	ice skate, eat soup
spring		
summer		
fall		

WRITE ABOUT THE SUN

<u>3.</u> Work with a partner. Take turns to tell each other how the Sun
helps people. Then tell each other how the Sun can be bad for
people, too. Write sentences to tell about the Sun.

EXAMPLE **3.** The Sun helps people grow crops.
The Sun is bad for your skin when you stay out too long.

Success in Science

▶ **Learn About Outer Space**

The Moon and Stars

The surface, or outside, of the Moon looks like this:

The bright places on the Moon are areas of **mountains**. The dark places are flat **plains**. Both have a lot of **craters**.

The **soil** and **rocks** on the Moon are made of minerals also found on Earth.

This is how a star is born:

A **nebula** is a cloud of dust and gas. If enough of the dust and gas come together, a **star** will form in the nebula.

Listen to the article. Then do the Review.

The Moon and the Stars

• **What are the Moon and the stars made of?**

Since the beginning of time, people have had questions about outer space. What is the Moon made of? Why do stars glow? Scientists on Earth are now answering some of the questions.

Astronauts have walked through the Moon's plains. They collected rocks and soil and brought them back to Earth. Here, scientists found that the rocks from the Moon have aluminum, silica, iron, and other minerals in them. There are also some gases trapped in the rocks. Scientists found that much of the Moon's soil is made up of small pieces of glass.

Scientists use telescopes and other special tools to study the stars. They learned that stars are huge balls of hot gases. They are not solid like the Moon or the Earth. The gases in the stars give off both heat and light.

We still have questions about the Moon and stars. Scientists are learning more about outer space every day.

The minerals in rocks from the Moon are also found on Earth.

We use **aluminum** in cans.

Glass is made of **silica**.

This pan is made of **iron**.

REVIEW

1. **Check Your Understanding** What did the scientists find out about the rocks and soil on the Moon? What are the stars made of?
2. **Vocabulary** What is on the surface of the Moon?

EXPLORING SPACE

Build Background for "Exploring Space"

SPACE

Outer space is the area beyond our planet. Many people study space. Some travel into outer space to learn more about our solar system.

◀ Scientists study the millions of stars in the night sky to learn about space.

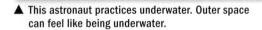

▲ This astronaut practices underwater. Outer space can feel like being underwater.

Learn Key Vocabulary

Rate and Study the Words Rate how well you know each word. Then:

1. Pronounce the word. Say it aloud several times. Spell it.
2. Study the example.
3. Tell more about the word.
4. Practice it. Make the word your own.

Key Words

space (spās) *noun*

Space is a big and unlimited area. Scientist use tools like this telescope to look into outer **space**.

solar system (sō-lur sis-tum) *noun*

The **solar system** is the sun and all the planets, moons, and comets that move around it. Earth is part of the **solar system**.

rocket (rok-it) *noun*

A **rocket** is a machine that burns fuel very quickly and moves very fast. **Rockets** can be used to send people into space.

moon (mūn) *noun*

A **moon** is any object that revolves, or turns, around a planet. Earth has one **moon**.

astronauts (as-tru-nots) *noun*

Astronauts are people who fly into space to study the solar system. Some **astronauts** live on space stations for weeks at a time.

Practice the Words With a partner, make a Vocabulary Study Card for each Key Word.

Write the word.

front

> rocket

Tell what the word means and use it in a sentence.

back

> fast spaceship
>
> Astronauts travel in rockets.

Use the cards to quiz your partner. Take turns answering.

Listen and Read Along

FOCUS ON GENRE

Science Article   A science article gives information about a science topic. It is nonfiction. This science article tells about space travel.

FOCUS ON COMPREHENSION

Goal and Outcome   Writers often tell about a goal, or something someone wanted to do. Then they tell about events, or what happens. Last, they tell if the goal was reached. This is called the outcome. As you read "Exploring Space," use a diagram like the one below to keep track of the goal, the events, and the outcome.

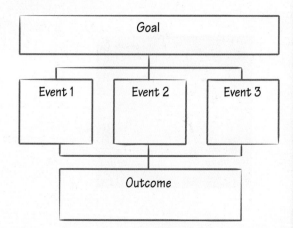

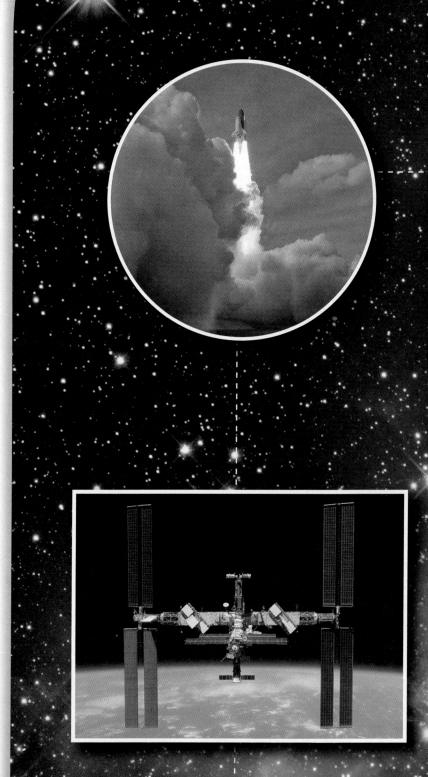

Rockets help people learn about outer space.

EXPLORING SPACE

Selection Recording

STUDYING SPACE

▲ Galileo used a small telescope to study the universe.

In the early 1600s, a scientist named Galileo Galilei used a telescope to study outer **space**. The telescope allowed him to see things 20 times larger than he could without it. He used the telescope to describe great things.

Hundreds of years passed. We learned more about the **solar system**. But we wanted to do more. We wanted to **blast off** into it, too.

▼ The space shuttle Atlantis blasts off into orbit.

Key Vocabulary

space *n.*, the empty area outside of Earth

solar system *n.*, the sun and planets that orbit the sun

In Other Words

blast off travel

BLASTING OFF

Science helped us reach our goal again. A **rocket** built in Russia carried the first **satellite** into space. It was called Sputnik. Sputnik is the Russian word for "traveler."

Then American scientists made a decision. They wanted to land a person on the **moon**. A rocket would need a lot of power to get all the way to the moon and back. Could they build a rocket engine powerful enough to make the trip?

▲ Sputnik was the first satellite launched into space.

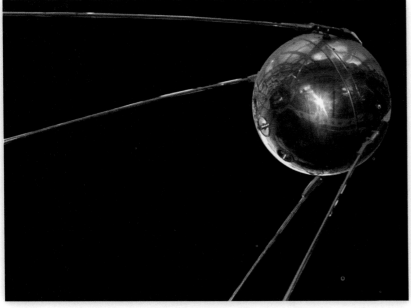

◀ Scientists use satellites like Sputnik to learn about space.

Key Vocabulary
  rocket *n.*, a vehicle that can travel into space
  moon *n.*, the natural satellite that orbits the earth

In Other Words
  satellite man-made thing that could orbit Earth

Before You Move On

1. **Details** Who was Galileo? What did he do?
2. **Goal and Outcome** What did American scientists decide to do?

REACHING THE GOAL

Scientists knew that a rocket would need a lot of **fuel** to reach the moon. They also knew that this much fuel would make the rocket too heavy to get there. They decided to use a multistage rocket. When the fuel in one stage of a multistage rocket is used up, that stage falls away. This makes the rocket lighter. The engine of the next stage pushes the rocket even faster and higher.

Astronauts Neil Armstrong and Buzz Aldrin flew a multistage rocket to the moon in 1969. They became the first people to walk on the moon. Since then, we have learned a lot more about our solar system.

▲ How do you think Buzz Aldrin felt when he stood on the moon?

The Saturn IV multistage rocket has three stages and a space capsule. ▶

Space Capsule

Stage 3

Stage 2

Stage 1

Key Vocabulary
astronaut *n.*, a person who travels into space

In Other Words
fuel gas

LIFE IN SPACE

So where do we go from here? One of the most exciting space explorations of all time is happening right now. It is called the International Space Station. Astronauts from many countries live and work there. They can stay there for **several** months at a time.

Astronauts have exciting jobs. They get to live in space. But their work is more than just fun. Astronauts help us learn about our planet. They help us learn about the solar system, too.

Astronauts float in space, even when they eat and sleep!

▼ International Space Station

In Other Words
several many

Before You Move On

1. **Goal and Outcome** What events happened before scientists reached their goal?
2. **Personal Opinion** Would you like to be an **astronaut**? Tell why or why not.

SPACE ADVENTURES

Scientists on the International Space Station do science **experiments**. They take pictures of Earth. They ask questions. What materials stay strong in space? How is our planet changing? How does space travel affect plants and animals? This information could be very important some day if we are going to take long trips into space. The adventure has just begun!

▲ working outside

▼ working inside

In Other Words
experiments tests

Stargazer

I heard that stars can fall and I want to catch one.

I want to watch its bright white light spin and swirl

    down,

       down,

          down,

to the waiting world

and into my open hands.

But as I stare up at the deep black sky

I remember the day's sun-filled heat and ask myself:

    Will that spinning star that burns bright white heat hurt my hand?

So I drop my hands to my side and stand straight,

    still watching the deep black sky.

Someone else can catch a star.

I'll just watch.

—Anne Kaske

Before You Move On

1. **Speculate** Where do you think we might try to explore in **space**?
2. **Author's Purpose** How did the author of the poem show the idea of something falling?

Think About "Exploring Space"

CHECK YOUR UNDERSTANDING

<u>1.–2.</u> Work with a partner to complete each item.

1. **Goal and Outcome** Make a diagram like the one below. Use information about **space** from the selection to complete the chart.

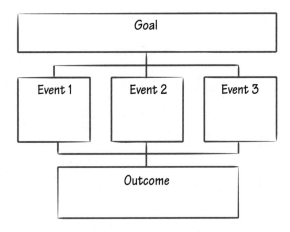

2. **Sum It Up** Use your diagram to summarize how scientists learned about our **solar system** and outer space.

REVIEW VOCABULARY

<u>3.–7.</u> Read the paragraph aloud. Add the vocabulary words.

Scientists study the _____. People who go to outer _____ are called _____. They have landed on the _____. They use _____ to get there.

Vocabulary

space

solar system

rockets

moon

astronauts

WRITE ABOUT OUTER SPACE

<u>8.</u> Write about what life would be like if you were an **astronaut** on a space station.

Diamante Poem

Poems use language to share thoughts, feelings, and memories. When you write poetry, choose each word carefully. Think about the sounds and beats of words.

- Some poems **rhyme**. Rhyming words end with the same sound.

- Sometimes other letter sounds are repeated in a poem. **Alliteration** is when the first sound of a word is repeated as the first sound of another word. Can you find the alliteration in line 2 of the diamante poem?

- Words in poems have **rhythm**, just like the beats in music. Rhythm is the beat of the words in a poem.

Some poems have special rules for words, syllables, rhythm and rhyme. Diamante poems even have special rules for the shape of the writing! A diamante poem uses nouns, adjectives, and verbs to compare two different objects. Each line uses a certain type of word. It only has 9 words.

DIAMANTE POEM

This is Jupiter.

1. <u>Jupiter</u>

2. <u>glowing</u>   <u>gaseous</u>

3. <u>turning</u>   <u>changing</u>   <u>reflecting</u>

4. <u>smaller</u>   <u>rocky</u>

5. <u>Earth</u>

Rules for a Diamante Poem

Line 1
Name the first object. Use a noun.

Line 2
Write 2 adjectives to describe the noun above.

Line 3
Write 3 verbs that end in *-ing*. The verbs must tell about both nouns.

Line 4
Write 2 adjectives to describe the noun below.

Line 5
Name the second object. Use a noun.

Write a Diamante Poem

WRITING PROMPT Find interesting facts about two things in outer space, then write a poem that compares them. Share the facts and your poem to inform and entertain your classmates.

Prewrite

When you prewrite, you gather ideas and choose your topic. You also make a plan for what you will write. Follow these steps.

❶ COLLECT IDEAS

Think about objects in outer space that are very different but can be compared in some way. List noun pairs. Think about which idea is best. Remember why you are writing. Remember who will read your poem. Now choose an idea.

Here is Jana's list. She chose to compare the Sun and the Moon.

> **Objects in Space**
> Saturn / Mercury
> comet / asteroid
> planet / star
> sun / moon

❷ GATHER INFORMATION

Start by finding interesting facts about your two objects. You can use the Internet and other research tools. Write the facts on cards.

> **Moon**
> cold; round; revolves around Earth; reflects light from the sun

> **Sun**
> hot; planets revolve around it; gives light and heat

Reflect
- Did you pick a good topic?
- Do you have a clear plan?

Draft

When you draft, you begin writing. Use the words you gathered to draft your poem.

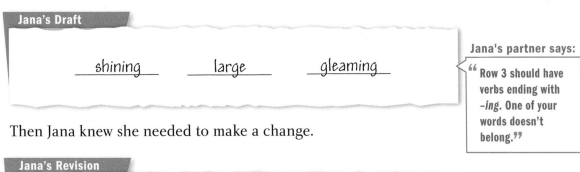

Revise

When you revise a draft, you make your writing better. First, you need to know what a reader thinks of your work. Jana read her paper to a partner.

Jana's Draft

shining   large   gleaming

Then Jana knew she needed to make a change.

Jana's partner says:

" Row 3 should have verbs ending with *-ing*. One of your words doesn't belong."

Jana's Revision

                 glowing.
shining   ⌃large   gleaming

She replaced a word that didn't belong and added a verb ending with *-ing*.

Now follow these steps to revise your poem.

1 DECIDE WHAT TO CHANGE

Read to a partner. Ask your partner to check the rules for a diamante poem. Do you need to make any changes?

2 MARK YOUR CHANGES

If you need to replace text, use this mark: ⌃‾.

Reflect

- Did you compare the two objects?

- Did you put the words in the correct places?

- Did you use interesting words?

Edit and Proofread

After you have revised your draft, check it for mistakes. Follow these steps.

1 CHECK YOUR ADJECTIVES

Adjectives make your poem more interesting. They give details about your topic and help the reader understand important things about it. Choose adjectives for your poem that help readers make a picture of your topic in their mind.

EXAMPLES   fiery   enormous

              distant   frozen

2 CHECK YOUR SPELLING

Circle each word that may be misspelled. Look it up in the dictionary or ask for help. Fix the spelling if you need to.

What errors did Jana correct in her poem?

3 MARK YOUR CHANGES

Now edit your poem. Use these marks to show your changes:

∧	✃	⌐	◯	≡	╱	¶
Add.	Take out.	Replace with this.	Check spelling.	Capitalize.	Make lowercase.	Make new paragraph.

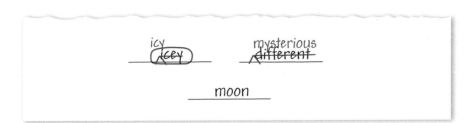

Reflect

• What kinds of errors did you find?

• What can you do to keep from making errors?

Publish, Share, and Reflect

You have finished your diamante poem. Now you are ready to publish your work! When you publish your writing, you put it in final form to share with others.

The moon formed at about the same time as Earth.

The sun will burn for millions and millions of years.

① FINISH AND DISPLAY

Think about how your writing looks.

- Write your poem on a piece of piece of paper cut into a special shape.

- Cut a star shape out of card stock or heavy paper. Copy your poem on one side. On the other side, write your facts.

- Add a rubber band and hang the star.

- Decorate your star.

- Read poems and facts on other stars from your classmates.

② READ ALOUD

There are many ways you can share your writing. For this poem, try reading it aloud. As you read aloud, think about your purpose.

- When you read your poem, read slowly to emphasize each word. Give listeners time to make a picture in their mind. Focus on the rhythm of the words and alliteration.

- Use a different voice and pace for reading the facts.

Also remember these tips.

Presenting Tips

If You Are the Speaker:	If You Are the Listener:
• Focus on rhythm and alliteration.	• Make a picture of the poem in your mind.
• Speak slowly.	• Enjoy the rhythm of the words.

Reflect

- How did researching your objects help you find interesting words?

- What did you like best about writing your poem?

Common Core

INSIDE

LANGUAGE · LITERACY · CONTENT

NATIONAL GEOGRAPHIC LEARNING

CENGAGE Learning

► Handbook

Strategies for Learning Language

These strategies can help you learn to use and understand the English language.

❶ Listen actively and try out language.

WHAT TO DO	EXAMPLES
Repeat what you hear.	You hear: "Way to go, Joe! Fantastic catch!" You say: "Way to go, Joe! Fantastic catch!"
Recite songs and poems.	My Family Tree Two grandmas, one brother, Two grandpas, one mother, One father, and then there's me. Eight of us together Make up my family tree. "Two grandmas, one brother,..."
Listen to others and use their language.	You hear: "When did you know that something was missing?" You say: "I knew that something was missing when I got to class."

❷ Ask for help.

WHAT TO DO	EXAMPLES
Ask questions about how to use language.	"Did I say that right?" "Did I use that word in the right way?" "Which is correct, "bringed" or "brought"?"
Use your native language or English to make sure that you understand.	You say: "Wait! Could you say that again more slowly, please?" Other options: "Does 'violet' mean 'purple'?" "Is 'enormous' another way to say 'big'?"

❸ Use gestures and body language, and watch for them.

WHAT TO DO	EXAMPLES
Use gestures and movements to help others understand your ideas.	I will hold up five fingers to show that I need five more minutes.
Watch people as they speak. The way they look or move can help you understand the meaning of their words.	Let's give him a hand. Everyone is clapping. "Give him a hand" must mean to clap for him.

❹ Think about what you are learning.

WHAT TO DO	EXAMPLES
Ask yourself: Are my language skills getting better? How can I improve?	Was it correct to use "they" when I talked about my grandparents? Did I add 's to show ownership?
Keep notes about what you've learned. Use your notes to practice using English.	How to Ask Questions • I can start a question with "who," "what," "where," "when," "how," or "why": What will the weather be like today? • I can also start a question with "do" or "does": Do you have my math book?

Sentences

A sentence is a group of words that expresses a complete thought.

TYPES OF SENTENCES	EXAMPLES
A **statement** tells something. It ends with a period.	The football game was on Friday. The coach made an important announcement.
A **question** asks for information. It ends with a question mark.	What did the coach say?

Kinds of Questions

Questions That Ask for a "Yes" or "No" Answer	Answers
Can you tell me what he said?	Yes.
Does everyone know the news?	No.
Is it about the team?	Yes.
Did the team win the game?	Yes.
Are the players sad?	No.
Were the fans surprised?	Yes.

Questions That Ask for Specific Information	
Who heard the announcement?	The team and the fans heard the announcement.
What did the coach say?	He said the team will play in a special game.
Where will the team play this game?	In Hawaii.
When did the coach find out?	Right before the game.
How did he feel?	He felt so happy!
Why was our team chosen?	Our team was chosen because we won a lot of games.
How many games did the team win this year?	All ten of them.
How much will the tickets to the game cost?	Fifteen dollars.

An **exclamation** shows surprise or strong feeling. It ends with an exclamation mark.	That's fantastic news! I can't believe it!

TYPES OF SENTENCES, continued	EXAMPLES
A **command** tells you what to do or what not to do. It usually begins with a verb. It often ends with a period.	Give the team my congratulations. Buy a ticket for me, too.
If a command shows strong emotion, it ends with an exclamation mark.	Don't forget!

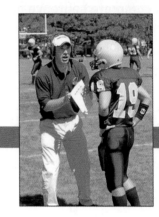

NEGATIVE SENTENCES	EXAMPLES
A **negative sentence** uses a **negative word** like *not*.	
• Add *not* after <u>am, is, are, was,</u> or *were*.	The game in Hawaii **was not** boring!
• Add *do not, does not,* or *did not* <u>before</u> all other verbs.	The other team **did not play** well.
• Combine the verb and *not* to make a **contraction**.	Our team **didn't make** any mistakes.

Contractions with *not*

To make a **contraction**, take out one or more letters and add an **apostrophe (')**.

are + not = aren't	The fans of the other team **aren't** happy.
is + not = isn't	Their coach **isn't** happy either.
can + not = can't	The other team **can't** believe they lost.
was + not = wasn't	The game **wasn't** fun for them.
were + not = weren't	The players **weren't** playing their best.
do + not = don't	They **don't** want to go to practice on Monday.
does + not = doesn't	The quarterback **doesn't** want to hear about his mistakes.
did + not = didn't	The other team **didn't** want to lose.

CAPITALIZATION IN SENTENCES	EXAMPLES
Every sentence begins with a **capital letter.**	**O**ur team was very proud. **W**hat do you think of all this? **I**t's a wonderful story!

COMPLETE SENTENCES	EXAMPLES
A **complete sentence** has a **subject** and a **predicate**. A complete sentence expresses a complete thought.	**Many people** **visit our National Parks**. Grand Canyon National Park, Arizona
A **fragment** is not a sentence. It is not a complete thought. You can add information to a fragment to turn it into a sentence.	**Fragment:** A fun vacation **Complete Sentences:** You can have a fun vacation. Will we have a fun vacation at the park? Go to a national park and have a fun vacation.

SUBJECT-VERB AGREEMENT	EXAMPLES

The verb must always agree with the subject of the sentence.

A **singular subject** names one person or thing. Use a **singular verb** with a singular subject.	Another popular **park** **is** the Grand Canyon. **It** **has** a powerful river.
A **plural subject** tells about more than one person or thing. Use a **plural verb** with a plural subject.	The **cliffs** **are** beautiful. **We** **were amazed** by their colors.

Singular and Plural Verbs

Singular	Plural
The park **is** big.	The parks **are** big.
The park **was** beautiful.	The parks **were** beautiful.
The park **has** campsites.	The parks **have** campsites.
The park **does** not **open** until spring.	The parks **do** not **open** until spring.

Punctuation Marks

Punctuation marks make words and sentences easier to understand.

PERIOD	EXAMPLES
Use a **period**:	
• at the end of a statement or a polite command	Georgia read the paper to her mom.
	Tell me if there are any interesting articles.
• after an abbreviation	There's a new restaurant on Stone St. near our house.
	It opens at 10 a.m. today.
	But: *Do not use a period in an acronym:*
	National Aeronautics and Space Administration **NASA**
	Do not use a period in the abbreviation of a state name written in a mailing address:
	Massachusetts **MA** Illinois **IL** Texas **TX**
	California **CA** Florida **FL** Virginia **VA**
• after an initial	The owner of J.J. Malone.
• to separate dollars and cents. The period is the decimal point.	The article says lunch today costs only $1.50.
• in an Internet address. The period is called a dot.	The restaurant has a Web site at www.jjmalone.org.

QUESTION MARK	EXAMPLES
Use a **question mark**:	
• at the end of a question	What kind of food do they serve**?**
• after a question that comes at the end of a statement	The food is good, isn't it**?**
	But: *Use a period after an indirect question. In an indirect question, you tell about a question you asked.*
	I asked how good the food could be for only $1.50.

Punctuation Marks, continued

EXCLAMATION MARK	EXAMPLES
Use an **exclamation mark**: • after an interjection • at the end of a sentence to show that you feel strongly about something	Wow**!** One-fifty is a really good price**!**

COMMA	EXAMPLES
Use a **comma**: • to separate three or more items in a series • when you write a number with four or more digits	Articles about the school, a big sale, and a new movie were also in the newspaper. The school will buy a new bus, 10 computers, and books for the library. There was $500,000 in the school budget.
Use a **comma** in these places in a letter: • between the city and the state • between the date and the year • after the greeting • after the closing	144 North Ave. Milpas, AK July 3, 2002 Dear Mr. Okada, I really like computers and am glad that we have them at school, but ours are out-of-date. As principal, can you ask the school board to buy us new ones for next year? Sincerely, Patrick Green

QUOTATION MARKS	EXAMPLES
Use **quotation marks** to show:	
• a speaker's exact words	"Listen to this!" Georgia said.
• the exact words quoted from a book or other printed material	The announcement in the paper was "The world-famous writer Josie Ramon will be at Milpas Library Friday night."
• the title of a song, poem, or short story	Her poem "Speaking" is famous.
• the title of a magazine article or newspaper article	It appeared in the magazine article "How to Talk to Your Teen."
• the title of a chapter from a book	On Friday night she'll be reading "Getting Along," a chapter from her new book.
• words used in a special way	We will be "all ears" at the reading.
Always put **periods** and **commas** inside quotation marks.	"She is such a great writer," Georgia said. "I'd love to meet her."

COLON	EXAMPLES
Use a **colon**:	356 Oak St. Milpas, AK Sept. 24, 2002 Features Editor *Milpas Post* 78 Main St. Milpas, AK Dear Sir or Madam:
• after the greeting in a business letter	Please place this announcement in the calendar section of your paper. Friday at 7:15 p.m., the writer Josie Ramón will be speaking at Milpas Library. When people come, they should bring:
• to separate hours and minutes	
• to start a list	1. Questions for Ms. Ramón. 2. Money to purchase her new book. 3. A cushion to sit on! Thank you. Sincerely, Hector Quintana

Capital Letters

A reader can tell that a word is special in some way if it begins with a capital letter.

PROPER NOUNS	EXAMPLES

A common noun names any person, place, thing, or idea.
A proper noun names one particular person, place, thing, or idea.

All the important words in a **proper noun** start with a capital letter.

	Common Noun	Proper Noun
Person	captain	Captain Meriwether Lewis
Place	land	Louisiana Territory
Thing	team	Corps of Discovery
Idea	destiny	Manifest Destiny

Proper nouns include:

• names of people and their titles

Laura Roberts
Captain Meriwether Lewis

But: Do not capitalize a title if it is used without a name:

The captain's co-leader on the expedition was William Clark.

• abbreviations of titles

Mr. Ramos
Mrs. Ramos
Dr. Schuyler
Ms. Nguyen

Abbreviations of Titles

Capt. for the captain of a boat or in the armed forces
Pres. for the president of a country, a company, a club, or an organization
Sen. for a member of the U.S. Senate
Rep. for a member of the U.S. House of Representatives

• words like **Mom** and **Dad** when they are used as names

"**Mom,** can you tell me more about the expedition?" said Laura.

But: Do not capitalize names if they follow a word like my.

I ask my **mom** a lot of questions.

• organizations

United Nations   Science Club   Wildlife Society   Lodi City Council

• names of languages, subject areas, and religions

Spanish   Mathematics   Buddhism
Vietnamese   Social Studies   Christianity

PROPER NOUNS, continued	EXAMPLES

- names of geographical places

Cities and States
Dallas, Texas
Miami, Florida
St. Louis, Missouri

Countries
Iran
Ecuador
Cambodia

Continents
Asia
South America
Africa

Streets and Roads
King Boulevard
Main Avenue
First Street

Landforms
Rocky Mountains
Sahara Desert
Grand Canyon

Public Spaces
Hemisfair Plaza
Central Park
Muir Camp

Bodies of Water
Yellowstone River
Pacific Ocean
Great Salt Lake
Gulf of Mexico

Buildings, Ships, and Monuments
Empire State Building
Titanic
Statue of Liberty

Planets and Heavenly Bodies
Earth
Jupiter
Milky Way

- abbreviations of geographic places

Words Used in Addresses

Avenue	Ave.	Highway	Hwy.	South	S.
Boulevard	Blvd.	Lane	Ln.	Square	Sq.
Court	Ct.	North	N.	Street	St.
Drive	Dr.	Place	Pl.	West	W.
East	E.	Road	Rd.		

Abbreviations for State Names in Mailing Addresses

Alabama	AL	Hawaii	HI	Massachusetts	MA	New Mexico	NM	South Dakota	SD
Alaska	AK	Idaho	ID	Michigan	MI	New York	NY	Tennessee	TN
Arizona	AZ	Illinois	IL	Minnesota	MN	North Carolina	NC	Texas	TX
Arkansas	AR	Indiana	IN	Mississippi	MS	North Dakota	ND	Utah	UT
California	CA	Iowa	IA	Missouri	MO	Ohio	OH	Vermont	VT
Colorado	CO	Kansas	KS	Montana	MT	Oklahoma	OK	Virginia	VA
Connecticut	CT	Kentucky	KY	Nebraska	NE	Oregon	OR	Washington	WA
Delaware	DE	Louisiana	LA	Nevada	NV	Pennsylvania	PA	West Virginia	WV
Florida	FL	Maine	ME	New Hampshire	NH	Rhode Island	RI	Wisconsin	WI
Georgia	GA	Maryland	MD	New Jersey	NJ	South Carolina	SC	Wyoming	WY

- months, days, special days and holidays

January	July	Sunday	New Year's Day
February	August	Monday	Mother's Day
March	September	Tuesday	Thanksgiving
April	October	Wednesday	Hanukkah
May	November	Thursday	Kwanzaa
June	December	Friday	
		Saturday	

IN LETTERS	EXAMPLES
Capitalize the first word used in the **greeting** or in the **closing** of a letter. Street, city, and state names in the address, as well as their abbreviations, are also capitalized.	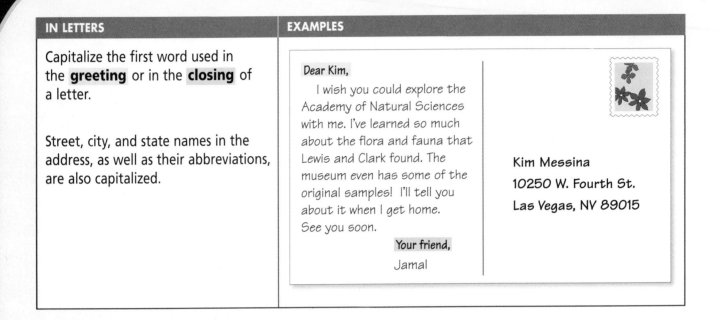

E-Mail

You can use e-mail to send a letter to a friend. E-mail is short for **electronic mail** and is sent by a computer. You can send letters to or receive messages from anyone in the world who has an e-mail address. Here's one kind of computer "mailbox" you might use.

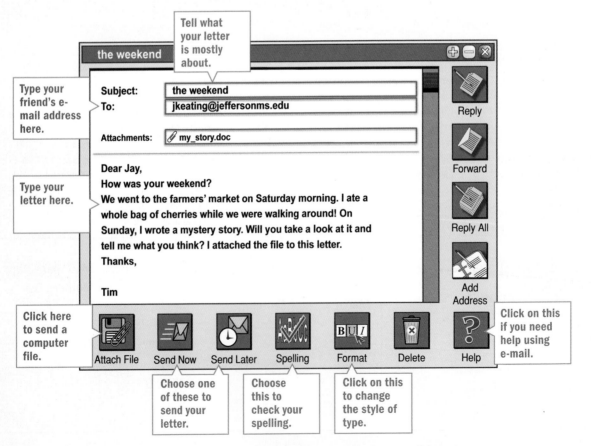

Nouns

A noun names a person, place, or thing.
There are different kinds of nouns.

COMMON AND PROPER NOUNS	EXAMPLES
A **common noun** names any person, place, or thing.	A **teenager** sat by the **ocean** and read a **book**.
A proper noun names one particular person, place, or thing. The important words in a proper noun start with a <u>capital letter</u>.	<u>**Daniel**</u> sat by the <u>**Atlantic Ocean**</u> and read _**Save the Manatee**_. A manatee

SINGULAR AND PLURAL NOUNS	EXAMPLES

A singular noun names one thing.
A plural noun names more than one thing.

	EXAMPLES				
Follow these rules to make a noun plural:					
• Add **-s** to most nouns.	desk desk**s**	book book**s**	teacher teacher**s**	apple apple**s**	line line**s**
• If the noun ends in **x**, **ch**, **sh**, **s**, or **z**, add **-es**.	box box**es**	lunch lunch**es**	dish dish**es**	glass glass**es**	waltz waltz**es**
• Some nouns change in different ways to show the plural.	child **children**	foot **feet**	tooth **teeth**	man **men**	woman **women**

POSSESSIVE NOUNS	EXAMPLES
A **possessive noun** shows ownership. It often ends in **'s**.	Daniel **'s** book was very interesting.

Nouns that Name People

Family Words

Girls/Women

great-grandmother
grandmother
mother
stepmother
sister
stepsister
half-sister
daughter
granddaughter
aunt
cousin
niece

Boys/Men

great-grandfather
grandfather
father
stepfather
brother
stepbrother
half-brother
son
grandson
uncle
cousin
nephew

My family includes my grandmother, mother, father, sister, cousins, aunts, uncles, and me.

People at Work

architect

artist
astronaut
athlete
baker
bank teller
barber
bus driver
business person
cab driver
cashier
coach
construction worker

cook
custodian

dancer

dentist
designer
doctor
editor
eye doctor
farmer
firefighter
flight attendant
florist

gardener
guard
historian
lawyer
letter carrier
librarian
mechanic

messenger

model
mover
musician
nurse
office worker

painter
photographer

pilot

plumber
police officer
reporter
sailor
salesperson
scientist
stylist
teacher
veterinarian
writer

Nouns that Name Places

At Home

bathroom
bedroom
dining room
garage
garden

kitchen

living room

yard

In Town

airport
bank
basketball court
beauty shop
bookstore

bus stop

cafe
city hall
clothing store

fire station
flower shop
garage
gas station

hardware store

hospital
intersection
jewelry store
library

mall
market
motel
movie theater
museum
music store
nursing home
office building
park
parking garage
parking lot
pet shop
police station
pool

post office
restaurant

school

shoe store
sports stadium
supermarket
theater
toy store
train station

On the Earth

beach
canyon
desert
forest
hill
island
lake

mountains

ocean

plains
pond
rain forest
river
sea
seashore
valley
wetland

Nouns, continued

SINGULAR AND PLURAL NOUNS	EXAMPLES
Noncount nouns are nouns that you cannot count. A noncount noun does not have a plural form.	My favorite museum has **furniture** and **art**. Sometimes I wonder how much **money** each item is worth.

Types of Noncount Nouns

Activities and Sports

baseball	camping	dancing	fishing
golf	singing	soccer	swimming

Examples

I love to play **soccer**.

Category Nouns

clothing	equipment	furniture	hardware	jewelry
machinery	mail	money	time	weather

My **equipment** is in the car.

Food

bread	cereal	cheese	corn	flour
lettuce	meat	milk	rice	salt
soup	sugar	tea	water	

You can count some food items by using a measurement word like **cup**, **slice**, **glass**, or **head** plus the word **of**. To show the plural form, just make the measurement word plural.

I'll drink some **water** on my way to the game.

I'll drink **two glasses of water** on my way to the game.

Ideas and Feelings

democracy	enthusiasm	freedom	fun	health
honesty	information	knowledge	luck	work

I'll also listen to the radio for **information** about the weather.

Materials

air	fuel	gasoline	gold
metal	paper	water	wood

The radio says the **air** is heavy. What does that mean?

Weather

fog	hail	heat	ice	lightning
rain	smog	snow	sunshine	thunder

Uh-oh! First came the **lightning** and the **thunder**. I want **sunshine** for my next soccer game!

Some words have more than one meaning. Add **-s** for the plural only if the noun means something you can count.	Throw me those **baseballs**. I want to learn to play **baseball**.

ARTICLES	EXAMPLES
An **article** is a word that helps identify a noun. An article often comes before a count noun.	After **the** game, we found **a** coat and **an** umbrella on **the** field.
Use **a** or **an** before **nouns** that are not specific. Use **the** before **nouns** that are specific.	A **boy** walked around the field. The coach's **son** walked around the field.
Use **a** before a word that starts with a consonant sound. Use **an** before a word that starts with a vowel sound.	a **b**all a **g**ate a **p**layer a **o**ne-way street (o is pronounced like w) a **c**ap a **k**ick a **n**et a **u**niform (u is pronounced like y) **a** **e** **i** **o** **u** silent **h** an **a**nt an **e**lbow an **i**nch an **o**live an **u**mbrella an **h**our an **a**pron an **e**el an **i**dea an **o**cean an **a**mount an **e**lection an **o**wl an **ar**tist an **or**ange
Do not use **a** or **an** before a noncount noun.	The soccer ball was made of ~~a~~ leather.
Do not use **the** before the name of: • a city or state • most countries • a language • a day, a month, or most holidays • a sport or activity • most businesses • a person	Our next game will be in **Dallas**. Games in **Texas** are always exciting. We will play a team from **Mexico**. People will be cheering in **Spanish** and **English**. The game will take place on **Monday**. Is that in **February**? Yes, on **President's Day**. That will be a good day to play **soccer**. The fans will have hot dogs to eat from **Sal's Market**. You may even see **Sal** himself.

Pronouns

A pronoun takes the place of a noun or refers to a noun.

PRONOUN AGREEMENT	EXAMPLES
Use the correct **pronoun** for a person or thing.	 I want to find out about careers.  What career are you interested in?
• To tell about yourself, use **I**.	
• When you speak to another person, use **you**.	
• To tell about a boy or man, use **he**.	Scott likes art. **He** wants to be a photographer.
• For a girl or woman, use **she**.	Anna likes animals. **She** wants to be a veterinarian.
• For a thing, use **it**.	What about music? Is **it** a good career?
• For yourself and other people, use **we**.	 Sam, Jill, and I like music. We might be good musicians.
• When you speak to more than one other person, use **you**.	 Joe and Maylin, what do you want to do?
• To tell about other people or things, use **they**.	Joe and Maylin love children. **They** want to be teachers.

SUBJECT PRONOUNS	EXAMPLES
Some pronouns tell who or what does the action. They are called **subject pronouns**.	Anna likes animals. **She** works at a pet shop. Ernesto works there, too. **He** is in charge of the fish section. **It** is a big area in the store. Anna takes care of the birds. **They** are in cages.

Subject Pronouns

Singular	Plural
I	we
you	you
he, she, it	they

OBJECT PRONOUNS	EXAMPLES
Some pronouns come after an action verb or after a word like *to*, *for*, or *with*. They are called **object pronouns**.	The parrots get hungry at 5 o'clock. Anna feeds **them** every day. The parrots are nice to **her**. One day, Ernesto fed the parrots. They didn't like **him**. The parrots took the food and threw **it** on the floor. Now only Anna can feed **them**.

Pronouns

Subject Pronouns		Object Pronouns
I	⟶	me
you	⟶	you
he	⟶	him
she	⟶	her
it	⟶	it
we	⟶	us
you	⟶	you
they	⟶	them

POSSESSIVE PRONOUNS	EXAMPLES
A **possessive pronoun** tells who or what owns something. It is sometimes called a **possessive adjective**.	Anna's favorite parrot is a red-and-blue male. **His** name is Repeat. Repeat knows how to say **her** name. Repeat knows Ernesto's name, too. The bird says **their** names over and over again.

Pronouns

Subject Pronouns		Object Pronouns
I	⟶	my
you	⟶	your
he	⟶	his
she	⟶	her
it	⟶	its
we	⟶	our
you	⟶	your
they	⟶	their

Adjectives

An adjective describes, or tells about, a noun. Many adjectives tell what something is like. An adjective can also tell "how many" or "which one".

ADJECTIVES	EXAMPLES
Usually an **adjective** comes <u>before</u> the **noun** it describes.	You can buy **fresh food** at the market. You can buy **colorful fruit**. You can buy **delicious vegetables**.
An **adjective** can come <u>after</u> the **noun** in sentences with verbs like *is, are, was,* or *were*.	The **bananas** are **yellow**. The **tomato** is **round**. The **market** was **busy**. The **shoppers** were **happy**.
Some **adjectives** tell "how many." They always come before the **noun**.	This farmer has **six kinds** of tomatoes. My mom wants **three tomatoes**. She has **five dollars**.
Some **adjectives** tell the order of persons or things in a group. They usually come before the **noun**. They can come after the noun in sentences with verbs like *is, are, was,* and *were*.	Mom looks at the tomatoes in the **first basket**. Then she looks at the tomatoes in the **second basket**. My **mom** is **first** in line to buy them!
Never add *-s* or *-es* to an **adjective,** even if the **noun** it describes is plural.	Look at the **green cucumbers**. Mom wants **two cucumbers**. The **vegetables** tonight will be **delicious**!

Sensory Adjectives

An adjective can tell how something looks, sounds, tastes, feels, or smells.

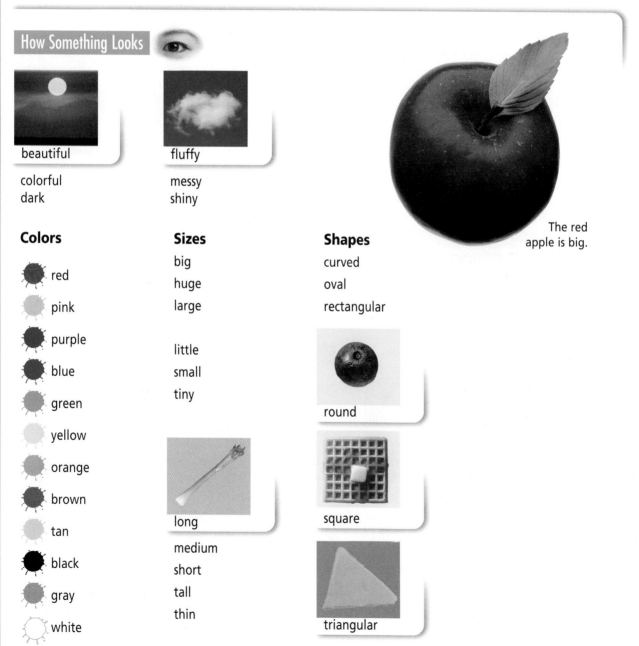

How Something Looks

beautiful

colorful
dark

fluffy

messy
shiny

The red
apple is big.

Colors
- red
- pink
- purple
- blue
- green
- yellow
- orange
- brown
- tan
- black
- gray
- white

Sizes
big
huge
large

little
small
tiny

long

medium
short
tall
thin

Shapes
curved
oval
rectangular

round

square

triangular

Adjectives, continued

How Something Sounds

blaring
crunchy
loud
noisy
quiet
soft
rattling

I like crunchy apples.

How Something Feels

bumpy
dry
hard
hot
rough
sharp
slimy
smooth
soft
sticky
warm

The outside of a pickle feels bumpy.

These cinnamon rolls are very sticky!

How Something Tastes

bitter
delicious
fresh
juicy
salty
sour
spicy
sweet
tasty

These vegetables will taste fresh.

Chili can be very spicy.

How Something Smells

fishy
fragrant
fresh
rotten
sweet

It smells very fragrant here!

Feelings

An adjective can tell how someone feels.

angry

embarrassed

sad

annoyed

excited

scared

bored

happy

shy

confused

nervous

surprised

curious

proud

worried

Numbers

Numbers are a special kind of adjective. They can tell how many.
They can also tell the order of things in a sequence.

Number Words

0	zero	30	thirty
1	one	40	forty
2	two	50	fifty
3	three	60	sixty
4	four	70	seventy
5	five	80	eighty
6	six	90	ninety
7	seven	100	one hundred
8	eight	500	five hundred
9	nine	1,000	one thousand
10	ten	5,000	five thousand
11	eleven	10,000	ten thousand
12	twelve	100,000	one hundred thousand
13	thirteen	500,000	five hundred thousand
14	fourteen	1,000,000	one million
15	fifteen		
16	sixteen		
17	seventeen		
18	eighteen		
19	nineteen		
20	twenty		

Order Words

1st	first
2nd	second
3rd	third
4th	fourth
5th	fifth
6th	sixth
7th	seventh
8th	eighth
9th	ninth
10th	tenth
11th	eleventh
12th	twelfth
13th	thirteenth
14th	fourteenth
15th	fifteenth
16th	sixteenth
17th	seventeenth
18th	eighteenth
19th	nineteenth
20th	twentieth

This woman is the first customer. She buys two heads of broccoli for $1.98.

Verbs

Every complete sentence has a verb.

THE FORMS OF *BE*	EXAMPLES	
The words **am, is,** and **are** are **verbs.** They are forms of the verb **be.** They tell about something that is happening now, or in the present.	I **am** in New York with my mom. She **is** here for the first time. We **are** excited to see the buildings. They **are** amazing!	**Forms of the Verb *be*** **Present** **Past** I **am** I **was** you **are** you **were** he, she, he, she, it **is** it **was** we **are** we **were** you **are** you **were** they **are** they **were**
The **verbs was** and **were** are also forms of the verb **be.** They tell about something that happened in the past.	I **was** in Central Park yesterday. It **was** beautiful. We **were** with some friends. They **were** very helpful.	

CONTRACTIONS WITH VERBS	EXAMPLES
You can shorten the verbs *am, is,* and *are* to make a **contraction.**	Today **we're** going to Lincoln Center.

> **Contractions with Verbs**
>
> To make a **contraction**, take out one or more letters and add an **apostrophe (').**
>
> I + ~~a~~m = I'm   **I'm** glad to be in New York.
>
> you + ~~a~~re = you're   **You're** going to meet my brother.
>
> he + ~~i~~s = he's   **He's** staying with my aunt.
>
> she + ~~i~~s = she's   **She's** in a performance at Lincoln Center.
>
> it + ~~i~~s = it's   **It's** a ballet.
>
> we + ~~a~~re = we're   **We're** going to watch a ballet practice.
>
> they + ~~a~~re = they're   **They're** coming to our hotel at 3:00.

ACTION VERBS	EXAMPLES
Most verbs are **action verbs.** They tell what a person or thing does.	The dancers **hop** and **spin.**
When you tell what another person or thing does, use **-s** or **-es** at the end of the **verb.**	The spotlight **shines** on them. One dancer **twirls** around and around. Then she **stretches** a leg and **leaps** gracefully.

Action Verbs

act
add
answer
arrive
ask
bake
bathe
boil
bounce
brush
burn
call

carry

change
check
chop
circle
clap

clean

climb
close
comb
cook
copy
count
cross
cry

dance

deliver
discuss
drop
dry
enter
erase

exercise

fill
finish
fix
fold
hammer
help
introduce
invite
jog
join

jump

kick
laugh

learn
listen
look

mail

mark
mix
mop
move

open

paint
plant
play
point
pour
pull
push
raise
rake
repair
repeat
skate
slice
spell
start
stir
stop
stretch

talk

tie
turn
type
underline
use
vote

walk

wash
watch
water
wipe

work

THE VERBS *CAN, COULD, MAY, MIGHT*	EXAMPLES
You can use the verbs **can, could, may,** or **might** with an **action verb** to express: • the ability to do something • a possibility, or the chance that something may happen	A hurricane **can cause** a lot of damage. Several inches of rain **might fall** in just a few minutes. The wind **may blow** at high speeds. It **might knock** over trees. It **could break** windows.

PRESENT TENSE VERBS	EXAMPLES

The tense of a verb shows when an action happens.

The **present tense** of a verb tells about an action that is happening now, or in the present.	My mom **looks** at her charts. She **checks** her computer screen. She **takes** notes.
The **present tense** of a verb can also tell about an action that happens regularly or all the time.	My mom **works** for the local TV station. She **is** a weather forecaster. She **reports** the weather every night at 5 p.m.
The **present progressive** form of a verb tells about an action as it is happening. It uses **am**, **is**, or **are** and a main verb. The main verb ends in **-ing**.	Right now, she **is getting** ready for the show. "I can't believe it!" she says. "I **am looking** at a terrible storm!" The high winds **are starting** to blow. Trees **are falling** down. Wind damage from Hurricane Floyd, 1999

Verbs, continued

PAST TENSE VERBS	EXAMPLES
The **past tense** of a verb tells about an action that happened earlier, or in the past.	Yesterday, my mom **warned** everyone about the hurricane. The storm **moved** over the ocean toward land. We **did** not **know** exactly when it would hit.
The past tense form of a **regular verb** ends with **-ed**.	The shop owners in our town **covered** their windows with wood. We **closed** our shutters and **stayed** inside.
Irregular verbs have special forms to show the past tense. See page 339 for more examples.	The storm **hit** land. The sky **grew** very dark. It **began** to rain.

Some Irregular Verbs

Present Tense	Past Tense
hit	hit
grow	grew
begin	began

FUTURE TENSE VERBS	EXAMPLES
The **future tense** of a verb tells about an action that will happen later, or in the future. To show future tense, use one of the following: • **will** plus another verb	After the storm, people **will come** out of their houses. They **will inspect** the damage.
• a **contraction** with **will** plus another verb	**They'll uncover** their windows. **They'll clean** up their yards. Some people **won't have** as much work as other people.
• the phrase **am going to, is going to,** or **are going to** plus a verb.	I **am going to take** the tree branches out of my yard. The city **is** not **going to clean** every street. We **are** all **going to help** each other.

Contractions with *will*

I + w~~ill~~ = I'll
you + w~~ill~~ = you'll
he + w~~ill~~ = he'll
she + w~~ill~~ = she'll
it + w~~ill~~ = it'll
we + w~~ill~~ = we'll
they + w~~ill~~ = they'll
will + not = won't

Irregular Verbs

These verbs have special forms to show the past tense.

Present	Past
become	became
begin	began
bend	bent
blow	blew
break	broke
build	built

Present	Past
buy	bought

Present	Past
catch	caught
come	came
cut	cut
do	did
draw	drew

Present	Past
drink	drank

Present	Past
eat	ate
fall	fell
feel	felt

Present	Past
find	found
fly	flew
get	got

Present	Past
give	gave

Present	Past
grow	grew
go	went
have	had
hear	heard
hide	hid
hit	hit

Present	Past
hold	held

Present	Past
keep	kept
know	known
lead	led
leave	left

Present	Past
make	made

Present	Past
pay	paid
put	put
read	read

Present	Past
run	ran

Present	Past
say	said
see	saw
sing	sang
sit	sat
speak	spoke
stand	stood
swim	swam
take	took
throw	threw
wear	wore

Present	Past
write	wrote

Handwriting

It's important to use your best **penmanship**, or handwriting. That way your audience will be able to read what your write.

HANDWRITING HINTS

You can **print** your words or write in **cursive**. Printing is sometimes called **manuscript**.

MANUSCRIPT

Manuscript is less formal than cursive and is usually easier to read at a glance. That makes manuscript good to use for filling out forms and for writing things like posters, ads, and short notes. When you write in manuscript, hold the pencil and paper this way.

Left-handed

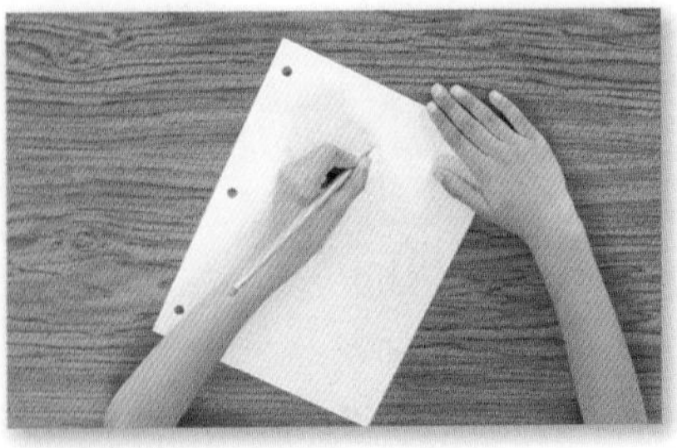

Right-handed

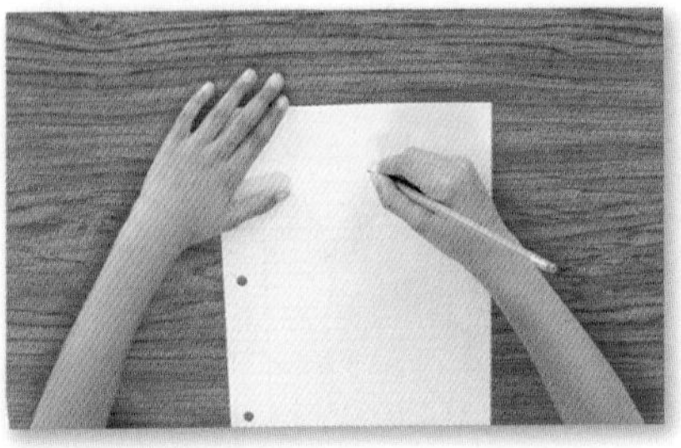

CURSIVE

Cursive is good to use for longer pieces, such as letters or stories, because you can write faster. You don't have to lift your pencil between letters. Also, cursive writing gives your finished pieces a polished look. When you write in cursive, hold the pencil and paper this way.

Left-handed

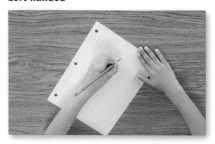

Right-handed

Manuscript Alphabet

CAPITAL LETTERS

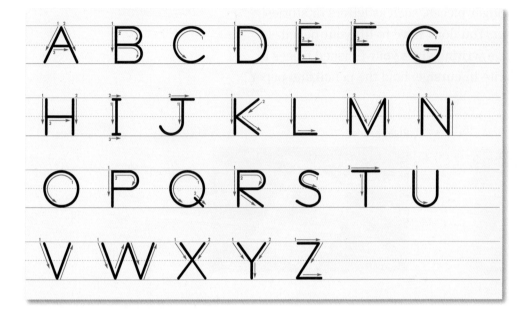

LOWERCASE LETTERS, NUMBERS, AND PUNCTUATION

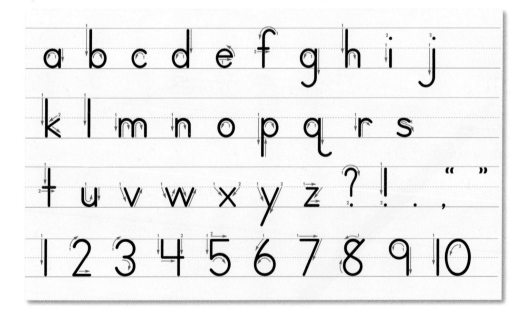

Writing Manuscript Letters

- Make letters sit on the **baseline**, or bottom line.
  Make letters the same size.

NOT OK

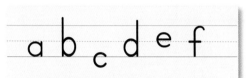

OK

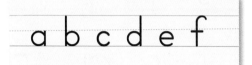

- Letters that go past the **midline**, or middle line, should all be the same height.

NOT OK

OK

- Make your capital letters touch the **headline**, or top line.
  Make half-size letters touch the midline.

NOT OK

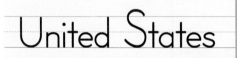

OK

- Letters should be **vertical**, or standing up straight.

NOT OK

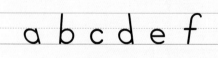

OK

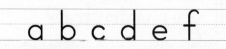

Handwriting, continued

WRITING WORDS AND SENTENCES

- Put the same amount of space between each word.

NOT OK

Votefor Juji for ClassPresident!

OK

Vote for Juji for Class President!

- Put the right amount of space between each letter.

NOT OK

She will work hard for our school.

OK

She will work hard for our school.

- Write smoothly. Do not press too hard or too light.
  Make your lines the same thickness.

NOT OK

Who will you **vo**te for?

OK

Who will you vote for?

Cursive Alphabet

CAPITAL LETTERS

LOWERCASE LETTERS

Writing Cursive Letters

Be careful not to make these common mistakes when you write in **cursive**.

MISTAKE	NOT OK	OK	IN A WORD
The **a** looks like a **u**.	*u*	*a*	*again*
The **d** looks like a **c** and an **l**.	*d*	*d*	*dad*
The **e** is too narrow.	*e*	*e*	*eagle*
The **h** looks like an **l** and an **i**.	*h*	*h*	*high*
The **i** has no dot.	*i*	*i*	*inside*
The **n** looks like a **w**.	*w*	*n*	*none*
The **o** looks like an **a**.	*a*	*o*	*onion*
The **r** looks like an **i** with no dot.	*i*	*r*	*roar*
The **t** is not crossed.	*l*	*t*	*title*
The **t** is crossed too high.	*t*	*t*	*that*

Writing Words and Sentences

• Slant your letters all the same way.

NOT OK

My Chinese-language class today was interesting.

OK

My Chinese-language class today was interesting.

• Put the right amount of space between words.

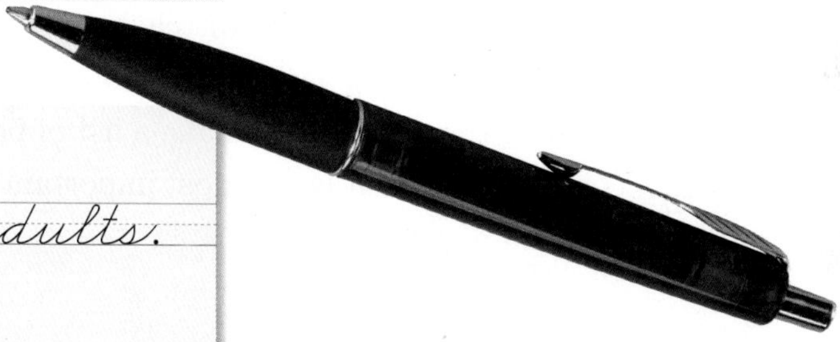

NOT OK

I learned how togreet   adults.

OK

I learned how to greet adults.

• Write smoothly. Do not press too hard or too lightly.

NOT OK

I practiced on my teacher. He was impressed.

OK

I practiced on my teacher. He was impressed.

The Writing Process

Writing is one of the best ways to express yourself. The steps in the Writing Process will help you say what you want to say clearly, correctly, and in your own unique way.

PREWRITE

Prewriting is what you do before you write. During this step, you collect ideas, choose a topic, make a plan, gather details, and organize your ideas.

❶ Collect Ideas Writing ideas are everywhere! Think about recent events or things you've read or seen. You can brainstorm more writing ideas with your classmates, friends, and family. Collect your ideas in a computer file, a notebook or a journal. Then when you're ready to write, check your idea collections.

❷ Choose a Topic Sometimes you have a lot of ideas you want to write about. Other times, your teacher may give you a writing prompt, or a writing assignment. You will still need to decide exactly what you write about. Make a list of possible writing ideas. Then circle the one that is the most important or interesting to you. That idea will be your topic.

I could write about...

a concert my friends and I went to

when my grandparents arrived in the U.S.

why we need more school dances

why the eagle is a popular symbol

❸ Plan Your Writing An FATP chart can help you organize your thoughts and focus on the details that you'll need for your writing.

The **form** tells you the type of writing. Study examples of the form to help you decide how to craft your writing.

A specific **topic** will help you collect only those details you need.

FATP Chart

HOW TO UNLOCK A PROMPT

Form: personal narrative

Audience: my teacher and classmates

Topic: when my grandparents arrived in the U.S.

Purpose: to describe a personal experience

If you know your **audience**, you can choose the appropriate style and tone. For example, if you are writing for your friends, you can use friendly, informal language.

The **purpose** is why you are writing. Your purpose can be to describe, to inform or explain, to persuade, or to express personal thoughts or feelings.

4 Gather Details To write about a personal experience, you can just list the things you remember about an event. For other kinds of writing, you may need to talk about your topic with others or do research to gather information.

There are many ways to show the details you've gathered. You can

- make charts, lists, or webs
- draw and label pictures
- take notes on notecards
- make a story map
- use a gathering grid to write down answers to your questions

Gathering Grid

Topic: Vietnam	Get to Know Vietnam (book)	Internet
What is the population?		
What fuels the economy?		

Show your details in a way that works best for you and for your topic.

5 Get Organized Review your details and plan an interesting way to write about your topic. Put the details in the best order for your writing.

- Sometimes you can organize the details as you write them down.
- Other times, you can use numbers to order events in time sequence or to order the details from the most to least important.
- You could also make an outline to show main ideas and supporting details.

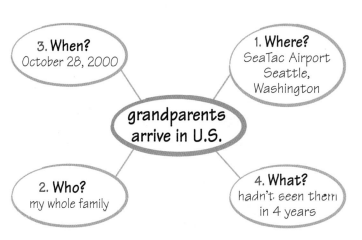

3. **When?** October 28, 2000

1. **Where?** SeaTac Airport Seattle, Washington

grandparents arrive in U.S.

2. **Who?** my whole family

4. **What?** hadn't seen them in 4 years

DRAFT

Now you are ready to start writing. At this stage, don't worry about making mistakes—just get your ideas down on paper! Turn your details into sentences and paragraphs. As you are writing, you'll probably think of new ideas. Add those to your draft.

Trang Bui's Draft

My family stood by the windows and watched the plane land at SeaTac airport in Seattle on October 28, 2007. We were so exsited to see the plane. The people started coming through the door, we lined up so we could see. I had to lift my little sister up so she could see. Suddenly everyone was hugging and crying. My little sister tried to hide. My sister didn't know my grandparents. She was feeling shy.

Write your ideas in a first draft.

REVISE

A first draft can always be improved. When you revise a draft, you make changes to it.

❶ Read Your Draft As you read your draft, ask yourself questions about the most important ideas. Make sure your ideas are clear, complete, and presented in the best way.

Revision Checklist

- ☑ Did I follow the plan on my FATP chart? Is the language appropriate for the writing form and audience? Did I stick to the topic?
- ☑ Does my writing have a beginning, a middle, and an ending?
- ☑ Are my details organized in the best way? Should I change the order of any details?
- ☑ Did I include details to make my ideas clear? Should I add or cut any details?
- ☑ Did I use the best words to say what I mean? Did I avoid using the same words over and over again?

❷ Mark Your Changes What changes do you want to make to your draft? Use the Revising Marks or special features in your computer's word-processing program to show the changes.

Trang Bui's Revisions

My family stood by the ^big, glass windows and

watched the plane land at SeaTac airport

in Seattle on October 28, 2007. We were

so exsited ^! to see the plane. ~~The people~~ ^When the passengers

started coming through the door, we lined

up so we could see. I had to lift my little

sister up so she could ^look over the heads of the people in front see. Suddenly

everyone was hugging and crying. My little

sister tried to hide ^because she My ~~sister~~ didn't know

my grandparents ^and ~~She~~ was feeling shy. ^

It took four long years, but my grandparents

finally arrived!

Revising Marks	
∧	Add.
↰	Move to here.
⌐	Replace with this.
⌐	Take out.

The Writing Process, continued

EDIT AND PROOFREAD

After you revise your draft for content, it's time to check it for mistakes.

❶ Check Your Sentences When you edit, check that your sentences are clear, complete, and correct. Ask yourself:

- Does each sentence have a subject and a predicate?

❷ Check for Mistakes Proofread to find and correct errors in capitalization, punctuation, grammar, and spelling. Look especially for:

- capital letters, end marks, apostrophes, and quotation marks
- subject-verb agreement
- use of pronouns
- misspelled words.

❸ Mark Your Corrections Use the Editing and Proofreading Marks to show your corrections or make the corrections when you find them in your document on the computer.

❹ Make a Final Copy Rewrite your work and make the corrections you marked. If you are using a computer, print your corrected copy.

Trang Bui's Proofread Draft

My family stood by the big, glass windows and watched the plane land at SeaTac airport in Seattle on October 28, 2007. We were so exsited When the passengers started coming through the door, we lined up so we could see. I had to lift my little sister up so she could look over the heads of the people in front. Suddenly everyone was hugging and crying. My little sister tried to hide because she didn't know my grandparents and was feeling shy. It took four long years, but my grandparents finally arrived!

Editing and Proofreading Marks	
∧	Add.
℘	Take out.
∧	Replace with this.
◯	Check Spelling.
≡	Capitalize.
/	Make lowercase.
¶	Make new paragraph

PUBLISH

Now that you have corrected your work, share it with others!

- E-mail it to a friend or family member.
- Make a home video of you reading it.
- Put it on a poster, add pictures, and display it in your classroom.
- Send it to your favorite magazine or publication.

The Best Day of My Life
by Trang Bui

My family stood by the big, glass windows and watched the plane land at SeaTac Airport in Seattle on October 28, 2007. We were so excited! When the passengers started coming through the door, we lined up so we could see. I had to lift up my little sister so she could look over the heads of the people in front. Suddenly everyone was hugging and crying. My little sister tried to hide because she didn't know my grandparents. It took four long years, but my grandparents finally arrived!

EVALUATE YOUR WRITING

Save examples of your writing. Date them and collect them in a portfolio. Look through your portfolio from time to time to see how you are doing as a writer.

❶ Organize Put your writing in order by date. Make sections for works written for the same purpose or audience. Group your writing by form—stories, research reports, or poems.

❷ Survey the Work Each time you add new work, ask yourself:

- How does this writing compare to other work I've done?
- Am I getting better in certain areas?
- Are there things that I didn't do as well this time? Why?

❸ Think About How You Write Think about the words you like to use, the kinds of sentences you write, and what you like to write about. All of those things together are your writing style.

I write with Style!

Using Information Resources

HOW TO FIND INFORMATION

You can use different resources to find information about your topic.
Resources can be experts, or people who know a lot about a topic.
Resources can also be nonfiction books, textbooks, magazines, newspapers,
or the Internet. You can find resources all around you.

Expert

Nonfiction Books

Magazines and Newspapers

Encyclopedia

Dictionary

Almanac

Atlas

Internet

Think about your research questions. Some resources may be more helpful than others, depending on what kind of information you need about your topic.

- Do you need to look up facts or scientific data?
- Do you want to know about something that happened recently?
- Are you interested in someone's opinion or experience?
- Do you want to see pictures?

These questions will help you decide which resources to use.

Whatever your topic is, try exploring the library first. There you'll discover a world of resources and information!

Using Information Resources, continued

DICTIONARY

Think of the **dictionary** as a tool you can use to learn everything you need to know about a word. Dictionaries tell you how to spell, say, and use words. From a dictionary you can learn how to divide a word into syllables, what part of speech a word is, and how to write different forms of a word. You can also learn the history of a word. Look for examples of all of these types of information on these dictionary pages.

 southwards ➤ space shuttle

ward slope of the mountain. Adjective.
south·ward (south′wərd) *adverb; adjective.*

southwards Another spelling of the adverb southward: *They drove southwards.* **south·wards** (south′wərdz) *adverb.*

southwest 1. The direction halfway between south and west. 2. The point of the compass showing this direction. 3. A region or place in this direction. 4. the Southwest. The region in the south and west of the United States. *Noun.*
  ◦ 1. Toward or in the southwest: *the southwest corner of the street.* 2. Coming from the southwest: *a southwest wind. Adjective.*
  ◦ Toward the southwest: *The ship sailed southwest. Adverb.*
south·west (south′west′) *noun; adjective; adverb.*

souvenir Something kept because it reminds one of a person, place, or event: *I bought a pennant as a souvenir of the baseball game.* **sou·ve·nir** (sü′və nîr′ *or* sü′və nîr′) *noun, plural* **souvenirs.**

sovereign A king or queen. *Noun.*
  ◦ 1. Having the greatest power or highest rank or authority: *The king and queen were the sovereign rulers of the country.* 2. Not controlled by others; independent: *Mexico is a sovereign nation. Adjective.*
sov·er·eign (sov′ər ən *or* sov′rən) *noun, plural* **sovereigns;** *adjective.*

Soviet Union Formerly, a large country in eastern Europe and northern Asia. It was composed of 15 republics and was also called the U.S.S.R. The largest and most important of the 15 republics was Russia.

sow¹ 1. To scatter seeds over the ground; plant: *The farmer will sow corn in this field.* 2. To spread or scatter: *The clown sowed happiness among the children.*
Other words that sound like this are sew and so. **sow** (sō) *verb,* **sowed, sown** *or* **sowed, sowing.**

sow² An adult female pig. **sow** (sou) *noun, plural* **sows.**

soybean A seed rich in oil and protein and used as food. Soybeans grow in pods on bushy plants. **soy·bean** (soi′bēn′) *noun, plural* **soybeans.**

space 1. The area in which the whole universe exists. It has no limits. The planet earth is in space. 2. The region beyond the earth's atmosphere; outer space: *The rocket was launched into space.* 3. A distance or area between things: *There is not much space between our house and theirs.* 4. An area reserved or available for some purpose: *a parking space.* 5. A period of time: *Both jets landed in the space of ten minutes. Noun.*
  ◦ To put space in between: *The architect spaced the houses far apart. Verb.*
space (spās) *noun, plural* **spaces;** *verb,* **spaced, spacing.**

spacecraft A vehicle used for flight in outer space. This is also called a spaceship. **space·craft** (spās′kraft′) *noun, plural* **spacecraft.**

space shuttle A spacecraft that carries a crew into space and returns to land on earth. The same

space shuttle

flight deck and crew's quarters — orbiter
remote-control arm
container for experiments
rudder
booster nozzle
main engines
— external fuel tank
— tank for liquid oxygen
— payload bay
— solid-rocket booster
— cargo bay door
— satellite inside protective cocoon
— wing
orbital maneuvering engine

space shuttle can be used again. A space shuttle is also called a shuttle.

space station A spaceship that orbits around the earth like a satellite and on which a crew can live for long periods of time.

spacesuit Special clothing worn by an astronaut in space. A spacesuit covers an astronaut's entire body and has equipment to help the astronaut breathe. **space·suit** (spās′süt′) *noun, plural* **spacesuits.**

Astronauts take spacewalks to repair satellites and vehicles.

spacewalk A period of activity during which an astronaut in space is outside a spacecraft. **space·walk** (spās′wôk′) *noun, plural* **spacewalks.**

spacious Having a lot of space or room; roomy; large. —**spa·cious** *adjective* —**spaciousness** *noun.*

spade¹ A tool used for digging. It has a long handle and a flat blade that can be pressed into the ground with the foot. *Noun.*
○ To dig with a spade: *We spaded the garden and then raked it. Verb.*
spade (spād) *noun, plural* **spades;** *verb,* **spaded, spading.**

spade² **1.** A playing card marked with one or more figures shaped like this. **2. spades.** The suit

thin strings. It is made of a mixture of flour and water. **spa·ghet·ti** (spə get′ē) *noun.*

Spain A country in southwest Europe. **Spain** (spān) *noun.*

spamming The sending of the same message to large numbers of e-mail addresses or to many newsgroups at the same time. Spamming is often thought of as impolite behavior on the Internet. **spam·ming** (spa′ming) *noun.*

span **1.** The distance or part between two supports: *The span of that bridge is very long.* **2.** The full reach or length of anything: *Some people accomplish a great deal in the span of their lives. Noun.*
○ To extend over or across. *Verb.*
span (span) *noun, plural* **spans;** *verb,* **spanned, spanning.**

This bridge spans a wide river.

spaniel Any of various dogs of small to medium size with long, drooping ears, a silky, wavy coat, and short legs. The larger types are used in hunting. **span·iel** (span′yəl) *noun, plural* **spaniels.**

Spanish **1.** The people of Spain. The word *Spanish* in this sense is used with a plural verb. **2.** The language spoken in Spain. It is also spoken in many countries south of the United States as well as in parts of the U.S. *Noun.*

Use the **guide words** at the top of each page to help you find the entry word you are looking up. The guide words are the first and last words on the page.

The **entry word** *spacesuit* falls between *space station* and *Spanish* in alphabetical order.

In this dictionary, words in **blue** have corresponding visuals. Special notes about how to use words also appear in blue.

357

THESAURUS

A **thesaurus** is similar to a dictionary, but instead of giving word meanings, it lists synonyms and antonyms. A thesaurus can be especially useful when you are looking for just the right word to use. For example, you might want to describe how *good* of an experience NASA's Space Camp® is for kids—but without using that tired, overworked adjective. You could look up *good* in a thesaurus and find an entry that looks like this:

Synonyms are words with almost the same meanings.

Antonyms are words with opposite meanings.

> fine
>
> **good** adjective **1** *a good product* FINE, superior, quality; excellent, superb, outstanding, magnificent, exceptional, marvelous, wonderful, first-rate, first-class, sterling; satisfactory, acceptable, not bad, all right; *informal* great, OK, A1, jake, hunky-dory, ace, terrific, fantastic, fabulous, fab, top-notch, blue-chip, blue-ribbon, bang-up, killer, class, awesome, wicked; smashing, brilliant. ANTONYM bad.
>
> **2** *a good person* VIRTUOUS, righteous, upright, [bad] nding, moral, ethical, high-minded, principled; e......lary,

from Oxford American Writer's Thesaurus. Christine A. Lundberg. By permission of Oxford University Press, Inc.

Which synonym would you decide to use?

A thesaurus can also be helpful when you are trying to decide how to express your thoughts about a big idea or topic. If you can't seem to come up with the right words, look up the subject—for example, *universe*—and see what you find.

> **universe** noun **1** *a collection of stars* COSMOS, creation, nature, heavens, luminaries, constellations, celestial, stellar.

These are only a few of the words listed in one thesaurus for that subject. Just think about how helpful these words might be.

A thesaurus might give more information than simple lists of words.

- This thesaurus looks very similar to a dictionary. It includes a definition for each **entry word**. The definition is followed by a **sample sentence** featuring the word. This thesaurus also includes **guide words** at the top of the page.

baby   **beautiful**

baby *n.* a very young child or animal: The *baby* is only ten months old.

Synonyms

infant a child too young to walk or talk: You need to carry an *infant*.

newborn a baby that has just been born: The *newborn* and her mother go home from the hospital.

beat *n.* a repeated sound, usually with a regular occurrence: Tap your foot to the *beat*.

Synonyms

pounding I could feel the *pounding* of my own heart.

rhythm The *rhythm* of the rain put me to sleep last night.

- This thesaurus does not include definitions, only sample sentences.

wakeful adjective **1** *he had been wakeful all night* AWAKE, restless, restive, tossing and turning. ANTONYM asleep.

2 *I was suddenly wakeful* ALERT, watchful, vigilant, on the lookout, on one's guard, attentive, heedful, wary. ANTONYM inattentive.

walk verb **1** *they walked along the road* STROLL, saunter, amble, trudge, plod, dawdle, hike, tramp, tromp, slog, stomp, trek, march, stride, sashay, glide, troop, patrol, wander, ramble, tread, prowl, promenade, roam, traipse; stretch one's legs; *informal* mosey, hoof it; *formal* perambulate.

PARTS OF A BOOK

There are many different kinds of books. All books share some features that make it easier for readers to find what they need. Let's look at the parts of a book.

Title Page

The **title page** is usually the first page in a book.

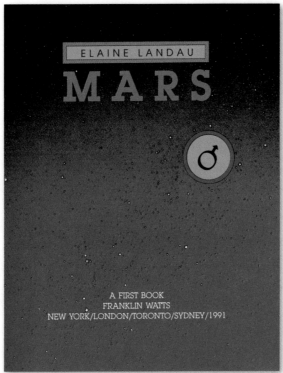

The **title page** gives the **title** of the book and the **author**.

It tells the **publisher** and often names the cities where the publisher has offices.

Copyright Page

The **copyright (©) page** gives the year when the book was published.

Check the **copyright** to see how current the information is.

```
Landau, Elaine
      Mars / by Elaine Landau
        p.cm. — (First book)
      Includes bibliographical references and index.
      Summary: Uses photographs and other recent findings to
        describe the atmosphere and geographic features of Mars.
      ISBN 0-531-20012-4 (lib. bdg)—ISBN 0-531-15773-3 (pbk)
      I. Mars (Planet)—Juvenile Literature. [1. Mars (Planet)]
    1. Title.    II. Series.
    QB641.L36 1991
    523.4'3—dc20                   90-13097  CIP AC

            Copyright © 1991 Elaine Landau
                  All rights reserved
           Printed in the United States of America
                      6  5  4  3
```

Table of Contents

The **table of contents** is in the front of a book. It shows how many chapters, or parts, are in a book. It tells the page numbers where those chapters begin. Look at the chapter names to see which ones might be useful to you.

A table of contents can be much more detailed than the one shown here. For example, it might list sections within chapters, important visuals, or special sections found in the book.

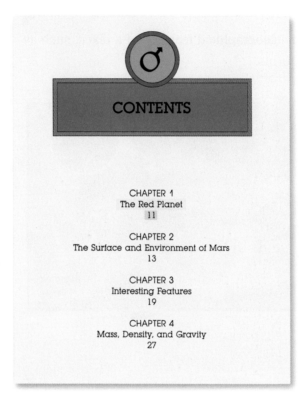

A **chapter title** tells what the chapter is mostly about.

The **page number** tells where the chapter begins.

Chapter Headings

Once you have found a chapter you are interested in using from the table of contents, you will turn to the chapter. The first page in the chapter will contain a header describing what you will find in the chapter. Often, chapters are numbered.

THE RED PLANET

CHAPTER ONE

The planet Mars appears as a rusty red ball in the nighttime sky. Because of its reddish color, the ancient Romans named the planet after their god of war—Mars. In fact, the fighting god's shield and spear are still used as the planet's symbol.

Mars is one of the nine planets that make up the *solar system*. The solar system consists of the sun and the planets, moons, and other objects that revolve around it. Mars is the fourth planet from the sun. Earth, Mars's neighbor, is the third planet from the sun.

You can find different types of maps inside atlases. You can use the different maps for different purposes. Let's see what some of them look like.

PHYSICAL MAPS

A **physical map** shows the geographical features of a place, such as bodies of water and landforms.

Mapmakers often use techniques that make mountains look like they are rising off the page.

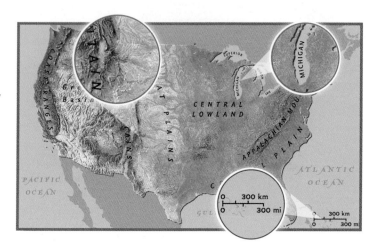

Landforms, like mountains or lakes, are often labeled.

The **scale** shows that this distance on the map is equal to 300 miles on land.

PRODUCT MAPS

A **product map** uses pictures and symbols to show where products come from or where natural resources are found.

The **compass rose** shows the directions north, south, east, and west.

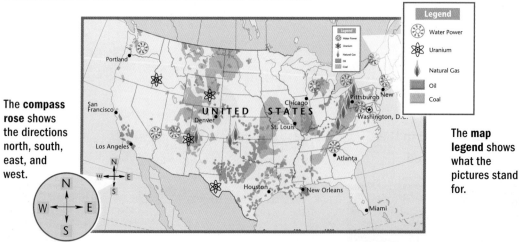

The **map legend** shows what the pictures stand for.

POLITICAL MAPS

A **political map** shows the boundaries between countries, states, and other areas. It also shows capitals and other major cities. **Road maps** are usually set up like political maps.

A **grid system** is used on these maps to make it easy to find a particular place. Look up the place name in the index to find the right map and a code to the exact location on the map. For example, L-6 for this map is the square at which the row L and the column 6 intersect. Can you find Orlando somewhere in the square?

GLOBE

A globe is a small model of the Earth. A globe has a round shape like the Earth does. It gives a better picture of Earth than a flat map does.

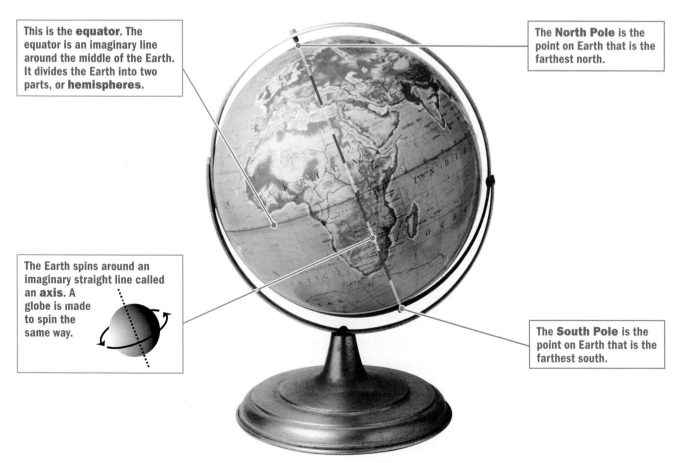

This is the **equator**. The equator is an imaginary line around the middle of the Earth. It divides the Earth into two parts, or **hemispheres**.

The **North Pole** is the point on Earth that is the farthest north.

The Earth spins around an imaginary straight line called an **axis**. A globe is made to spin the same way.

The **South Pole** is the point on Earth that is the farthest south.

Finding Information on the World Wide Web

The Internet is an international network, or connection, of computers that share information with one another. The World Wide Web allows you to find, read, go through, and organize information. The Internet is like a giant library, and the World Wide Web is everything in the library including the books, the librarian, and the computer catalog. The Internet is a fast way to get the most current information about your topic! You'll find resources like encyclopedias and dictionaries, as well as amazing pictures, movies, and sounds.

HOW TO GET STARTED

Check with your teacher for how to access the Internet from your school. Usually you can just double click on the icon, or picture, to get access to the Internet and you're on your way!

DOING THE RESEARCH

Once the search page comes up, you can begin the research process. Just follow these steps.

❶ Type your subject in the search box and then click on the Search button.

If you already know the address of a Web site, you can type it in the address box, instead of a search box, at the top of the screen. A Web site address is also called the URL (Uniform Resource Locator).

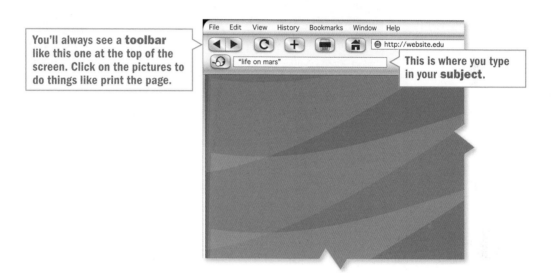

You'll always see a **toolbar** like this one at the top of the screen. Click on the pictures to do things like print the page.

This is where you type in your **subject**.

❷ Read the search results.

All underlined, colored words are links, or connections, to other sites. They help you get from page to page quickly.

If you want to go directly to a **Web page**, click on a site.

Science: Astronomy: Solar System: Planets: Mars:

Life on Mars?

• Science Magazine: **Life on Mars** Special

• Is there **life on Mars**? - an interview with top scientists

• Scientists think there might be **life on Mars**

• **Life on Mars** - from the Astronomy Association

• **Life on Mars**: Interpreting the meteorite

Entertainment: Music: Artists: Rock and Pop

• **Life On Mars** - an alternative rock band

Click on a **category** to see more options for information related to the words you typed.

Read the descriptions of the sites to save time. This site could be very interesting, but it probably won't help with your report.

3 **Select a site, and read the article.**

You might want to pick a new site or start a new search. If so, click on the **back arrow** to go back a page to the search results.

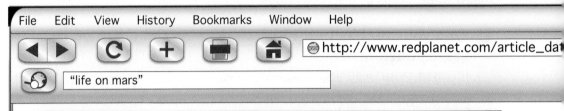

"life on mars"

Anything you ever wanted to know about the planet Mars is on this site! Is it really red? Does it really have water? Information about the appearance of the planet is only the beginning. Articles are about the planet's history, from its discovery to the most recent evidence scientists have gathered about this interesting planet. Search the list by title or by topic.

If you want to go to another Web page, click on a **link**.

MORE ON MARS:

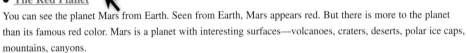

● The Red Planet
You can see the planet Mars from Earth. Seen from Earth, Mars appears red. But there is more to the planet than its famous red color. Mars is a planet with interesting surfaces—volcanoes, craters, deserts, polar ice caps, mountains, canyons.

● Mariner 4
In 1965, scientists believed Mars was covered with liquid similar to our oceans. In recent years, scientists have been able to gather evidence about the liquid history of Mars.

● Orbiting Mars
Mars has more spacecraft circling it than any other planet: Mars Odyssey, Mars Express, and Mars Reconnaissance Orbiter. Mars also has two Exploration Rovers: *Spririt* and *Opportunity*.

● Phobos and Deimos—Mars has Two Moons
Some people believe these are not really moons. Some think they are asteroids.

● Life on Mars?
What would life be like on Mars? Scientists thought they had the answer.

● Models of Mars Missions
Experience a mission to Mars! Click the link to watch video and read scientific analysis of the planet's properties.

4 **You may choose to print the article if it is helpful for your research. Later on, you can use the article to take notes.**

CHOOSING DATA FROM THE INTERNET

You may find much more information on the Internet than you need.
Follow these steps to help you choose data for your research.

❶ Choose your key words carefully.

If your words are too general, the search results
might show hundreds or even thousands of sites
to choose from. Narrow your search by choosing
specific key words.

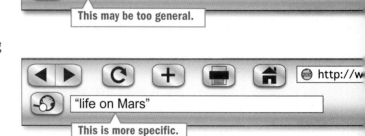

❷ Look back at your research questions.

Skim and scan a Web site to see if it answers
at least some of your questions. If it does,
save it under "Favorites" or "Bookmarks." You can come
back to it later to read
more carefully.

❸ Check facts and sources.

Use more than one source to **verify your
facts**, or make sure they are true. Try to find
the same fact in at least two Web sites or in
an encyclopedia. Think about the source, too.
A well-known scientific Web site probably has
more **reliable**, or true, information than a
personal Web site.

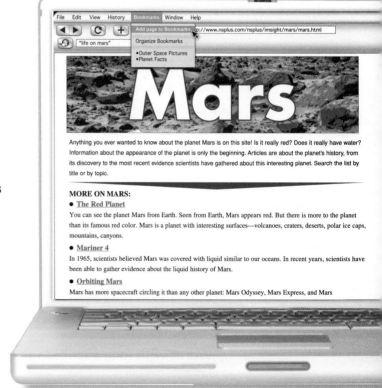

Bright Dogs

Do you know a person that cannot see well? If you do, you might know a service dog, too. This is a dog that helps people with bad sight. A helping dog can do many things to help these people. He tries to see just what the person needs. A helping dog is a real friend to the sight impaired.

Sight dogs are very bright animals. A sight dog can help someone get around. The dog knows the right way to go. Just tie a tight harness on the dog, and he will lead you on the right path. The dog will stop if it is not safe to cross a street. Then he will go when it is safe.

If a person needs to get a box from a high shelf, a helping dog tries with all his might to reach it. If the dog hears even a slight sound at night, he will bark to tell his owner about it. A sight dog might even switch on a light—no lie!

A sight dog tries his best to please his owner. He wants to do the right thing all the time. And it does not take much to reward the dog. He might sit upright and put his paw on your thigh just to get a pat on the head or a small treat. Then he sighs with delight. He knows that he did just the right thing.

Words with long *i* spelled *ie*					
lie	tie	tries			

Words with long *i* spelled *igh*					
bright	light	night	sighs	slight	tight
delight	might	right	sight	thigh	upright
high					

Unit 1 High Frequency Words
sound

Rescue Teams

Rescue teams are the best! Rescue teams come when a person needs help. A rescue team brings tools to help. Rescue teams use boats, trucks, and even planes in their jobs. Rescue teams wear suits that keep them safe. A rescue team tries to do its job each day of the week.

If you get stuck on a high cliff or in a tight spot, a rescue team can help. The rescue team might bring equipment like ropes to save you. If you are on a cruise ship and the ship runs out of fuel, a rescue team might bring fuel to fill the fuel tank. If a car quits on a street full of trucks, a rescue team might push the car off the road and away from traffic.

Men and women on rescue teams know just what to do. Don't disagree with a rescue team when they come to help. Do just what the rescue team tells you to do. Then you will be in good hands. A rescue team will not fail to tell you the right thing.

Rescue teams continue with their jobs each day. They help people in need no matter what. You can depend on rescue teams. People value rescue teams because they make life safe. If you know someone on a rescue team, tell the person that you are glad he or she does that job. It is good to feel so safe!

Words with long *u* spelled *ui*

cruise   suits

Words with long *u* spelled *ue*

continue   fuel   rescue   value

Unit 1 High Frequency Words

life

Out of Harm's Way

Karl loves to teach kids how to be safe. Karl went on a walk and thought about many things that could harm kids.

Inside their houses, kids can slip on wet floors. Sharp knives can cut a kid's hand. Kids can trip on cords or rugs in the dark. Karl says, "Think smart to stay safe at home. Never run on wet floors. Switch on a bright light at night. Stay away from sharp knives and tools."

Karl went to a park. Most kids like to play in parks and backyards. Karl tells kids how to stay safe in parks and yards. Karl says, "Don't play with strange dogs. If a dog starts to bark, march away."

Kids can be harmed in a park when they ride bikes or play sports. Karl says, "Pads should be worn when you ride bikes or play sports. A hard fall can harm you." Sometimes, cars drive past fast. Karl says, "On the way to the park, listen for horns, and wait for the cars to pass. At the park, play far away from busy streets."

Kids need to know how to be safe in a storm. Trees might drop sharp branches that can cut an arm. A bad cut will leave a mark or a scar. Karl says, "To stay safe, stay inside during a storm."

Karl helps a lot of kids.

Words with *r*-controlled vowels spelled *ar*

arm	dark	harmed	march	parks	smart
backyards	far	harm's	mark	scar	starts
bark	hard	Karl	park	sharp	yards
cars	harm				

Words with *r*-controlled vowels spelled *or*

horns	or	sports	storm	worn

Units 1–2 High Frequency Words

house	know	never	should

Teens Who Serve

It is not true that guys and girls who are teens don't care. No, sir! Just look around, and you will see teens that serve night and day, often for no pay.

First, a girl named Gert works as a clerk in a pet shelter. She is there day after day. Dirt on her skirt is okay with her. She loves cats and dogs. But, she loves bats, snakes, and birds that chirp, too. She believes they all deserve warm beds, fresh food to eat, and fresh water to stop their thirst. Her best T-shirt says, "I Support Animals!"

Then a boy named Kirk thinks about fir trees a lot. He even thinks of fir trees that grow in far-away parts of the world. He works hard to help preserve old fir forests. The shirt I will get him for his birthday will say, "Fir Trees First!"

Third, my sister helps a doctor for no pay. She squirts liquid cleaner day after day. No dirt is left behind after she gets through! Her motto is, "Get Stern with Dirt!"

And last, teams of teens work on trails in parks. They clean the trails where people hike all day. They sweep rocks off to the side. Their shirts may say, "Save Our Parks!"

Today's teens deserve a lot of praise for their hard work. They serve us in so many ways. They make the world a better place. Let's pay them with our praise. We should give teens like Gert, Kirk, and my sister a pat on the back.

Words with *r*-controlled vowels spelled *er*

better	clerk	Gert	preserve	sister	stern
cleaner	deserve	her	serve		

Words with *r*-controlled vowels spelled *ir*

birds	dirt	girl	shirts	squirts	thirst
birthday	fir	girls	sir	third	T-shirt
chirp	first	Kirk	skirt		

Units 1–2 High Frequency Words

often	should

Be Fair to Bears

Bears are big solid mammals with strong legs, long noses, short tails, and thick fur. Bears are the same kind of animals as seals and walruses.

Despite their large size and lumbering walk, bears have a flair for swimming and scaling trees. Sharp claws help bears grip and tear. Bears are active during the evenings. Their sharp sense of smell helps them navigate and find food.

A bear's diet includes fish, insects, rodents, and grasses. Bears also eat scraps that people leave behind at campsites. Bears don't spend much time in pairs. They prefer to live and hunt alone.

Bears survive the cold, harsh winters by sleeping. They shelter themselves in caves or dens and hibernate until spring returns. They don't eat, drink, or wake the entire winter. When spring arrives, starving bears come out of their lairs to hunt.

Your favorite teddy bear may be soft and sweet, but real bears can be very threatening. Female bears defend their cubs at all costs. People have taken over much of the bear's natural habitat, leaving bears little room to roam free. Laws have been passed to protect bears' habitats and give them a fair chance at survival.

Bears often perform in traveling shows. Trained bears may wear costumes or perform feats such as standing on chairs, walking across wires, or twirling. Many think making bears perform stunts and tricks is unfair. Bears are not stuffed dolls. They need fresh air and room to roam. Be fair. Let bears run free. Pick up litter. Keep the bear's habitat clean!

Words with *r*-controlled vowels spelled *air, ear*

air	chairs	flair	lairs	tear	wear
bears	fair	hair	pairs	unfair	

Units 1–2 High Frequency Words

also	been	often

Be a Volunteer

At times, do you wish you could make this planet a better home for everyone? If so, maybe you can be a volunteer and donate time to helping others.

If you can't think of the kinds of things to do as a volunteer, look for projects near your home, such as at a school or a church. Ask your mom and dad to tell you when they hear of a project that you might like.

There are lots of things a kid can do as a volunteer. If you prefer being in nature, help clean up the shoreline of a lake, bay, or river, or volunteer in a wildlife shelter. Maybe you will help heal a sick bird or help a deer with a broken leg.

Perhaps you have a clear talent for music or art. If so, offer to help teach these skills to other kids. You can volunteer each year on Thanksgiving to prepare supper and cheer up the homeless.

Helping in any way is important. Don't be afraid that you lack the skills to be a volunteer. Mentors will be grateful and glad to teach you the things you need to know. And be proud as a volunteer! Peers may sneer when you say that you work hard for no pay, but just tell them that the sheer joy of giving is enough payment.

Words with *r*-controlled vowels spelled *ear, eer*

cheer	deer	hear	peer	sneer	year
clear	fear	near	sheer	volunteer	

Units 1–2 High Frequency Words

could	know

Penny Candy

It is funny to think about life in the years before we were born. My great granddad told me that many types of candy were a penny when he was young. Things were different then—candy was cheap, but life was hard.

In those years, there were more farms and fewer stores. People on farms had to make most of the items they needed by hand. They stitched quilts, spun wool into yarn, and made berry or peach jelly and saved it for the winter. Cows provided milk for butter, cheese, and yogurt. Hens gave eggs, and two big oxen joined with a yoke pulled a plow to prepare the rocky land for crops. Each day, whether sunny, windy, or rainy, the whole family got up at sunrise to work.

Today, things sound easy compared to then. We don't ride for days in horse-pulled carts along bumpy, dusty roads. We can fly in planes and arrive in much less time. Today, we might have a puppy in a yard rather than an ox in a field.

My great granddad missed the open sky of the farm. He joked that there was plenty of fresh air for everyone back on the farm.

I am happy to have the things that modern life offers us. We're lucky that we can buy jelly or yogurt instead of having to make it by hand. Would I go back in time to visit an old farm if I could? Sure, why not! But just for a visit.

Words with _y_

berry	dusty	jelly	puppy	types	yarn
bumpy	easy	lucky	rainy	why	years
by	fly	my	rocky	windy	yogurt
candy	funny	penny	sky	yard	yoke
day	happy	plenty	sunny		

Units 1–4 High Frequency Words

along	before	life	much	why
back	could	miss	sound	would

Pointers from an Employed Mom

When I was a boy, my mother went back to work and my dad stayed at home. Mom worried that we would not survive without her, so she left us reminders … everywhere!

Inside the cupboard, a note said, "TOO MANY SNACKS WILL SPOIL DINNER." In the refrigerator, notes on the sirloin steaks said, "FOR DINNER," on the green beans, "PLEASE BOIL," and on the soy sauce, "FOR SALTY FLAVOR." A note that said, "USE FOIL IN THE PAN WHEN YOU BROIL THE MEAT" was on the stove. The same note was in the drawer with the foil.

On the back door were three notes: for Dad to remember to oil the squeaking hinge, for me to coil the hose after watering the garden, and for all of us to wipe the soil off our feet before coming inside.

When she ran out of short reminders to point out on notes, she began to send postcards with more details. She told my sister to avoid waiting until late to do homework. She sent me one to say not to annoy my sister or make too much noise, and to help her with homework. She even sent a postcard to the dog! She asked him to please just chew his toys instead of destroying the furniture.

I missed my mom when she went back to work, but with all the notes, it was like she was still there … everywhere!

Words with diphthongs and variant vowels spelled *oi, oy*

annoy	boy	destroying	noise	pointers	soy
avoid	broil	employed	oil	sirloin	spoil
boil	coil	foil	point	soil	toys

Units 1–5 High Frequency Words

back	but	much	oil	until	would
before					

How to Speak "Cow"

Most of the time, we speak to say things with words. But sometimes we express feelings in other ways. A frown or pout can mean "I'm unhappy." A smile or shout may show joy. But what about an animal? How does it tell us its feelings? How does it tell another animal how it feels? It uses more than just its mouth!

Animals may use sounds or movements to communicate. You may have a dog or cat in your house. Can you tell when it is content or upset? Does the cat bound to the door to show it is happy to see you? Does the dog growl when you take away its bone? When your cat drops a mouse at your feet, it may meow to say that it is proud of this gift.

Animals that dwell outside may communicate better with other animals than with humans. Researchers have found that the sound a cow makes can tell other cows its age, whether it is male or female, and how it ranks in the herd. To find their rank, cows may butt their heads together to see who is stronger.

Water fowl like ducks and geese call to each other as they prepare to fly. A loud call can mean the bird is excited or angry. The calls are distinct if the bird is in the air flying or down on the ground.

Animals can say a lot without words. If we open our ears and eyes, they may teach us a lot.

Words with diphthongs and variant vowels spelled *ou, ow*

about	down	frown	how	mouth	shout
bound	foul	ground	loud	outside	sound
cow	fowl	growl	meow	pout	sounds
cows	found	house	mouse	proud	without

Units 1–5 High Frequency Words

as	but	found	house	sound	words
away	each				

The View from Space

Major Cooper looked out the window at the view below. The Earth gleamed like wet dew on a very large jewel. Thin wisps of clouds floated by a yellow moon.

The major squeezed the stuffed kangaroo that Lewis gave her before she left. Suddenly, she missed her two boys. Her crew's mission was good for her career. Still, sometimes it was hard to be away from her kids. It seemed like they grew like bamboo shoots while she was away. Soon, she would be home.

Major Cooper turned on her computer and saw that she had a new message. She hooted when she saw that it was an e-mail from Lewis.

Dear Mom,

We hope you have a blast in space. It's so cool that you could go.

Tonight we think we saw your space craft. It wasn't a star, because it did not blink. It wasn't a planet, either. IT HAD TO BE YOU!

We miss you so much, but Dad has been taking good care of us. We have not had one fast food meal yet. (Boo hoo!) Dad made stew, and we couldn't chew it!

Boots got into real trouble. We went to the beach today. Boots got loose and ate a rotten fish, or maybe a crab. It stank! None of us would let her kiss us after that! We had to shampoo her when we got home.

It's time for bed. We send you big hugs and hope you have a smooth trip.

Lewis

Words with diphthongs and variant vowels spelled *oo, ew*

bamboo	Cooper	grew	Lewis	stew	smooth
Boo hoo	crew	hooted	loose	shampoo	soon
Boots	dew	jewel	moon	shoots	view
chew	food	kangaroo	new		

Units 1–5 High Frequency Words

away	been	but	into	miss	seemed
because	before	could	made	much	would

Reptile Jigsaws

Dinosaurs were reptiles, the same type of animals as snakes, lizards, and turtles. They came in all shapes and sizes. Some were tall, and some were small. Some had sharp teeth and claws. Their bones help us find out about these reptiles that lived in the past.

After scientists dig up the bones, they must set them together like a jigsaw puzzle. This isn't an easy job because many bones may be missing or broken. At times, there may be just one or two bones, like an arm bone or a jaw fragment.

Scientists study the parts they find. They check the teeth to see how the dinosaur chewed its food. They study the leg bones to see how it walked. Then they work in teams to make the jigsaw puzzle. Artists draw what the reptile may have looked like. They craft the missing bones from glass and install bolts to join all the parts. The finished puzzle is a model of what the real dinosaur looked like.

The puzzle may end up with flaws because no one has seen a real dinosaur. But if you pause and study a display about them, there is still so much you can learn.

We may never find out what these extinct reptiles looked like, but the jigsaw puzzles show us a lot. We can tell which ones glided like hawks or were as harmless as fawns. It's interesting and fun to learn as much as we can about the past.

Words with diphthongs and variant vowels spelled *au, aw; al, all*					
all	Dinosaurs	flaws	jaw	pause	tall
because	draw	hawks	jigsaw	small	walked
claws	fawns	install	jigsaws		

Units 1–5 High Frequency Words					
as	because	but	lived	much	never

Dance Practice

Grace sat at the table as Mom diced celery and added it to the rice in the pot. Grace looked concerned, so Mom asked why she had a worried face. "I want to audition for the dance team," Grace said, "but I can't do the fast steps. The song has a fast pace, and I have a hard time keeping up."

"Maybe you just have to practice some more," Mom said as she added spices to the rice. "Why don't you call Pam? She is on the city dance team. I bet she can watch you and give you some good advice."

"Great plan, Mom!" Grace said. "I'll ask her tomorrow."

After school the next day, Pam came to Grace's house. She helped Grace practice her dance steps. When Grace rushed to keep up with the pace, Pam slowed her down. "It's not a race!" she said. "Make each step precise. You'll get faster as you learn the steps."

Grace practiced with Pam after school twice a week. As she learned the steps, she made sure to place her feet just right. Finally, it was time to audition. Grace did her best. After all her practice, keeping the pace was easy, just like Pam said it would be.

On Friday, the list of girls who made the dance team was posted. Grace's name was on the list. She had made the dance team! She called Mom.

"Your hard work paid off!" Mom said in an excited voice. "I'll cancel my meeting. Let's pick up Pam and go get some ice cream to celebrate!"

Words with soft c

advice	city	excited	pace	precise	spices
cancel	concerned	face	place	race	twice
celebrate	dance	Grace	practice	rice	voice
celery	diced	ice			

Units 1–6 High Frequency Words

as	but	each	made	why	would
asked	called	house			

A Gem of Advice

Bruce was not good at winning races or contests of any kind. He lost almost all the challenges he entered.

"Another contest?" Ginger asked. "I don't think you've noticed, but you're no ace at winning. You'll lose for sure."

"You don't know that," Bruce answered. "It sounds strange, but even when I finish in last place, I learn something that I can change next time."

"What did you learn when you lost the road race?" Ginger asked.

"I learned that I had to check my shoe laces so I wouldn't trip and fall," Bruce answered. "So I made sure to check my laces in my next race."

"But you didn't win that race either!" Ginger said. "Your pace was too slow. You lost by a huge margin."

"You're right, I didn't win. But I learned that I had to practice more. And I practiced a lot for the dance contest. I was so graceful."

Ginger cringed. "Was that the time you fell off the stage and hurt your face?"

"Yes," Bruce admitted, "and my leg, too. I wore a bandage and a brace for six weeks. But I bounced back, and I learned something. Now I stay in the center of the stage when I dance."

"I'll win this time," said Bruce. "It will be a cinch. I just need to use everything I've learned since I was young!"

And that's when Bruce won his first contest.

"Any gem of advice?" the principal asked Bruce as he handed him a huge medal.

"Gee, yes. Just keep trying!" Bruce said with a giant grin.

Words with soft *g*					
challenge	cringed	exchanging	Ginger	large	strange
change	exchange	gem	huge		

Units 1–6 High Frequency Words					
another	learn	said	something	wouldn't	young
answered	now				

A Gem on Ice

Sage got her first pair of ice skates when she was very young. She loved the ice like mice love cheese. On the ice, her face lit up in a huge smile. Her eyes lit up, too. "This is my place!" she thought. Time on ice was a magic time. Her urge to skate was huge! And she skated with grace. "You are a gem on ice," her mother and father said.

One day, Sage said, "I want to learn to do something new. I want to learn to ice dance. It is all the rage. This is my choice. When I am on the ice, I am at peace. It is like being on a stage." Her mother and father thought it was a great idea.

Now, here she was at the finals. She laced up her skates and thought, "This is my chance to take charge." She forced herself to smile as she glided onto the ice in front of the large crowd.

Sage took her place in the center of the ice rink. Gems shone from her costume. The people in the crowd ceased clapping. She gave a nod, and her music started.

Sage moved with grace along the ice. She leaned into her first jump. She twirled around once, twice, and landed on her blade. "Perfect!" she thought, as she glided on. She braced herself for the next jump. It was an important one, and it would count a lot with the judges. She forced herself to concentrate. Then she spun and leaped into space! The noise of the crowd told her that she had aced the jump.

The judges held up their cards: 10, 10, 10! This was Sage's best dance ever!

Words with soft *g* spelled *g*

charge	gems	large	rage	stage	urge
gem	huge	magic	Sage		

Words with soft *c* spelled *c*

aced	center	dance	grace	mice	space
braced	chance	face	ice	peace	twice
ceased	choice	forced	laced	place	

Units 1–6 High Frequency Words

along	ever	idea	into	now	would
as					

A Summer by the Brook

Jon and Les were very different. Jon preferred to be in the woods, and Les loved reading books inside. They were both having a lonely summer. Every day, Jon took his fishing rod and hooks and went alone to the brook in the woods. Sometimes he sat on a log to catch fish, and sometimes he stood on a rock. Most of the fish were too small, so he would unhook them and throw them back. While Jon was in the woods, Les sat inside all day in a window nook and read good books. It was the only place he liked to sit and read because he could look out the window.

When their father saw that they never spent time together, he shook his head with dismay. He understood that his sons were different, but he was sad that they would spend so much of their childhood apart. "Look, boys," he said. "Why don't we do something together? Why don't we build something that you can both use and enjoy?"

So, they all went to the lumberyard to buy wood. Les went to the library to find books on carpentry while Jon and his dad took the tools out of the basement. Together, the three of them worked hard to build a new bench. It was a beautiful bench, and they put it in the woods near the brook. It was big enough for both Jon and Les to sit on. Jon fished while Les read aloud from books about fish and other creatures in the brook. The brothers spent the rest of the summer together. On the back of the bench, they painted the words, "Built by Jon and Les—Brothers and Good Friends."

Words with variant vowels spelled _oo_

books	good	nook	stood	understood	wood
brook	hooks	shook	took	unhook	woods
childhood	look				

Units 1–6 High Frequency Words

back	could	much	put	why	would
because	friends	never	while	words	

Design for Recovery

It was a snowstorm for the ages. Jami Goldman drove home from a skiing trip in the mountains, when she took a wrong turn. Hours later, she was stuck in a snowstorm for days. After many days, she and her friend were rescued, but then she got some bad news from the doctors. She lost both her legs to frostbite. They were amputated below both knees.

Being an amputee was not something Jami had ever thought about. She was only in her twenties, and her whole life loomed ahead. She knew she had to work hard. The first thing she did was go to college to get a degree. Then she started to race.

Like many amputees, Jami was fitted with artificial limbs. When she raced on a track, she used special legs called "Cheetahs." They cost $3,000, but they gave her freedom to become what she wanted—an athlete and a competitor.

Not content to just run races, Jami wrote a book about her life called "Up and Running." She tells about being stuck in the snowstorm and how she worked to make herself strong again. Her story inspires anyone who has ever had problems. Her life is a design for recovery.

Words with variant vowels and consonants spelled *gn, kn; wr; dge; mb*					
design	knees	knew	limbs	wrong	wrote

Units 1–6 High Frequency Words					
but	ever	life	mountains	news	story
called					

Glossary

The definitions in this glossary are for words as they are used in the Language and Content selections in this book.

ancient (**ān**-chent) *adj. old or from a long time ago*

Stories have survived from **ancient** Greece.

astronaut (**as**-trə-not) *n. a person who travels into space*

Some **astronauts** live on space stations.

athlete (**ath**-lēt) *n. a person who exercises or plays a sport*

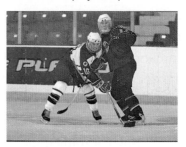

These **athletes** play hockey.

beautiful (**byū**-ti-ful) *adj. pretty*

These **beautiful** flowers are plants.

characters (**ka**-rak-turz) *n.*
people or animals in a story or play

Many times in Greek myths the
characters are gods.

cowboy (**kow**-boi) *n. a person*
who takes care of cattle

Here you see a **cowboy** riding a bull.

compete (cum-**pēt**) *v. to try to*
do better than another person

These athletes **compete** against
each other in speed skating.

culture (**kul**-chur) *n. ways of life,*
including food, music, and language

People with different **cultures** live
together in the Southwest.

content (kun-**tent**) *adj. happy*
with what you have; not wanting more

King Midas should have been
content to live in a big castle.

declared (dē-**klaird**) *v. spoken clearly*
and with strength

These people **declared** what they wanted.

earthquake (**urth**-kwāk) *n. when the earth's surface moves and causes disaster, like fallen buildings*

Here you see what an **earthquake** can do to an area.

ecosystem (**ēk**-oh-sis-tum) *n. all the things that live together in one area*

Animals and plants live together in **ecosystems**.

emergencies (ē-**mur**-gen-sēz) *n. sudden and unexpected events that need action*

SAR dogs can help during water rescues and other **emergencies**.

energy (**eh**-nur-jē) *n. the power to move and do things*

This squirrel eats plants to get **energy** to move!

explore (ek-**splôr**) *v. to look around and find out things about a place*

People come to the Southwest to **explore** the land and rivers.

female (**fē**-māl) *adj.* having to do with a girl or woman

This **female** athlete has trained hard in the sport of snowboarding.

forest (**fōr**-est) *n.* a big area of land covered with trees

Many animals live in the trees of this **forest**.

freedom (**frē**-dum) *n.* to have choices and not to be ruled by others

The Washington Monument honors George Washington, who led his people to **freedom**.

government (**guh**-vern-ment) *n.* the group of leaders who direct a group of people

The members of Congress are one part of the U.S. **government**.

greedy (**grē**-dē) *adj.* not happy with what you have; always wanting more

King Midas was **greedy** for more gold.

healthy (**hel**-thē) *adj.* being well and not sick

People stay **healthy** by eating vegetables like broccoli.

laws (lôz) *n. the rules in a society*

A judge decides whether someone is guilty of breaking a **law**.

miles (mīlz) *n. great distances*

There are **miles** of desert land in the Southwest.

life (līf) *n. a living being; being alive*

This SAR dog sniffs for clues to help save a **life**.

moon (mün) *n. the natural satellite that orbits the earth*

Earth's **moon** is round and white.

male (māl) *adj. having to do with a boy or man*

The players on this team are all **male**.

oxygen (ok-si-jen) *n. a kind of gas that is in the air*

Plants make the **oxygen** that is in the air.

photograph (fō-tō-graf) *n. an image produced by a camera*

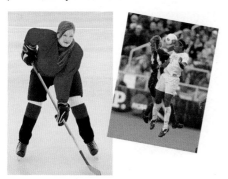

These are **photographs** of women athletes.

plot (plot) *n. the plan or what is mainly happening in stories or plays*

The **plot** of King Midas includes the king's love for his daughter.

police officers (pō-lēs o-fi-serz) *n. people who enforce the laws and keep order*

This dogs helps a **police officer** look for a missing person.

pond (pond) *n. a body of water that is smaller than a lake*

Frogs and fish live in this **pond**.

power (pow-ur) *n. strength*

The Three Branches
of U.S. Government

Legislative Branch   Executive Branch

Judicial Branch

The first leaders of the United States wanted to balance the **power** across the government.

protest (**prō**-test) *v. to show that you do not like something*

These people are **protesting**.

rescue (**res**-cyū) *v. to save or free someone*

Here, a dog helps **rescue** people after the attacks on September 11, 2001.

right (**rīt**) *n. something all people have the freedom to do*

Martin Luther King, Jr., wanted equal **rights** for all people.

rocket (**rok**-it) *n. a vehicle that can travel into space*

A **rocket** is used to send people into space.

sign (**sīn**) *n. a message printed large enough for many people to read*

These women are holding **signs**.

solar system (**sō**-lər **sis**-tem) *n. the sun and planets that orbit the sun*

Our planet Earth is part of the **solar system**.

soil (soyl) *n. the ground where things grow*

Crops like corn can grow in **soil**.

space (spās) *n. the empty area outside of Earth*

Scientists use tools to look into outer **space**.

states (stāts) *n. a part of a political union, like the United States of America*

Four big **states** make up the Southwest.

survive (ser-vīv) *v. to keep on living*

Bears need plants, water, and air to **survive**.

vitamins (vī-tuh-minz) *n. substances that make you grow and be healthy*

Fruits like blueberries have the **vitamins** that people need.

women (**wi-mun**) *n. mature females*

These **women** lived in 1917.

vote (vōt) *v. to choose or select someone or something, as in an election*

This woman is **voting** for the next President of the U.S.

Index of Skills

VOCABULARY

Academic vocabulary 19, 40, 53, 70, 73–74, 87, 106–107, 123, 142–144, 157, 176, 191, 210, 212, 225, 245, 259, 280, 293

Antonyms 11, 143

Basic vocabulary

Abbreviations 320–322

Actions 335–336

Animals 70–71, 73, 75, 84–87, 92–97

Body parts 176, 180–181

Cardinal numbers *See* Numbers and basic operations.

Careers 3, 8, 18, 245, 246, 324

Colors 331

Commands 145, 315

Comparison words 86, 107, 112–113, 248–249, 258

Days of the week 321

Describing words 73, 75, 143, 247, 330–334

Direction words 39, 212

Family 324

Farming 242, 245, 248–249

Feelings 333

Food 243–244, 246–249, 326

Habitats 73–76, 82–87, 89–93, 325

Homes and household objects 325

Landforms 212–213, 220–225, 325

Location words 325

Money 244, 330, 334

Months of the year 321

Negative words 279, 315

Neighborhood 325

Numbers and basic operations 53, 244, 330, 334

Opinion words 72, 209

Opposites 11, 143, 146, 252–253

Order words 334

Ordinal numbers *See* Order words.

People 4, 12, 16, 18, 107–108, 123, 157, 210–211 *See also* Careers *and* Family.

Plants 73–75, 248–249, 252, 254–259

Question words 211, 244, 312–314

Restaurant words 246

Rooms in a house *See* Homes and household objects.

Sensory words 75, 247, 331–332

Shapes 331

Sizes 331

Social courtesies 178

Sports 175, 177–179, 186–191, 194–202

Story elements 142–144, 146–147, 156

Telling time 5, 144

Weather 75, 82–85, 225, 251, 256–258

Classify words 8, 18, 42, 73–74, 76, 89, 112, 146, 176, 180, 210, 214, 248, 280, 282

Content-area words *See* **Academic vocabulary.**

High frequency words 10–11, 13–18, 44–45, 47–52, 78–79, 81–86, 114–115, 117–122, 148–149, 151–156, 182–183, 185–190, 216–217, 219–224, 250–251, 253–258, 284–285, 287–292

Key vocabulary 21, 30, 55, 64, 89, 98, 125, 134, 159, 168, 193, 202, 227, 236, 261, 270, 295, 304

Multiple-meaning words 284–285

Prefixes 252–253, 286–287

Relate words 10–11, 13, 18, 47, 81, 117, 151, 156, 190, 214–215, 219, 248–249, 253, 258

Suffixes 252–253, 286–287

Synonyms 11, 72, 107, 156, 190

Word maps and webs 8, 42, 44–45, 76, 112, 146, 159, 180, 182–183, 214, 248, 282

LANGUAGE FUNCTIONS

Agree and disagree 278

Ask and answer questions 210–211, 244–245

Ask for and accept a favor 143

Ask for and give advice 142

Ask for and give information 106, 176, 244–245

Buy or sell an item 244

Describe 73, 75, 86, 144, 156, 224, 246–247, 277, 281

Express feelings 40, 99

Express needs, wants, and thoughts 40, 99

Express probability 4–5

Express social courtesies 178

Give and carry out commands 145

Give directions 39, 212

Give information 38, 43, 77, 113, 176–177, 181, 215, 245, 249 *See also* **Ask for and give information.**

Give opinions 72

Have a discussion 106, 113, 224

Make a suggestion 74

Make comparisons 86, 107, 113, 248–249, 258

Read aloud and recite 4, 10–12, 38, 44–46, 72, 78–80, 106, 114–116, 142, 148–150, 176, 182–184, 210, 216–218, 224, 244, 250–252, 278, 284–286

Retell a story 8–9, 146–147, 282–283

Tell an original story 144

READING AND LEARNING STRATEGIES, CRITICAL THINKING, AND COMPREHENSION

Text Structures and Literary Concepts

LISTENING, SPEAKING, VIEWING, AND REPRESENTING

WRITING

RESEARCH SKILLS

Acknowledgments, continued from page ii

iii Gail Mooney/Masterfile. **iii** (bl) Tom Bean/Terra/Corbis. **iii** (b) Panoramic Images/Getty Images. **iii** (br) ©Adam Burton/Photolibrary/Getty Images. **xvi** (b) Rolf Kopfle/ KOPFL. **xvii** (t) Ron Watts/Corbis. **002** (fgd) Cartesia. **002** (fgd) NGS/HB/Liz Garza-Williams. **004** (c) NGS/HB/Liz Garza-Williams. **005** (tl) David Young-Wolff/PhotoEdit. **005** (cl) NGS/HB/Liz Garza-Williams. **005** (c) NGS/HB/Digital Studios. **005** (cl) NGS/HB/Liz Garza-Williams. **005** (c) NGS/HB/Liz Garza-Williams. **005** (cr) NGS/HB/Liz Garza-Williams. **005** (br) NGS/HB/Liz Garza-Williams. **005** (cr) NGS/HB/New Century Graphics. **006** (tl) NGS/HB/Liz Garza-Williams. **006** (c) NGS/HB/Liz Garza-Williams. **007** (tl) NGS/HB/Liz Garza-Williams. **007** (bl) NGS/HB/Liz Garza-Williams. **007** (br) NGS/HB/Liz Garza-Williams. **008** (c) NGS/HB/New Century Graphics. **009** ©Dusan Jankovic/ Shutterstock. **009** (c) NGS/HB/Liz Garza-Williams. **010** bkgd Creatas/Jupiterimages. **010** (fgd) NGS/HB. **010** bkgd Urban CGI/Alamy. **012** (tr) NGS/HB/Liz Garza-Williams. **014** (b) Ancil Nance/Getty Images. **014** (c) Ellen Denuto/ The Image Bank/Getty Images. **014** (bl) NGS/HB. **014** (br) NGS/HB. **014** (bl) NGS/HB/New Century Graphics. **015** (b) NGS/HB/Barbara Kelley. **016** bkgd YinYang/iStockphoto. com. **016** (cl) NGS/HB. **016** (c) NGS/HB. **016** (cr) NGS/HB/ Liz Garza-Williams. **017** (bc) NGS/HB/Digital Studios. **017** (tl) NGS/HB/Liz Garza-Williams. **017** (br) NGS/HB/Liz Garza-Williams. **017** (bl) Siede Preis/Photodisc/Getty Images. **017** (b) Siede Preis/Photodisc/Getty Images. **018** (tl) NGS/HB/Liz Garza-Williams. **019** (cl) Artville Produce. **020** (cl) Baerbel Schmidt/Stone/Getty Images. **020** (br) Inti St Clair/Digital Vision/Getty Images. **020** (tr) Elie Bernager/Stone/Getty Images. **021** (tl) David Young-Wolff/ Photographer's Choice/. **021** (cl) David Young-Wolff/ Stone/ Getty Images. **021** (bl) Hola Images/Getty Images. **021** (cr) John-Francis Bourke/The Image Bank/Getty Images. **021** (tr) NGS/HB/Luisa Henoo. **022** (r) Elie Bernager/Stone/ Getty Images. **022** bkgd NGS/HB/GGS. **024** (fgd) David Young-Wolff/ Stone/Getty Images. **025** (fgd) Inti St Clair/ Digital Vision/Getty Images. **025** bkgd NGS/HB/GGS. **026** (fgd) Baerbel Schmidt/Stone/Getty Images. **027** bkgd NGS/ HB/GGS. **027** (fgd) Michael Newman/PhotoEdit. **028** (t) Hola Images/Getty Images. **028** bkgd NGS/HB/GGS. **028** (c) Image Source/Jupiter Images. **029** (r) Amos Morgan/ Photodisc/Getty Images. **029** (tl) SW Productions/ Photodisc/Getty Images. **031** (b) Pat Doyle/Encyclopedia/ Corbis. **032** (b) PhotoDisc/Getty Images. **034** (c) G.K. & Vikki Hart/PhotoDisc/Getty Images. **034** (fgd) NGS/HB/ Ray Godfrey. **036** (c) NGS/HB/Lori Loestoeter. **037** (c) Artville Food Icons. **037** (cl) Artville Produce. **037** (b) Artville Produce. **037** (tl) Artville Produce. **037** (c) Artville Produce. **037** (t) NGS/HB/New Century Graphics. **037** (t) NGS/HB/New Century Graphics. **037** (tr) NGS/HB/New Century Graphics. **037** (cr) NGS/HB/New Century Graphics. **037** (bl) NGS/HB/New Century Graphics. **037** (br) NGS/HB/New Century Graphics. **037** (b) Stockbyte/ Getty Images. **038** (c) NGS/HB/Tom Casmer. **039** (tl) NGS/ HB/Liz Garza-Williams. **039** (c) NGS/HB/Liz Garza-Williams. **040** (r) NGS/Andy Adams. **040** (c) NGS/HB. **041** (fgd) NGS/Andy Adams. **042** (tr) Ian O'Leary/Stone/Getty Images. **042** (cr) NGS/Rachel Geswaldo. **043** (cr) NGS/ Rachel Geswaldo. **044** (c) NGS/HB/Lori Loestoeter. **044** (b) NGS/HB/New Century Graphics. **044** (br) Nick Koudis/ Photodisc/Getty Images. **044** (bl) John A. Rizzo/ Photodisc/Getty Images. **044** (b) Siede Preis/Photodisc/ Getty Images. **044** (br) Nick Koudis/Photodisc/Getty Images. **045** (b) NGS/HB/Barbara Kelley. **046** (fgd) Finn O'Hara/Getty Images. **046** (r) NGS/HB/GGS. **047** (b) NGS/ HB/Liz Garza-Williams. **047** (tl) NGS/HB/Liz Garza-Williams. **047** (br) NGS/HB/Liz Garza-Williams. **047** (bl) Jules Frazier/Photodisc/Getty Images. **047** (b) C Squared Studios/Photodisc/Getty Images. **048** (b) Artville Produce. **048** (cl) Artville fast food. **048** (tl) NGS/HB/Norm Bendell. **048** (cr) Siede Preis/Photodisc/Getty Images. **048** (br) C Squared Studios/Photodisc/Getty Images. **048** (bl) Stockbyte/Getty Images. **049** (t) NGS/Bud Endress. **049** John E. Kelly/Stone/Getty Images. **049** (t) ©Lew Robertson/Brand X Pictures/Getty Images. **049** ©Dennis Gottlieb/FoodPix/Getty Images. **049** (tc) ©PhotoDisc/ Getty Images. **049** (tc) ©Multi-bits/Photodisc/Getty Images. **049** (t) PhotoDisc/Getty Images. **050** (cr) Purestock/Getty Images. **050** (c) Hugh Threlfall/Alamy. **050** (cl) Tim Hill/Alamy. **050** (br) Chuck Savage/Cusp/ Corbis. **050** Mikael Andersson/Nordic Photos/Getty Images. **050** (tr) Jonathan Kantor/The Image Bank/Getty Images. **050** ©aleaimage/E+/Getty Images. **050** ©aleaimage/E+/Getty Images. **051** (tr) David Young-Wolff/ PhotoEdit. **051** (bl) Ariel Skelley/Taxi/Getty Images. **051** (c) Burazin/ Photographer's Choice/Getty Images. **051** (tr) Simone Metz/ StockFood Creative/Getty Images. **051** (cr) Siede Preis/Photodisc/Getty Images. **051** (cr) Lusoimages/ iStockphoto.com. **051** (cl) Image Source/Jupiterimages. **052** (bc) Tim Hill/Alamy. **052** (tr) Jonathan Kantor/The Image Bank/Getty Images. **052** Mikael Andersson/Nordic Photos/Getty Images. **053** (t) Hugh Threlfall/Alamy. **053** (bc) Purestock/Getty Images. **053** ©aleaimage/E+/Getty Images. **053** bkgd NGS/HB. **054** (cl) Tom Bean/Terra/ Corbis. **054** (l) NGS/HB/GGS. **054** (b) Image Source/ Jupiterimages. **054** (t) Image Source/Jupiter Images. **054** (t) Image Source/Jupiterimages. **054** (tl) Image Source/ Jupiter Images. **054** ©Jupiterimages. **055** (tr) Digital Vision/Alamy. **055** (t) lee hacker/Alamy. **055** (tl) Stockbyte/ Alamy. **055** (c) Wayne Hutchinson/Alamy. **055** (t) Maximilian Stock Ltd/photocuisine/Corbis. **055** (b) Rosemary Calvert/ Photographer's Choice/Getty Images. **055** (l) NGS/HB/GGS. **055** (cr) Exactostock / SuperStock. **055** (cr) Purestock/Getty Images. **056** (t) Stockbyte/Alamy. **056** (tl) Burazin/ Photographer's Choice/Getty Images. **056** (tr) Foodcollection /Getty Images. **056** (br) Christina Peters/StockFood Creative/Getty Images. **056** (t) Siede Preis/Photodisc/Getty Images. **056** (t) NGS/HB/GGS. **056** (t) Lusoimages/iStockphoto.com. **056** (cl) ©Vincenzo Lombardo/Photodisc/Getty Images. **057** (tl) MaRoDee Photography/Alamy. **057** (br) Simone Metz/ StockFood Creative/Getty Images. **057** (t) NGS/HB/GGS. **057** (tr) Jostein Hauge/iStockphoto. **057** (t) Kevin Russ/ iStockphoto. **057** (t) Image Source/Jupiter Images. **057** (t) Purestock/Jupiter Images. **057** (c) David Young-Wolff/ PhotoEdit. **058** (tl) Aleksandr Ugorenkov/Alamy. **058** (t) Geoffrey Kidd/Alamy. **058** (cr) Wilmar Photography/Alamy. **058** (cl) Lynda Richardson/Terra/Corbis. **058** (t) Eising/ Photodisc/Getty Images. **058** (t) Renee Comet/ StockFood Creative /Getty Images. **058** (t) Stockbyte/Getty Images. **058** (t) NGS/HB/GGS. **058** (tr) Jernej Borovin ek/ iStockphoto. **058** (c) Chuck Savage/Cusp/Corbis. **061** (c) NGS/HB/GGS. **063** (br) NGS/HB/Bud Endress. **064** (tl) Angela Maynard/PhotoDisc/Getty Images. **064** (c) Squared Studios/Photodisc/Getty Images. **064** (c) C. Borland/ PhotoDisc/Getty Images. **064** (bl) Bob Rowan/Progressive Image/Historical/Corbis. **064** (br) Gabe Palmer/ Cusp/ Corbis. **064** David Hiller/Photodisc/Getty Images. **064** (tr) Dick Luria/Taxi/Getty Images. **064** (br) Hugh Sitton/Stone/ Getty Images. **064** (c) Michael Krasowitz/Taxi/Getty Images. **064** ©Digital Vision/Alamy. **064** (fgd) Stephen Derr/Getty Images. **064** (c) Stephen Derr/Stone/Getty Images. **064** (tl) Jack Star/PhotoDisc/Getty Images. **064** (tl) Joshua Ets-Hokin/ Photodisc/Getty Images. **064** (fgd) NGS/HB/Digital Stock/New York City. **064** (cl) PhotoDisc/ Getty Images. **064** (c) Adam Crowley/ Photodisc/Getty Images. **064** (bl) Don Tremain/Photodisc/Getty Images. **064** (tc) Scott T. Baxter/Photodisc/Getty Images. **064** (bl) PhotoDisc/Getty Images. **064** (br) Adam Crowley/ Photodisc/Getty Images. **064** (cr) Adam Crowley/ Photodisc/Getty Images. **064** (tr) Arthur S. Aubry/ Photodisc/Getty Images. **064** (bl) Skip Nall/ Photodisc/ Getty Images. **064** (b) Arthur S. Aubry/Photodisc/Getty Images. **064** (tr) PhotoDisc/Getty Images. **064** (tl) David Buffington/Photodisc/Getty Images. **064** (bc) Arthur S. Aubry/Photodisc/Getty Images. **064** (cr) Hisham Ibrahim/ Photodisc/Getty Images. **064** (cl) Keith Brofsky/Photodisc/ Getty Images. **064** (t) PhotoDisc/Getty Images. **064** (tl) Don Tremain/Photodisc/Getty Images. **064** (cl) Keith Brofsky/ Photodisc/Getty Images. **064** (tl) PhotoDisc/Getty Images. **064** (c) "David Young-Wolff/PhotoEdit Inc." **064** (cr) Russell Illig/PhotoDisc/Getty Image. **064** Stockbyte/ Getty Images. **064** (tr) Stockbyte/Getty Images. **066** (bc) Ed Bock/Cusp/Corbis. **066** (cl) Andrea Pistolesi/ The Image Bank/Getty Images. **066** (tl) David Young-Wolff/Stone/ Getty Images. **066** (cl) ©Digital Vision/Alamy. **066** (b) NGS/HB. **066** (bl) Paul Conklin/PhotoEdit. **066** (br) Jeff Greenberg/PhotoEdit. **066** (br) Stockbyte/Getty Images. **067** (tl) JDC/LWA/Cusp/Corbis. **067** ©Angelo Cavalli/Tips Images/age fotostock. **067** (bc) Ancil Nance/Getty Images. **067** (cl) ©Thinkstock Images/Comstock Images/Getty Images. **067** (bl) David Toase/PhotoDisc/Getty Images. **067** (br) Michelle D. Bridwell/PhotoEdit. **068** (cr) "Jose Luis Pelaez Inc/Cusp/Corbis." **068** (cl) © Steve Chenn/ Corbis. **068** (tl) NGS/HB/Liz Garza-Williams. **068** (bl) Jonathan Nourok / PhotoEdit. **068** (br) "Bonnie Kamin/ PhotoEdit IncPhotoEdit." **068** (c) Dana White/PhotoEdit. **068** (bc) Michael Newman/PhotoEdit. **069** (cl) NGS/HB/ Robert Hynes. **069** (cr) NGS/HB/Robert Hynes. **070** (fgd) NGS/HB. **070** bkgd Mark Garlick / Science Source/Photo Researchers. **071** (b) NGS/HB/Micheal Slack. **072** (t) Ales Fevzer/ Documentary/Corbis. **072** (c) Rachel Geswaldo. **073** (b) NGS/Rachel Geswaldo. **074** (bl) David Frazier/ Spirit/Corbis. **074** Phillip Wallick/Corbis. **074** (cl) Kevin Laubacher/Taxi/Getty Images. **074** (b) NGS/HB/John Paul Endress. **074** (bl) NGS/HB—Digital Stock/transportation. **074** (tr) PhotoDisc/Getty Images. **074** (tc) PhotoDisc/Getty Images. **074** (bl) PhotoDisc/Getty Images. **074** (br) PhotoDisc/Getty Images. **074** (br) PhotoDisc/Getty Images. **074** (bc) Tony Freeman/PhotoEdit. **074** (l) Stockbyte/Getty Images. **075** (b) NGS/HB/Barbara Kelley. **076** (t) Superstudio/ The Image Bank/Getty Images. **076** (cl) NGS/ HB/John Paul Endress. **076** (br) Rudi Von Briel / PhotoEdit. **077** (fgd) Mark Weiss/Taxi/Getty Images. **078** (tl) Rudi Von Briel / PhotoEdit. **079** (tc) NGS/HB/Liz Garza-Williams. **079** (tr) NGS/HB/Liz Garza-Williams. **079** (t) NGS/HB/Liz Garza-Williams. **079** (t) NGS/HB/Liz Garza-Williams. **079** (c) NGS/HB/New Century Graphics. **079** (tl) NGS/HB/New Century Graphics. **080** (tr) BILL HATCHER/National Geographic Stock. **080** (cl) Grant Faint/The Image Bank / Getty Images. **080** (br) Royalty-Free/Corbis. **081** (cl) James L. Amos/ Documentary/Corbis. **081** (bl) Richard T. Nowitz/ Terra/Corbis. **081** (cr) "Michael Newman/PhotoEdit Inc." **081** (tl) Will Hart/PhotoEdit. **081** (cr) ©Robert Adrian Hillman/Shutterstock. **082** (r) BILL HATCHER/National Geographic Stock. **084** bkgd Grant Faint/The Image Bank / Getty Images. **084** (t) ©Adam Burton/Photolibrary/Getty Images. **085** (b) ©CLM/Shutterstock. **086** (br) Tom Bean/ Corbis. **086** (br) NGS/HB. **086** (tr) Robert Marien/Corbis. **087** (fgd) Robert Glusic/Corbis. **088** (cr) Albert J. Copley/ Stockbyte/Getty Images. **088** (bl) Steve Cole/Photodisc/ Getty Images. **088** (tr) MarcelClemens. **089** (b) James L. Amos/ Documentary/Corbis. **089** (t) Siede Preis/Photodisc/ Getty Images. **089** (tr) Siede Preis/Photodisc/Getty Images. **091** (b) PhotoDisc/Getty Images. **091** (t) NGS/HB/Liz Garza-Williams. **094** (tc) Corbis Images/PictureQuest. **094** (bl) Corbis Images/PictureQuest. **094** (cr) Corbis Images/ PictureQuest. **094** (cr) Image Ideas Inc./PictureQuest. **094** (br) Kent Knudson/PictureQuest. **094** (cl) Nick Koudis/ PictureQuest. **094** (c) PhotoLink. **094** (tl) S. Meltzer/ PhotoLink/Getty. **096** (cl) NGS/HB/Liz Garza-Williams. **096** (c) Ray McVay/PhotoDisc/Getty Images. **097** (cl) Alan Pappe/RubberBall Productions/PictureQuest. **097** (cr) Corbis Images/PictureQuest. **097** (tc) Michael McQueen/ Stone/Getty Images. **097** (bl) NGS/HB. **098** (br) Dag Sundberg/ The Image Bank /Getty Images. **098** (t) NGS/HB/ Norm Bendell. **099** NGS/HB/Norm Bendell. **100** (r) Robert Harding Picture Library Ltd/Alamy. **100** credit unknown. **102** (tr) David Young-Wolff/PhotoEdit. **102** (br) NGS/ Rachel Geswaldo. **104** (tr) Corbis Images/PictureQuest. **104** (c) Jake Rajs/ Stone/Getty Images. **104** (bc) NGS/HB/ John Paul Endress. **104** (tl) ©Jeremy Swinborne/ Shutterstock. **104** (br) C Squared Studios/Photodisc/Getty Images. **104** (tc) PhotoDisc/Getty Images. **104** (bc) Photodisc/Getty Images/Houghton Mifflin Harcourt. **104** (cr) Jules Frazier/Getty Images. **104** (bl) Ryan McVay/ Photodisc/Getty Images. **104** (cl) Siede Preis/Photodisc/ Getty Images. **104** (tr) PhotoLink/PhotoDisc/PictureQuest. **104** (c) Stockbyte/Getty Images. **106** (tr) ©Alan Schein Photography/Corbis/. **106** (tr) Gregor Schuster/ Flirt/ Corbis. **106** (br) Paul Colangelo/Terra/Corbis. **106** (cl) Stockbyte/Getty Images. **107** (t) NGS/HB/Norm Bendell. **108** (tl) NGS/HB/Norm Bendell. **109** (cr) Jeremy Horner/ Corbis. **109** (c) ©AND Inc/Shutterstock. **109** (cl) Harvey Lloyd/Taxi/Getty Images. **110** (tr) KENNETH GARRETT/ National Geographic Image Collection. **110** (c) KENNETH GARRETT/National Geographic Stock. **110** (br) NGS/HB/ National Geographic Maps. **111** (tr) Nic Cleave Photography / Alamy. **111** (bl) Danny Lehman/ Documentary Value/Corbis. **111** (tl) NGS/HB/National Geographic Maps. **111** (cr) Gabriela Medina/Superstock. **113** (c) KENNETH GARRETT/National Geographic Image Collection. **114** (tl) J Marshall - Tribaleye Images / Alamy. **114** (c) KENNETH GARRETT/National Geographic Stock. **114** (tr) NGS/HB/National Geographic Maps. **115** (c) Mural reconstruction by Heather Hurst. **116** (c) Jordi Camí/Age Fotostock. **116** (tl) J Marshall - Tribaleye Images / Alamy. **117** (t) ©Tom Schwabel/Flickr/Getty Images. **117** (cr) NGS/HB/National Geographic Maps. **118** (tr) NGS/HB/ National Geographic Maps. **118** (tl) J Marshall - Tribaleye Images / Alamy. **118** (c) Gabriela Medina/Superstock. **119** (t) Jorge Silva/Reuters. **122** (cr) David Young-Wolff/Stone/ Getty Images. **124** (bl) Ed Young/AgStock Images/Corbis. **124** (c) Getty Images/ Digital Stock Animals. **124** (tl) NGS/ HB. **124** NGS/HB/Liz Garza-Williams. **124** (br) Marty Honig/Photodisc/Getty Images. **124** (bl) PhotoDisc/Getty Images. **124** (tr) C Squared Studios/Photodisc/Getty Images. **124** (t) John Wang/Photodisc/Getty Images. **126** (cl) NGS/HB/Norm Bendell. **127** (bl) Chris Birck. **127** (bc) NGS/Chris Birck. **127** (c) Kevin Fleming/Corbis. **127** (tl) Courtesy of Brown Publishing Network. **127** (tc) Courtesy of Brown Publishing Network. **127** (tc) Courtesy of Brown Publishing Network. **127** (tr) Courtesy of Brown Publishing Network. **127** (br) Courtesy of Brown Publishing Network. **127** (bc) David Young-Wolff/Stone/Getty Images. **127** (c) Susan Van Etten/PhotoEdit. **128** (c) NGS/HB/Norm Bendell. **129** (tl) NGS/HB/Liz Garza-Williams. **129** (tc) NGS/HB/Liz Garza-Williams. **129** (cl) NGS/HB/Liz Garza-Williams. **129** (cl) NGS/HB/Liz Garza-Williams. **129** (cr) NGS/HB/Liz Garza-Williams. **129** (cr) NGS/HB/Liz Garza-Williams. **129** (bl) NGS/HB/Liz Garza-Williams—Royalty-Free. **129** (bl) NGS/HB/Liz Garza-Williams—Royalty-Free. **129** (br) NGS/HB/Liz Garza-Williams. **129** (br) NGS/HB/Liz Garza-Williams. **130** (br) Rob Gage/Taxi/ Getty Images. **130** (tl) David Young-Wolff/PhotoEdit. **131** (bl) Joseph Sohm; Visions of America/Encyclopedia/ CORBIS. **131** (tl) Michael Newman/PhotoEdit. **131** (br) "PhotoEdit Inc." **132** (r) Mario Tama/ Getty Images News / Getty Images. **132** (r) NGS/HB—publisher owned art. **134** (tr) John A. Rizzo/Photodisc/Getty Images. **134** (tr) NGS/ Rachel Geswaldo. **135** (cr) NGS/Rachel Geswaldo—work for hire art. **136** (tl) Digital Stock New York City. **136** (c) NGS/HB/Liz Garza-Williams. **136** (bc) C Squared Studios/ Photodisc/Getty Images. **138** (r) Peter M. Fisher/ Flirt/ Corbis. **138** (cl) Tim Ridley/Dorling Kindersley/Getty Images. **138** (cl) Brand X Pictures/Jupiterimages. **138** (tr) Don Farrall/Digital Vision/Getty Images. **138** (cl) NGS/HB/ Liz Garza-Williams. **138** (tc) NGS/HB/Liz Garza-Williams. **138** (cr) NGS/HB/Liz Garza-Williams. **139** (cl) NGS/HB/Liz Garza-Williams. **139** (tr) NGS/HB/Liz Garza-Williams. **140** (tl) Bonnie Kamin/PhotoEdit. **141** (bc) Colin Garratt; Milepost 92 _/ Historical/CORBIS. **141** (tr) Ryan McVay/ Photodisc/Getty Images. **141** (bc) NGS/HB—publisher owned art. **141** (tl) NGS/HB—publisher owned art. **141** (cl) NGS/HB—publisher owned art. **142** (cl) Bill Heinsohn/ Photographer's Choice /Getty Images. **142** (tr) John Kelly/ Stone /Getty Images. **142** Gail Mooney/Masterfile. **143** (tr) Ellen Isaacs/Alamy. **143** (cl) NGS/Michael Hortens. **143** (tl) Age fotostock/SuperStock. **143** (bl) Sal Maimone/ SuperStock. **143** (cr) ©Advertising Archive/Courtesy Everett Collection. **144** (r) John Kelly/ Stone /Getty Images. **146** (b) NGS/Michael Hortens—publisher owned art. **146** (tr) Sal Maimone/SuperStock. **147** (b) ©Huntington Library / SuperStock/1060-896. **147** (cr) Photolibrary/Index Stock. **147** (tr) ©Advertising Archive/Courtesy Everett Collection.

Common Core State Standards

Inside Fundamentals is designed to build foundational skills to help you succeed in middle school. The lessons meet the Common Core Anchor standards in all strands. Additional correlations are provided for grade-level Reading Foundational Skills and Language standards to show how those specific foundational skills are covered.

Unit 1 Here to Help

Language Development

SE Pages	Lesson	Code	Standards Text
2–3	Unit Launch	CCRA.SL.2	Integrate and evaluate information presented in diverse media and formats, including visually, quantitatively, and orally.
4	Language: Tell What May Happen	CCRA.SL.1	Prepare for and participate effectively in a range of conversations and collaborations with diverse partners, building on others' ideas and expressing their own clearly and persuasively.
		CCRA.SL.6	Adapt speech to a variety of contexts and communicative tasks, demonstrating command of formal English when indicated or appropriate.
5	Vocabulary: Time	CCRA.SL.1	Prepare for and participate effectively in a range of conversations and collaborations with diverse partners, building on others' ideas and expressing their own clearly and persuasively.
	Language: Tell What May Happen	CCRA.L.6	Acquire and use accurately a range of general academic and domain-specific words and phrases sufficient for reading, writing, speaking, and listening at the college and career readiness level; demonstrate independence in gathering vocabulary knowledge when encountering an unknown term important to comprehension or expression.
6	Grammar: Phrases With *Have To* and *Need To*	CCRA.SL.1	Prepare for and participate effectively in a range of conversations and collaborations with diverse partners, building on others' ideas and expressing their own clearly and persuasively.
			Demonstrate command of the conventions of standard English grammar and usage when writing or speaking.
		L.3.1d	Form and use regular and irregular verbs.
7	Grammar: Possessive Adjectives		Demonstrate command of the conventions of standard English grammar and usage when writing or speaking.
		L.1.1d	Use personal, possessive, and indefinite pronouns (e.g., *I, me, my; they, them, their, anyone, everything*).
		L.1.1f	Use frequently occurring adjectives.
8	Listen and Read Along: *Power Out!*	CCRA.R.4	Interpret words and phrases as they are used in a text, including determining technical, connotative, and figurative meanings, and analyze how specific word choices shape meaning or tone.
		CCRA.R.10	Read and comprehend complex literary and informational texts independently and proficiently.
			With guidance and support from adults, demonstrate understanding of word relationships and nuances in word meanings.
		L.1.5a	Sort words into categories (e.g., colors, clothing) to gain a sense of the concepts the categories represent.
9	Comprehension: Identify Cause and Effect	CCRA.R.3	Analyze how and why individuals, events, or ideas develop and interact over the course of a text.

Common Core State Standards, continued

Language Development, continued

SE Pages	Lesson	Code	Standards Text
9	**Comprehension: Identify Cause and Effect,** continued	• CCRA.R.5	Analyze the structure of texts, including how specific sentences, paragraphs, and larger portions of the text (e.g., a section, chapter, scene, or stanza) relate to each other and the whole.
		• CCRA.SL.1	Prepare for and participate effectively in a range of conversations and collaborations with diverse partners, building on others' ideas and expressing their own clearly and persuasively.

Language and Literacy

SE Pages	Lesson	Code	Standards Text
10–11	**High Frequency Words**		Know and apply grade-level phonics and word analysis skills in decoding words.
		• RF.K.3c	Read common high-frequency words by sight (e.g., *the, of, to, you, she, my, is, are, do, does*).
		• RF.1.3g • RF.2.3f	Recognize and read grade-appropriate irregularly spelled words.
		• CCRA.SL.1	Prepare for and participate effectively in a range of conversations and collaborations with diverse partners, building on others' ideas and expressing their own clearly and persuasively.
			Demonstrate command of the conventions of standard English capitalization, punctuation, and spelling when writing.
		• L.1.2d	Use conventional spelling for words with common spelling patterns and for frequently occurring irregular words.
		• L.3.2e	Use conventional spelling for high-frequency and other studied words and for adding suffixes to base words (e.g., *sitting, smiled, cries, happiness*).
		• L.4.2d • L.5.2e	Spell grade-appropriate words correctly, consulting references as needed.
12–13	**Reading and Spelling: Long Vowels:** *ie, igh; ui, ue*		Know and apply grade-level phonics and word analysis skills in decoding words.
		• RF.K.3a	Demonstrate basic knowledge of one-to-one letter-sound correspondences by producing the primary sound or many of the most frequent sounds for each consonant.
		• RF.K.3b	Associate the long and short sounds with the common spellings (graphemes) for the five major vowels.
		• RF.1.3b	Decode regularly spelled one-syllable words.
		• RF.2.3a	Distinguish long and short vowels when reading regularly spelled one-syllable words.
		• CCRA.L.1	Demonstrate command of the conventions of standard English grammar and usage when writing or speaking.
			Demonstrate command of the conventions of standard English capitalization, punctuation, and spelling when writing
		• L.1.2d	Use conventional spelling for words with common spelling patterns and for frequently occurring irregular words.

Language and Literacy, continued

SE Pages	Lesson	Code	Standards Text
14–17	**Read on Your Own: "Hot Crumbs Cause Fire"**	● CCRA.R.3	Analyze how and why individuals, events, or ideas develop and interact over the course of a text.
		● CCRA.R.5	Analyze the structure of texts, including how specific sentences, paragraphs, and larger portions of the text (e.g., a section, chapter, scene, or stanza) relate to each other and the whole.
		● CCRA.R.10	Read and comprehend complex literary and informational texts independently and proficiently.
			Know and apply grade-level phonics and word analysis skills in decoding words.
		● RF.1.3b	Decode regularly spelled one-syllable words.
		● RF.1.3c	Know final -e and common vowel team conventions for representing long vowel sounds.
		● RF.1.3g ● RF.2.3f	Recognize and read grade-appropriate irregularly spelled words.
			Read with sufficient accuracy and fluency to support comprehension.
		● RF.1.4a ● RF.2.4a	Read grade-level text with purpose and understanding.
		● RF.1.4b ● RF.2.4b	Read grade-level text orally with accuracy, appropriate rate, and expression on successive readings.
18	**Check Your Understanding**	● CCRA.W.9	Draw evidence from literary or informational texts to support analysis, reflection, and research.
	Expand Your Vocabulary	● CCRA.SL.1	Prepare for and participate effectively in a range of conversations and collaborations with diverse partners, building on others' ideas and expressing their own clearly and persuasively.
		● CCRA.L.6	Acquire and use accurately a range of general academic and domain-specific words and phrases sufficient for reading, writing, speaking, and listening at the college and career readiness level; demonstrate independence in gathering vocabulary knowledge when encountering an unknown term important to comprehension or expression.
	Write About Community Workers	● CCRA.W.2	Write informative/explanatory texts to examine and convey complex ideas and information clearly and accurately through the effective selection, organization, and analysis of content.
		● CCRA.W.10	Write routinely over extended time frames (time for research, reflection, and revision) and shorter time frames (a single sitting or a day or two) for a range of tasks, purposes, and audiences.

Language and Content

SE Pages	Lesson	Code	Standards Text
19	**Success in Language Arts: Learn About Paragraphs**	● CCRA.R.2	Determine central ideas or themes of a text and analyze their development; summarize the key supporting details and ideas.
		● CCRA.R.5	Analyze the structure of texts, including how specific sentences, paragraphs, and larger portions of the text (e.g., a section, chapter, scene, or stanza) relate to each other and the whole.

Common Core State Standards, continued

Language and Content, continued

SE Pages	Lesson	Code	Standards Text
19	Success in Language Arts: Learn About Paragraphs	● CCRA.R.10	Read and comprehend complex literary and informational texts independently and proficiently.
		● CCRA.W.3	Write narratives to develop real or imagined experiences or events using effective technique, well-chosen details and well-structured event sequences.
		● CCRA.W.10	Write routinely over extended time frames (time for research, reflection, and revision) and shorter time frames (a single sitting or a day or two) for a range of tasks, purposes, and audiences.
20–21	Build Background and Vocabulary	● CCRA.R.7	Integrate and evaluate content presented in diverse media and formats, including visually and quantitatively, as well as in words.
		● CCRA.SL.1	Prepare for and participate effectively in a range of conversations and collaborations with diverse partners, building on others' ideas and expressing their own clearly and persuasively.
		● CCRA.L.6	Acquire and use accurately a range of general academic and domain-specific words and phrases sufficient for reading, writing, speaking, and listening at the college and career readiness level; demonstrate independence in gathering vocabulary knowledge when encountering an unknown term important to comprehension or expression.
			Determine or clarify the meaning of unknown and multiple-meaning words and phrases based on grade-level reading and content, choosing flexibly from a range of strategies.
		● L.1.4a ● L.2.4a ● L.3.4a	Use sentence-level context as a clue to the meaning of a word or phrase.
		● L.4.4a	Use context (e.g., definitions, examples, or restatements in text) as a clue to the meaning of a word or phrase.
22–29	Listen and Read Along: "Dog Detectives"	● CCRA.R.2	Determine central ideas or themes of a text and analyze their development; summarize the key supporting details and ideas.
		● CCRA.R.3	Analyze how and why individuals, events, or ideas develop and interact over the course of a text.
		● CCRA.R.4	Interpret words and phrases as they are used in a text, including determining technical, connotative, and figurative meanings, and analyze how specific word choices shape meaning or tone.
		● CCRA.L.6	Acquire and use accurately a range of general academic and domain-specific words and phrases sufficient for reading, writing, speaking, and listening at the college and career readiness level; demonstrate independence in gathering vocabulary knowledge when encountering an unknown term important to comprehension or expression.
30	Check Your Understanding	● CCRA.R.3	Analyze how and why individuals, events, or ideas develop and interact over the course of a text.
		● CCRA.SL.1	Prepare for and participate effectively in a range of conversations and collaborations with diverse partners, building on others' ideas and expressing their own clearly and persuasively.
	Review Vocabulary	● CCRA.R.4	Interpret words and phrases as they are used in a text, including determining technical, connotative, and figurative meanings, and analyze how specific word choices shape meaning or tone.

Language and Content, continued

SE Pages	Lesson	Code	Standards Text
30	**Write About Helping A Friend**	• CCRA.W.2	Write informative/explanatory texts to examine and convey complex ideas and information clearly and accurately through the effective selection, organization, and analysis of content.
		• CCRA.W.4	Produce clear and coherent writing in which the development, organization, and style are appropriate to task, purpose, and audience.
		• CCRA.W.10	Write routinely over extended time frames (time for research, reflection, and revision) and shorter time frames (a single sitting or a day or two) for a range of tasks, purposes, and audiences.

Writing Project

SE Pages	Lesson	Code	Standards Text
31	**Model Study: Friendly Letter**	• CCRA.R.5	Analyze the structure of texts, including how specific sentences, paragraphs, and larger portions of the text (e.g., a section, chapter, scene, or stanza) relate to each other and the whole.
32	**Prewrite**	• CCRA.W.4	Produce clear and coherent writing in which the development, organization, and style are appropriate to task, purpose, and audience.
33	**Draft**	• CCRA.W.3	Write narratives to develop real or imagined experiences or events using effective technique, well-chosen details and well-structured event sequences.
		• CCRA.W.5	Develop and strengthen writing as needed by planning, revising, editing, rewriting, or trying a new approach.
33	**Revise**	• CCRA.W.4	Produce clear and coherent writing in which the development, organization, and style are appropriate to task, purpose, and audience.
		• CCRA.W.5	Develop and strengthen writing as needed by planning, revising, editing, rewriting, or trying a new approach.
		• CCRA.L.1	Demonstrate command of the conventions of standard English grammar and usage when writing or speaking.
34	**Edit and Proofread**	• CCRA.W.5	Develop and strengthen writing as needed by planning, revising, editing, rewriting, or trying a new approach.
			Demonstrate command of the conventions of standard English grammar and usage when writing or speaking.
		• L.1.1b	Use common, proper, and possessive nouns.
		• L.2.1e	Use adjectives and adverbs, and choose between them depending on what is to be modified.
			Demonstrate command of the conventions of standard English capitalization, punctuation, and spelling when writing.
		• L.1.2a	Capitalize dates and names of people.
		• L.2.2b	Use commas in greetings and closings of letters.
		• L.2.2e • L.3.2g	Consult reference materials, including beginning dictionaries, as needed to check and correct spellings.
		• L.4.2a	Use correct capitalization.
		• L.4.2d • L.5.2e	Spell grade-appropriate words correctly, consulting references as needed.

Common Core State Standards, continued

Writing Project, continued

SE Pages	Lesson	Code	Standards Text
35	Publish, Share, and Present	• CCRA.W.10	Write routinely over extended time frames (time for research, reflection, and revision) and shorter time frames (a single sitting or a day or two) for a range of tasks, purposes, and audiences.
		• CCRA.SL.6	Adapt speech to a variety of contexts and communicative tasks, demonstrating command of formal English when indicated or appropriate.

Unit 2 Make a Difference!

Language Development

SE Pages	Lesson	Code	Standards Text
36–37	Unit Launch	• CCRA.SL.2	Integrate and evaluate information presented in diverse media and formats, including visually, quantitatively, and orally.
38	Language: Give Information	• CCRA.SL.1	Prepare for and participate effectively in a range of conversations and collaborations with diverse partners, building on others' ideas and expressing their own clearly and persuasively.
		• CCRA.SL.6	Adapt speech to a variety of contexts and communicative tasks, demonstrating command of formal English when indicated or appropriate.
39	Vocabulary: Direction words	• CCRA.SL.1	Prepare for and participate effectively in a range of conversations and collaborations with diverse partners, building on others' ideas and expressing their own clearly and persuasively.
	Language: Give Directions	• CCRA.L.6	Acquire and use accurately a range of general academic and domain-specific words and phrases sufficient for reading, writing, speaking, and listening at the college and career readiness level; demonstrate independence in gathering vocabulary knowledge when encountering an unknown term important to comprehension or expression.
40	Vocabulary: Civil Rights	• CCRA.W.2	Write informative/explanatory texts to examine and convey complex ideas and information clearly and accurately through the effective selection, organization, and analysis of content.
	Language: Express Wants and Feelings	• CCRA.SL.2	Integrate and evaluate information presented in diverse media and formats, including visually, quantitatively, and orally.
		• CCRA.L.6	Acquire and use accurately a range of general academic and domain-specific words and phrases sufficient for reading, writing, speaking, and listening at the college and career readiness level; demonstrate independence in gathering vocabulary knowledge when encountering an unknown term important to comprehension or expression.
41	Grammar: Irregular Past Tense Verbs	• CCRA.SL.1	Prepare for and participate effectively in a range of conversations and collaborations with diverse partners, building on others' ideas and expressing their own clearly and persuasively.
			Demonstrate command of the conventions of standard English grammar and usage when writing or speaking.
		• L.1.1e	Use verbs to convey a sense of past, present, and future (e.g., *Yesterday I walked home; Today I walk home; Tomorrow I will walk home*).
		• L.2.1d	Form and use the past tense of frequently occurring irregular verbs (e.g., *sat, hid, told*).
		• L.3.1d	Form and use regular and irregular verbs.
		• L.5.1c	Use verb tense to convey various times, sequences, states, and conditions.

Language Development, continued

SE Pages	Lesson	Code	Standards Text
42	**Listen and Read Along:** *"Who Was Martin Luther King, Jr.?"*	• CCRA.R.4	Interpret words and phrases as they are used in a text, including determining technical, connotative, and figurative meanings, and analyze how specific word choices shape meaning or tone.
		• CCRA.R.10	Read and comprehend complex literary and informational texts independently and proficiently.
		• L.1.5a	With guidance and support from adults, demonstrate understanding of word relationships and nuances in word meanings. Sort words into categories (e.g., colors, clothing) to gain a sense of the concepts the categories represent.
43	**Comprehension: Identify Sequence**	• CCRA.R.3	Analyze how and why individuals, events, or ideas develop and interact over the course of a text.
		• CCRA.R.5	Analyze the structure of texts, including how specific sentences, paragraphs, and larger portions of the text (e.g., a section, chapter, scene, or stanza) relate to each other and the whole.
		• CCRA.SL.1	Prepare for and participate effectively in a range of conversations and collaborations with diverse partners, building on others' ideas and expressing their own clearly and persuasively.

Language and Literacy

SE Pages	Lesson	Code	Standards Text
44–45	**High Frequency Words**		Know and apply grade-level phonics and word analysis skills in decoding words.
		• RF.K.3c	Read common high-frequency words by sight (e.g., *the, of, to, you, she, my, is, are, do, does*).
		• RF.1.3g • RF.2.3f	Recognize and read grade-appropriate irregularly spelled words.
			Demonstrate command of the conventions of standard English capitalization, punctuation, and spelling when writing.
		• L.1.2d	Use conventional spelling for words with common spelling patterns and for frequently occurring irregular words.
		• L.3.2e	Use conventional spelling for high-frequency and other studied words and for adding suffixes to base words (e.g., *sitting, smiled, cries, happiness*).
		• L.4.2d • L.5.2e	Spell grade-appropriate words correctly, consulting references as needed.
46–47	**Reading and Spelling:** *R*-**Controlled Vowels**		Know and apply grade-level phonics and word analysis skills in decoding words.
		• RF.K.3a	Demonstrate basic knowledge of one-to-one letter-sound correspondences by producing the primary sound or many of the most frequent sounds for each consonant.
		• RF.1.3b	Decode regularly spelled one-syllable words.
		• RF.2.3b	Know spelling-sound correspondences for additional common vowel teams.
		• CCRA.L.1	Demonstrate command of the conventions of standard English grammar and usage when writing or speaking.

Common Core State Standards, continued

Language and Literacy, continued

SE Pages	Lesson	Code	Standards Text
46–47	**Reading and Spelling:** ***R*-Controlled Vowels,** continued		Demonstrate command of the conventions of standard English capitalization, punctuation, and spelling when writing.
		• L.1.2d	Use conventional spelling for words with common spelling patterns and for frequently occurring irregular words.
48–51	**Read on Your Own:** **"Kids Are Helping Kids"**	• CCRA.R.10	Read and comprehend complex literary and informational texts independently and proficiently.
			Know and apply grade-level phonics and word analysis skills in decoding words.
		• RF.1.3b	Decode regularly spelled one-syllable words.
		• RF.1.3g • RF.2.3f	Recognize and read grade-appropriate irregularly spelled words.
		• RF.2.3b	Know spelling-sound correspondences for additional common vowel teams.
			Read with sufficient accuracy and fluency to support comprehension.
		• RF.1.4a • RF.2.4a	Read grade-level text with purpose and understanding.
		• RF.1.4b • RF.2.4b	Read grade-level text orally with accuracy, appropriate rate, and expression on successive readings.
		• CCRA.L.6	Acquire and use accurately a range of general academic and domain-specific words and phrases sufficient for reading, writing, speaking, and listening at the college and career readiness level; demonstrate independence in gathering vocabulary knowledge when encountering an unknown term important to comprehension or expression.
52	**Check Your Understanding**	• CCRA.SL.1	Prepare for and participate effectively in a range of conversations and collaborations with diverse partners, building on others' ideas and expressing their own clearly and persuasively.
		• CCRA.W.9	Draw evidence from literary or informational texts to support analysis, reflection, and research.
	Expand Your Vocabulary	• CCRA.L.6	Acquire and use accurately a range of general academic and domain-specific words and phrases sufficient for reading, writing, speaking, and listening at the college and career readiness level; demonstrate independence in gathering vocabulary knowledge when encountering an unknown term important to comprehension or expression.
	Write About People	• CCRA.W.2	Write informative/explanatory texts to examine and convey complex ideas and information clearly and accurately through the effective selection, organization, and analysis of content.
		• CCRA.W.10	Write routinely over extended time frames (time for research, reflection, and revision) and shorter time frames (a single sitting or a day or two) for a range of tasks, purposes, and audiences.

Language and Content

SE Pages	Lesson	Code	Standards Text
53	**Success in Social Science:** **Interpret Data**	• CCRA.R.4	Interpret words and phrases as they are used in a text, including determining technical, connotative, and figurative meanings, and analyze how specific word choices shape meaning or tone.
		• CCRA.R.7	Integrate and evaluate content presented in diverse media and formats, including visually and quantitatively, as well as in words.

Language and Content, continued

SE Pages	Lesson	Code	Standards Text
53	**Success in Social Science: Interpret Data,** continued	• CCRA.R.10	Read and comprehend complex literary and informational texts independently and proficiently
		• CCRA.L.4	Determine or clarify the meaning of unknown and multiple-meaning words and phrases by using context clues, analyzing meaningful word parts, and consulting general and specialized reference materials, as appropriate.
54–55	**Build Background and Vocabulary**	• CCRA.R.7	Integrate and evaluate content presented in diverse media and formats, including visually and quantitatively, as well as in words.
		• CCRA.SL.1	Prepare for and participate effectively in a range of conversations and collaborations with diverse partners, building on others' ideas and expressing their own clearly and persuasively.
		• CCRA.L.6	Acquire and use accurately a range of general academic and domain-specific words and phrases sufficient for reading, writing, speaking, and listening at the college and career readiness level; demonstrate independence in gathering vocabulary knowledge when encountering an unknown term important to comprehension or expression.
			Determine or clarify the meaning of unknown and multiple-meaning words and phrases based on grade-level reading and content, choosing flexibly from a range of strategies.
		• L.1.4a • L.2.4a • L.3.4a	Use sentence-level context as a clue to the meaning of a word or phrase.
		• L.4.4a	Use context (e.g., definitions, examples, or restatements in text) as a clue to the meaning of a word or phrase.
56–63	**Listen and Read Along: "Striving for Change"**	• CCRA.R.3	Analyze how and why individuals, events, or ideas develop and interact over the course of a text.
		• CCRA.R.4	Interpret words and phrases as they are used in a text, including determining technical, connotative, and figurative meanings, and analyze how specific word choices shape meaning or tone.
		• CCRA.R.7	Integrate and evaluate content presented in diverse media and formats, including visually and quantitatively, as well as in words.
		• CCRA.L.6	Acquire and use accurately a range of general academic and domain-specific words and phrases sufficient for reading, writing, speaking, and listening at the college and career readiness level; demonstrate independence in gathering vocabulary knowledge when encountering an unknown term important to comprehension or expression.
64	**Check Your Understanding**	• CCRA.R.2	Determine central ideas or themes of a text and analyze their development; summarize the key supporting details and ideas.
		• CCRA.R.5	Analyze the structure of texts, including how specific sentences, paragraphs, and larger portions of the text (e.g., a section, chapter, scene, or stanza) relate to each other and the whole.
		• CCRA.SL.1	Prepare for and participate effectively in a range of conversations and collaborations with diverse partners, building on others' ideas and expressing their own clearly and persuasively.

Common Core State Standards, continued

Language and Content, continued

SE Pages	Lesson	Code	Standards Text
64	Review Vocabulary	• CCRA.R.4	Interpret words and phrases as they are used in a text, including determining technical, connotative, and figurative meanings, and analyze how specific word choices shape meaning or tone.
		• CCRA.L.6	Acquire and use accurately a range of general academic and domain-specific words and phrases sufficient for reading, writing, speaking, and listening at the college and career readiness level; demonstrate independence in gathering vocabulary knowledge when encountering an unknown term important to comprehension or expression.
	Write About Change	• CCRA.W.1	Write arguments to support claims in an analysis of substantive topics or texts using valid reasoning and relevant and sufficient evidence. Students are to write about something they think should be changed.
		• CCRA.W.10	Write routinely over extended time frames (time for research, reflection, and revision) and shorter time frames (a single sitting or a day or two) for a range of tasks, purposes, and audiences.

Writing Project

SE Pages	Lesson	Code	Standards Text
65	Model Study: Personal Narrative	• CCRA.R.5	Analyze the structure of texts, including how specific sentences, paragraphs, and larger portions of the text (e.g., a section, chapter, scene, or stanza) relate to each other and the whole.
66	Prewrite	• CCRA.W.4	Produce clear and coherent writing in which the development, organization, and style are appropriate to task, purpose, and audience.
67	Draft	• CCRA.W.3	Write narratives to develop real or imagined experiences or events using effective technique, well-chosen details and well-structured event sequences.
		• CCRA.W.4	Produce clear and coherent writing in which the development, organization, and style are appropriate to task, purpose, and audience.
67	Revise	• CCRA.W.4	Produce clear and coherent writing in which the development, organization, and style are appropriate to task, purpose, and audience.
		• CCRA.W.5	Develop and strengthen writing as needed by planning, revising, editing, rewriting, or trying a new approach.
68	Edit and Proofread	• CCRA.W.5	Develop and strengthen writing as needed by planning, revising, editing, rewriting, or trying a new approach.
			Demonstrate command of the conventions of standard English grammar and usage when writing or speaking.
		• L.1.1b	Use common, proper, and possessive nouns.
		• L1.1e	Use verbs to convey a sense of past, present, and future (e.g., *Yesterday I walked home; Today I walk home; Tomorrow I will walk home*).
		• L.2.1d	Form and use the past tense of frequently occurring irregular verbs (e.g., *sat, hid, told*).
		• L.3.1d	Form and use regular and irregular verbs.
		• L.3.1e	Form and use the simple (e.g., *I walked; I walk; I will walk*) verb tenses.
		• L.5.1c	Use verb tense to convey various times, sequences, states, and conditions.

Writing Project, continued

SE Pages	Lesson	Code	Standards Text
68	**Edit and Proofread,** continued		Demonstrate command of the conventions of standard English capitalization, punctuation, and spelling when writing.
		● L.2.2e ● L.3.2g	Consult reference materials, including beginning dictionaries, as needed to check and correct spellings.
		● L.4.2d ● L.5.2e	Spell grade-appropriate words correctly, consulting references as needed.
69	**Publish, Share, and Reflect**	● CCRA.W.10	Write routinely over extended time frames (time for research, reflection, and revision) and shorter time frames (a single sitting or a day or two) for a range of tasks, purposes, and audiences.
		● CCRA.SL.4	Present information, findings, and supporting evidence such that listeners can follow the line of reasoning and the organization, development, and style are appropriate to task, purpose, and audience.

Unit 3   Our Living Planet

Language Development

SE Pages	Lesson	Code	Standards Text
70–71	**Unit Launch**	● CCRA.SL.2	Integrate and evaluate information presented in diverse media and formats, including visually, quantitatively, and orally.
72	**Language: Give Your Opinion**	● CCRA.SL.1	Prepare for and participate effectively in a range of conversations and collaborations with diverse partners, building on others' ideas and expressing their own clearly and persuasively.
		● CCRA.SL.4	Present information, findings, and supporting evidence such that listeners can follow the line of reasoning and the organization, development, and style are appropriate to task, purpose, and audience.
73	**Vocabulary: Animals and Habitats**	● CCRA.SL.1	Prepare for and participate effectively in a range of conversations and collaborations with diverse partners, building on others' ideas and expressing their own clearly and persuasively.
	Language: Describe Places	● CCRA.L.6	Acquire and use accurately a range of general academic and domain-specific words and phrases sufficient for reading, writing, speaking, and listening at the college and career readiness level; demonstrate independence in gathering vocabulary knowledge when encountering an unknown term important to comprehension or expression.
			Demonstrate command of the conventions of standard English grammar and usage when writing or speaking.
		● L.1.1f	Use frequently occurring adjectives.
		● L.4.1d	Order adjectives within sentences according to conventional patterns (e.g., *a small red bag* rather than *a red small bag*).
74	**Vocabulary: Plants and Habitats** **Language: Make a Suggestion**	● CCRA.L.6	Acquire and use accurately a range of general academic and domain-specific words and phrases sufficient for reading, writing, speaking, and listening at the college and career readiness level; demonstrate independence in gathering vocabulary knowledge when encountering an unknown term important to comprehension or expression.
		● CCRA.SL.1	Prepare for and participate effectively in a range of conversations and collaborations with diverse partners, building on others' ideas and expressing their own clearly and persuasively.

Common Core State Standards, continued

Language Development, continued

SE Pages	Lesson	Code	Standards Text
75	**Grammar: Sensory Adjectives**	• CCRA.W.10	Write routinely over extended time frames (time for research, reflection, and revision) and shorter time frames (a single sitting or a day or two) for a range of tasks, purposes, and audiences.
			Demonstrate command of the conventions of standard English grammar and usage when writing or speaking.
		• L.1.1f	Use frequently occurring adjectives.
76	**Listen and Read Along: *Rachel Carson***	• CCRA.R.4	Interpret words and phrases as they are used in a text, including determining technical, connotative, and figurative meanings, and analyze how specific word choices shape meaning or tone.
		• CCRA.R.10	Read and comprehend complex literary and informational texts independently and proficiently.
		• CCRA.L.5	Demonstrate understanding of figurative language, word relationships, and nuances in word meanings.
77	**Comprehension: Identify Details**	• CCRA.R.2	Determine central ideas or themes of a text and analyze their development; summarize the key supporting details and ideas.
		• CCRA.R.3	Analyze how and why individuals, events, or ideas develop and interact over the course of a text.
		• CCRA.R.5	Analyze the structure of texts, including how specific sentences, paragraphs, and larger portions of the text (e.g., a section, chapter, scene, or stanza) relate to each other and the whole.
		• CCRA.SL.1	Prepare for and participate effectively in a range of conversations and collaborations with diverse partners, building on others' ideas and expressing their own clearly and persuasively.

Language and Literacy

SE Pages	Lesson	Code	Standards Text
78–79	**High Frequency Words**		Know and apply grade-level phonics and word analysis skills in decoding words.
		• RF.K.3c	Read common high-frequency words by sight (e.g., *the, of, to, you, she, my, is, are, do, does*).
		• RF.1.3g • RF.2.3f	Recognize and read grade-appropriate irregularly spelled words.
			Demonstrate command of the conventions of standard English capitalization, punctuation, and spelling when writing.
		• L.1.2d	Use conventional spelling for words with common spelling patterns and for frequently occurring irregular words.
		• L.3.2e	Use conventional spelling for high-frequency and other studied words and for adding suffixes to base words (e.g., *sitting, smiled, cries, happiness*).
		• L.4.2d • L.5.2e	Spell grade-appropriate words correctly, consulting references as needed.

Language and Literacy, continued

SE Pages	Lesson	Code	Standards Text
80–81	Reading and Spelling: Syllable Types		Know and apply grade-level phonics and word analysis skills in decoding words.
		RF.K.3a	Demonstrate basic knowledge of one-to-one letter-sound correspondences by producing the primary sound or many of the most frequent sounds for each consonant.
		RF.1.3b	Decode regularly spelled one-syllable words.
		RF.1.3e	Decode two-syllable words following basic patterns by breaking the words into syllables.
			Demonstrate command of the conventions of standard English capitalization, punctuation, and spelling when writing.
		L.1.2d	Use conventional spelling for words with common spelling patterns and for frequently occurring irregular words.
		L.3.2f	Use spelling patterns and generalizations (e.g., word families, position-based spellings, syllable patterns, ending rules, meaningful word parts) in writing words.
		L.4.2d	Spell grade-appropriate words correctly, consulting references as needed.
		L.5.2e	
82–85	Read on Your Own: "Animals in the Wild"	CCRA.R.10	Read and comprehend complex literary and informational texts independently and proficiently.
			Know and apply grade-level phonics and word analysis skills in decoding words.
		RF.1.3g	Recognize and read grade-appropriate irregularly spelled words.
		RF.2.3f	
		RF.1.3e	Decode two-syllable words following basic patterns by breaking the words into syllables.
			Read with sufficient accuracy and fluency to support comprehension.
		RF.1.4a	Read grade-level text with purpose and understanding.
		RF.2.4a	
		RF.1.4b	Read grade-level text orally with accuracy, appropriate rate, and expression on successive readings.
		RF.2.4b	
		RF.1.4c	Use context to confirm or self-correct word recognition and understanding, rereading as necessary.
		RF.2.4c	
86	Check Your Understanding	CCRA.W.9	Draw evidence from literary or informational texts to support analysis, reflection, and research.
	Expand Your Vocabulary	CCRA.SL.1	Prepare for and participate effectively in a range of conversations and collaborations with diverse partners, building on others' ideas and expressing their own clearly and persuasively.
		CCRA.L.6	Acquire and use accurately a range of general academic and domain-specific words and phrases sufficient for reading, writing, speaking, and listening at the college and career readiness level; demonstrate independence in gathering vocabulary knowledge when encountering an unknown term important to comprehension or expression.

Common Core State Standards, continued

Language and Literacy, continued

SE Pages	Lesson	Code	Standards Text
86	**Write About Animals**	• CCRA.W.2	Write informative/explanatory texts to examine and convey complex ideas and information clearly and accurately through the effective selection, organization, and analysis of content.
		• CCRA.W.10	Write routinely over extended time frames (time for research, reflection, and revision) and shorter time frames (a single sitting or a day or two) for a range of tasks, purposes, and audiences.

Language and Content

SE Pages	Lesson	Code	Standards Text
87	**Success in Science and Mathematics: Learn About Line Graphs**	• CCRA.R.2	Determine central ideas or themes of a text and analyze their development; summarize the key supporting details and ideas.
		• CCRA.R.4	Interpret words and phrases as they are used in a text, including determining technical, connotative, and figurative meanings, and analyze how specific word choices shape meaning or tone.
		• CCRA.R.7	Integrate and evaluate content presented in diverse media and formats, including visually and quantitatively, as well as in words.
		• CCRA.R.10	Read and comprehend complex literary and informational texts independently and proficiently.
88–89	**Build Background and Vocabulary**	• CCRA.R.7	Integrate and evaluate content presented in diverse media and formats, including visually and quantitatively, as well as in words.
		• CCRA.SL.1	Prepare for and participate effectively in a range of conversations and collaborations with diverse partners, building on others' ideas and expressing their own clearly and persuasively.
		• CCRA.L.6	Acquire and use accurately a range of general academic and domain-specific words and phrases sufficient for reading, writing, speaking, and listening at the college and career readiness level; demonstrate independence in gathering vocabulary knowledge when encountering an unknown term important to comprehension or expression.
			Determine or clarify the meaning of unknown and multiple-meaning words and phrases based on grade-level reading and content, choosing flexibly from a range of strategies.
		• L.1.4a • L.2.4a • L.3.4a	Use sentence-level context as a clue to the meaning of a word or phrase.
		• L.4.4a	Use context (e.g., definitions, examples, or restatements in text) as a clue to the meaning of a word or phrase.
90–97	**Listen and Read Along: "Animal Ecosystems"**	• CCRA.R.2	Determine central ideas or themes of a text and analyze their development; summarize the key supporting details and ideas.
		• CCRA.R.4	Interpret words and phrases as they are used in a text, including determining technical, connotative, and figurative meanings, and analyze how specific word choices shape meaning or tone.
		• CCRA.R.7	Integrate and evaluate content presented in diverse media and formats, including visually and quantitatively, as well as in words.
		• CCRA.L.6	Acquire and use accurately a range of general academic and domain-specific words and phrases sufficient for reading, writing, speaking, and listening at the college and career readiness level; demonstrate independence in gathering vocabulary knowledge when encountering an unknown term important to comprehension or expression.

Language and Content, continued

SE Pages	Lesson	Code	Standards Text
98	**Check Your Understanding**	• CCRA.R.2	Determine central ideas or themes of a text and analyze their development; summarize the key supporting details and ideas.
		• CCRA.SL.1	Prepare for and participate effectively in a range of conversations and collaborations with diverse partners, building on others' ideas and expressing their own clearly and persuasively.
		• CCRA.SL.2	Integrate and evaluate information presented in diverse media and formats, including visually, quantitatively, and orally.
		• CCRA.SL.4	Present information, findings, and supporting evidence such that listeners can follow the line of reasoning and the organization, development, and style are appropriate to task, purpose, and audience.
	Review Vocabulary	• CCRA.R.4	Interpret words and phrases as they are used in a text, including determining technical, connotative, and figurative meanings, and analyze how specific word choices shape meaning or tone.
	Write About Life On Earth	• CCRA.W.2	Write informative/explanatory texts to examine and convey complex ideas and information clearly and accurately through the effective selection, organization, and analysis of content.
		• CCRA.W.4	Produce clear and coherent writing in which the development, organization, and style are appropriate to task, purpose, and audience.
		• CCRA.W.10	Write routinely over extended time frames (time for research, reflection, and revision) and shorter time frames (a single sitting or a day or two) for a range of tasks, purposes, and audiences.

Writing Project

SE Pages	Lesson	Code	Standards Text
99	**Model Study: Fact-and-Opinion Article**	• CCRA.R.5	Analyze the structure of texts, including how specific sentences, paragraphs, and larger portions of the text (e.g., a section, chapter, scene, or stanza) relate to each other and the whole.
100	**Prewrite**	• CCRA.W.4	Produce clear and coherent writing in which the development, organization, and style are appropriate to task, purpose, and audience.
			Demonstrate command of the conventions of standard English grammar and usage when writing or speaking.
		• L.1.1f	Use frequently occurring adjectives.
101	**Draft**	• CCRA.W.1	Write arguments to support claims in an analysis of substantive topics or texts using valid reasoning and relevant and sufficient evidence.
101	**Revise**	• CCRA.W.4	Produce clear and coherent writing in which the development, organization, and style are appropriate to task, purpose, and audience.
		• CCRA.W.5	Develop and strengthen writing as needed by planning, revising, editing, rewriting, or trying a new approach.
102	**Edit and Proofread**	• CCRA.W.5	Develop and strengthen writing as needed by planning, revising, editing, rewriting, or trying a new approach.
		• CCRA.L.2	Demonstrate command of the conventions of standard English capitalization, punctuation, and spelling when writing.

Common Core State Standards, continued

Writing Project, continued

SE Pages	Lesson	Code	Standards Text
102	**Edit and Proofread,** continued		Demonstrate command of the conventions of standard English grammar and usage when writing or speaking.
		• L.1.1f	Use frequently occurring adjectives.
		• L.4.1d	Order adjectives within sentences according to conventional patterns (e.g., *a small red bag* rather than *a red small bag).*
			Demonstrate command of the conventions of standard English capitalization, punctuation, and spelling when writing.
		• L.2.2e • L3.2g	Consult reference materials, including beginning dictionaries, as needed to check and correct spellings.
		• L.4.2d • L.5.2e	Spell grade-appropriate words correctly, consulting references as needed.
103	**Publish, Share, and Present**	• CCRA.W.10	Write routinely over extended time frames (time for research, reflection, and revision) and shorter time frames (a single sitting or a day or two) for a range of tasks, purposes, and audiences.
		• CCRA.SL.4	Present information, findings, and supporting evidence such that listeners can follow the line of reasoning and the organization, development, and style are appropriate to task, purpose, and audience.
		• CCRA.SL.5	Make strategic use of digital media and visual displays of data to express information and enhance understanding of presentations.
		• CCRA.SL.6	Adapt speech to a variety of contexts and communicative tasks, demonstrating command of formal English when indicated or appropriate.

Unit 4 Past and Present

Language Development

SE Pages	Lesson	Code	Standards Text
104–105	**Unit Launch**	• CCRA.SL.2	Integrate and evaluate information presented in diverse media and formats, including visually, quantitatively, and orally.
106	**Language: Have a Discussion**	• CCRA.SL.1	Prepare for and participate effectively in a range of conversations and collaborations with diverse partners, building on others' ideas and expressing their own clearly and persuasively.
107	**Vocabulary: Historical Records**	• CCRA.L.6	Acquire and use accurately a range of general academic and domain-specific words and phrases sufficient for reading, writing, speaking, and listening at the college and career readiness level; demonstrate independence in gathering vocabulary knowledge when encountering an unknown term important to comprehension or expression.
	Language: Make Comparisons	• CCRA.L.3	Apply knowledge of language to understand how language functions in different contexts, to make effective choices for meaning or style, and to comprehend more fully when reading or listening.
108	**Grammar: Nouns**		Demonstrate command of the conventions of standard English grammar and usage when writing or speaking.
		• L.1.1b	Use common, proper, and possessive nouns.
		• L.3.1b	Form and use regular and irregular plural nouns.

Language Development, continued

SE Pages	Lesson	Code	Standards Text
109	**Grammar:** **Present and Past Tense Verbs**		Demonstrate command of the conventions of standard English grammar and usage when writing or speaking.
		● L.1.1e	Use verbs to convey a sense of past, present, and future (e.g., *Yesterday I walked home; Today I walk home; Tomorrow I will walk home*).
		● L.2.1d	Form and use the past tense of frequently occurring irregular verbs (e.g., *sat, hid, told*).
		● L.3.1d	Form and use regular and irregular verbs.
		● L.3.1f	Ensure subject-verb and pronoun-antecedent agreement.
		● L.5.1c	Use verb tense to convey various times, sequences, states, and conditions.
110–111	**Grammar:** **Object Pronouns**	● CCRA.W.10	Write routinely over extended time frames (time for research, reflection, and revision) and shorter time frames (a single sitting or a day or two) for a range of tasks, purposes, and audiences.
			Demonstrate command of the conventions of standard English grammar and usage when writing or speaking.
		● L.1.1d	Use personal, possessive, and indefinite pronouns (e.g., *I, me, my; they, them, their, anyone, everything*).
		● L.3.1f	Ensure subject-verb and pronoun-antecedent agreement.
112	**Listen and Read Along:** ***The Children We Remember***	● CCRA.R.4	Interpret words and phrases as they are used in a text, including determining technical, connotative, and figurative meanings, and analyze how specific word choices shape meaning or tone.
		● CCRA.R.10	Read and comprehend complex literary and informational texts independently and proficiently.
113	**Comprehension:** **Make Comparisons**	● CCRA.R.1	Read closely to determine what the text says explicitly and to make logical inferences from it; cite specific textual evidence when writing or speaking to support conclusions drawn from the text.
		● CCRA.SL.1	Prepare for and participate effectively in a range of conversations and collaborations with diverse partners, building on others' ideas and expressing their own clearly and persuasively.

Language and Literacy

SE Pages	Lesson	Code	Standards Text
114–115	**High Frequency Words**		Know and apply grade-level phonics and word analysis skills in decoding words.
		● RF.K.3c	Read common high-frequency words by sight (e.g., *the, of, to, you, she, my, is, are, do, does*).
		● RF.1.3g ● RF.2.3f	Recognize and read grade-appropriate irregularly spelled words.
			Demonstrate command of the conventions of standard English capitalization, punctuation, and spelling when writing.
		● L.1.2d	Use conventional spelling for words with common spelling patterns and for frequently occurring irregular words.
		● L.3.2e	Use conventional spelling for high-frequency and other studied words and for adding suffixes to base words (e.g., *sitting, smiled, cries, happiness*).
		● L.4.2d ● L.5.2e	Spell grade-appropriate words correctly, consulting references as needed.

Common Core State Standards, continued

Language and Literacy, continued

SE Pages	Lesson	Code	Standards Text
116–117	Reading and Spelling: Words with y		Know and apply grade-level phonics and word analysis skills in decoding words.
		RF.K.3a	Demonstrate basic knowledge of one-to-one letter-sound correspondences by producing the primary sound or many of the most most frequent sounds for each consonant.
		RF.1.3g RF.2.3f	Recognize and read grade-appropriate irregularly spelled words.
			Demonstrate command of the conventions of standard English capitalization, punctuation, and spelling when writing.
		L.1.2d	Use conventional spelling for words with common spelling patterns and for frequently occurring irregular words.
		L.4.2d L.5.2e	Spell grade-appropriate words correctly, consulting references as needed.
118–121	Read on Your Own: "Kidworks for Peace"	CCRA.R.10	Read and comprehend complex literary and informational texts independently and proficiently.
			Know and apply grade-level phonics and word analysis skills in decoding words.
		RF.1.3g RF.2.3f	Recognize and read grade-appropriate irregularly spelled words.
			Read with sufficient accuracy and fluency to support comprehension.
		RF.1.4a RF.2.4a	Read grade-level text with purpose and understanding.
		RF.1.4b RF.2.4b	Read grade-level text orally with accuracy, appropriate rate, and expression on successive readings.
122	Check Your Understanding	CCRA.W.9	Draw evidence from literary or informational texts to support analysis, reflection, and research.
	Expand Your Vocabulary	CCRA.L.6	Acquire and use accurately a range of general academic and domain-specific words and phrases sufficient for reading, writing, speaking, and listening at the college and career readiness level; demonstrate independence in gathering vocabulary knowledge when encountering an unknown term important to comprehension or expression.
	Write About Kids and History	CCRA.W.1	Write arguments to support claims in an analysis of substantive topics or texts using valid reasoning and relevant and sufficient evidence.
		CCRA.W.10	Write routinely over extended time frames (time for research, reflection, and revision) and shorter time frames (a single sitting or a day or two) for a range of tasks, purposes, and audiences.

Language and Content

SE Pages	Lesson	Code	Standards Text
123	Success in Social Studies: Learn About the U.S. Government	CCRA.R.2	Determine central ideas or themes of a text and analyze their development; summarize the key supporting details and ideas.
		CCRA.R.7	Integrate and evaluate content presented in diverse media and formats, including visually and quantitatively, as well as in words.

Language and Content, continued

SE Pages	Lesson	Code	Standards Text
123	**Success in Social Studies: Learn About the U.S. Government,** continued	• CCRA.R.10	Read and comprehend complex literary and informational texts independently and proficiently.
		• CCRA.L.4	Determine or clarify the meaning of unknown and multiple-meaning words and phrases by using context clues, analyzing meaningful word parts, and consulting general and specialized reference materials, as appropriate.
124–125	**Build Background and Vocabulary**	• CCRA.R.7	Integrate and evaluate content presented in diverse media and formats, including visually and quantitatively, as well as in words.
		• CCRA.SL.1	Prepare for and participate effectively in a range of conversations and collaborations with diverse partners, building on others' ideas and expressing their own clearly and persuasively.
		• CCRA.L.6	Acquire and use accurately a range of general academic and domain-specific words and phrases sufficient for reading, writing, speaking, and listening at the college and career readiness level; demonstrate independence in gathering vocabulary knowledge when encountering an unknown term important to comprehension or expression.
			Determine or clarify the meaning of unknown and multiple-meaning words and phrases based on grade-level reading and content, choosing flexibly from a range of strategies.
		• L.1.4a • L.2.4a • L.3.4a	Use sentence-level context as a clue to the meaning of a word or phrase.
		• L.4.4a	Use context (e.g., definitions, examples, or restatements in text) as a clue to the meaning of a word or phrase.
126–133	**Listen and Read Along: "Our Government"**	• CCRA.R.2	Determine central ideas or themes of a text and analyze their development; summarize the key supporting details and ideas.
		• CCRA.R.4	Interpret words and phrases as they are used in a text, including determining technical, connotative, and figurative meanings, and analyze how specific word choices shape meaning or tone.
		• CCRA.L.6	Acquire and use accurately a range of general academic and domain-specific words and phrases sufficient for reading, writing, speaking, and listening at the college and career readiness level; demonstrate independence in gathering vocabulary knowledge when encountering an unknown term important to comprehension or expression.
134	**Check Your Understanding**	• CCRA.R.2	Determine central ideas or themes of a text and analyze their development; summarize the key supporting details and ideas.
		• CCRA.SL.1	Prepare for and participate effectively in a range of conversations and collaborations with diverse partners, building on others' ideas and expressing their own clearly and persuasively.
	Review Vocabulary	• CCRA.R.4	Interpret words and phrases as they are used in a text, including determining technical, connotative, and figurative meanings, and analyze how specific word choices shape meaning or tone.
		• CCRA.L.6	Acquire and use accurately a range of general academic and domain-specific words and phrases sufficient for reading, writing, speaking, and listening at the college and career readiness level; demonstrate independence in gathering vocabulary knowledge when encountering an unknown term important to comprehension or expression.

Common Core State Standards, continued

Language and Content, continued

SE Pages	Lesson	Code	Standards Text
134	Write About Jobs	• CCRA.W.2	Write informative/explanatory texts to examine and convey complex ideas and information clearly and accurately through the effective selection, organization, and analysis of content.
		• CCRA.W.10	Write routinely over extended time frames (time for research, reflection, and revision) and shorter time frames (a single sitting or a day or two) for a range of tasks, purposes, and audiences.

Writing Project

SE Pages	Lesson	Code	Standards Text
135	Model Study: Comparison Paragraph	• CCRA.R.5	Analyze the structure of texts, including how specific sentences, paragraphs, and larger portions of the text (e.g., a section, chapter, scene, or stanza) relate to each other and the whole.
136	Prewrite	• CCRA.W.4	Produce clear and coherent writing in which the development, organization, and style are appropriate to task, purpose, and audience.
137	Draft	• CCRA.W.2	Write informative/explanatory texts to examine and convey complex ideas and information clearly and accurately through the effective selection, organization, and analysis of content.
137	Revise	• CCRA.W.4	Produce clear and coherent writing in which the development, organization, and style are appropriate to task, purpose, and audience.
		• CCRA.W.5	Develop and strengthen writing as needed by planning, revising, editing, rewriting, or trying a new approach.
		• CCRA.SL.1	Prepare for and participate effectively in a range of conversations and collaborations with diverse partners, building on others' ideas and expressing their own clearly and persuasively.
138	Edit and Proofread	• CCRA.W.5	Develop and strengthen writing as needed by planning, revising, editing, rewriting, or trying a new approach.
			Demonstrate command of the conventions of standard English grammar and usage when writing or speaking.
		• L.1.1e	Use verbs to convey a sense of past, present, and future (e.g., *Yesterday I walked home; Today I walk home; Tomorrow I will walk home*).
		• L.2.1d	Form and use the past tense of frequently occurring irregular verbs (e.g., *sat, hid, told*).
		• L.3.1d	Form and use regular and irregular verbs.
			Demonstrate command of the conventions of standard English capitalization, punctuation, and spelling when writing.
		• L.1.2c	Use commas in dates and to separate single words in a series.
		• L.2.2e • L3.2g	Consult reference materials, including beginning dictionaries, as needed to check and correct spellings.
		• L.4.2d	Spell grade-appropriate words correctly, consulting references as needed.
		• L.5.2a • L.5.2e	Use punctuation to separate items in a series.

Writing Project, continued

SE Pages	Lesson	Code	Standards Text
139	Publish, Share, and Present	• CCRA.W.10	Write routinely over extended time frames (time for research, reflection, and revision) and shorter time frames (a single sitting or a day or two) for a range of tasks, purposes, and audiences.
		• CCRA.SL.4	Present information, findings, and supporting evidence such that listeners can follow the line of reasoning and the organization, development, and style are appropriate to task, purpose, and audience.
		• CCRA.SL.6	Adapt speech to a variety of contexts and communicative tasks, demonstrating command of formal English when indicated or appropriate.

Unit 5   Tell Me More

Language Development

SE Pages	Lesson	Code	Standards Text
140–141	Unit Launch	• CCRA.SL.2	Integrate and evaluate information presented in diverse media and formats, including visually, quantitatively, and orally.
142	Language: Ask for and Give Advice	• CCRA.SL.1	Prepare for and participate effectively in a range of conversations and collaborations with diverse partners, building on others' ideas and expressing their own clearly and persuasively.
		• CCRA.SL.6	Adapt speech to a variety of contexts and communicative tasks, demonstrating command of formal English when indicated or appropriate.
143	Vocabulary: Opposites	• CCRA.L.6	Acquire and use accurately a range of general academic and domain-specific words and phrases sufficient for reading, writing, speaking, and listening at the college and career readiness level; demonstrate independence in gathering vocabulary knowledge when encountering an unknown term important to comprehension or expression.
	Language: Ask for and Accept a Favor	• CCRA.W.10	Write routinely over extended time frames (time for research, reflection, and revision) and shorter time frames (a single sitting or a day or two) for a range of tasks, purposes, and audiences.
		• CCRA.SL.1	Prepare for and participate effectively in a range of conversations and collaborations with diverse partners, building on others' ideas and expressing their own clearly and persuasively.
		• CCRA.L.6	Acquire and use accurately a range of general academic and domain-specific words and phrases sufficient for reading, writing, speaking, and listening at the college and career readiness level; demonstrate independence in gathering vocabulary knowledge when encountering an unknown term important to comprehension or expression.
			Demonstrate understanding of figurative language, word relationships and nuances in word meanings.
		• L.4.5c	Demonstrate understanding of words by relating them to their opposites (antonyms) and to words with similar but not identical meanings (synonyms).
		• L.5.5c	Use the relationship between particular words (e.g., synonyms, antonyms, homographs) to better understand each of the words.
144	Vocabulary: Phrases for Times and Places	• CCRA.W.10	Write routinely over extended time frames (time for research, reflection, and revision) and shorter time frames (a single sitting or a day or two) for a range of tasks, purposes, and audiences.
	Language: Describe Actions	• CCRA.L.6	Acquire and use accurately a range of general academic and domain-specific words and phrases sufficient for reading, writing, speaking, and listening at the college and career readiness level; demonstrate independence in gathering vocabulary knowledge when encountering an unknown term important to comprehension or expression.

Common Core State Standards, continued

Language Development, continued

SE Pages	Lesson	Code	Standards Text
145	**Grammar: Commands**	• CCRA.W.10	Write routinely over extended time frames (time for research, reflection, and revision) and shorter time frames (a single sitting or a day or two) for a range of tasks, purposes, and audiences.
		• CCRA.SL.1	Prepare for and participate effectively in a range of conversations and collaborations with diverse partners, building on others' ideas and expressing their own clearly and persuasively.
		• L.1.2b	Demonstrate command of the conventions of standard English capitalization, punctuation, and spelling when writing. Use end punctuation for sentences.
		• L.4.3b	Use knowledge of language and its conventions when writing, speaking, reading, or listening. Choose punctuation for effect.
146	**Listen and Read Along: *The Eagle and the Moon Gold***	• CCRA.R.4	Interpret words and phrases as they are used in a text, including determining technical, connotative, and figurative meanings, and analyze how specific word choices shape meaning or tone.
		• CCRA.R.10	Read and comprehend complex literary and informational texts independently and proficiently.
		• L.4.5c	Demonstrate understanding of figurative language, word relationships and nuances in word meanings. Demonstrate understanding of words by relating them to their opposites (antonyms) and to words with similar but not identical meanings (synonyms).
		• L.5.5c	Use the relationship between particular words (e.g., synonyms, antonyms, homographs) to better understand each of the words.
147	**Think About *The Eagle and the Moon Gold***	• CCRA.R.3	Analyze how and why individuals, events, or ideas develop and interact over the course of a text.
		• CCRA.SL.1	Prepare for and participate effectively in a range of conversations and collaborations with diverse partners, building on others' ideas and expressing their own clearly and persuasively.

Language and Literacy

SE Pages	Lesson	Code	Standards Text
148–149	**High Frequency Words**	• RF.K.3c	Know and apply grade-level phonics and word analysis skills in decoding words. Read common high-frequency words by sight (e.g., *the, of, to, you, she, my, is, are, do, does*).
		• RF.1.3g • RF.2.3f	Recognize and read grade-appropriate irregularly spelled words.
		• L.1.2d	Demonstrate command of the conventions of standard English capitalization, punctuation, and spelling when writing. Use conventional spelling for words with common spelling patterns and for frequently occurring irregular words.
		• L.3.2e	Use conventional spelling for high-frequency and other studied words and for adding suffixes to base words (e.g., *sitting, smiled, cries, happiness*).
		• L.4.2d • L.5.2e	Spell grade-appropriate words correctly, consulting references as needed.

Language and Literacy, continued

SE Pages	Lesson	Code	Standards Text
150–151	Reading and Spelling: Diphthongs and Variant Vowels		Know and apply grade-level phonics and word analysis skills in decoding words.
		RF.K.3a	Demonstrate basic knowledge of one-to-one letter-sound correspondences by producing the primary sound or many of the most frequent sounds for each consonant.
		RF.2.3b	Know spelling-sound correspondences for additional common vowel teams.
			Demonstrate command of the conventions of standard English capitalization, punctuation, and spelling when writing.
		L.1.2d	Use conventional spelling for words with common spelling patterns and for frequently occurring irregular words.
152–155	Read on Your Own: "A Chill in the Air"	CCRA.R.10	Read and comprehend complex literary and informational texts independently and proficiently.
			Know and apply grade-level phonics and word analysis skills in decoding words.
		RF.1.3g RF.2.3f	Recognize and read grade-appropriate irregularly spelled words.
		RF.2.3b	Know spelling-sound correspondences for additional common vowel teams.
			Read with sufficient accuracy and fluency to support comprehension.
		RF.1.4a RF.2.4a	Read grade-level text with purpose and understanding.
		RF.1.4b RF.2.4b	Read grade-level text orally with accuracy, appropriate rate, and expression on successive readings.
156	Check Your Understanding	CCRA.W.9	Draw evidence from literary or informational texts to support analysis, reflection, and research.
	Expand Your Vocabulary	CCRA.SL.1	Prepare for and participate effectively in a range of conversations and collaborations with diverse partners, building on others' ideas and expressing their own clearly and persuasively.
		CCRA.L.6	Acquire and use accurately a range of general academic and domain-specific words and phrases sufficient for reading, writing, speaking, and listening at the college and career readiness level; demonstrate independence in gathering vocabulary knowledge when encountering an unknown term important to comprehension or expression.
			Demonstrate understanding of figurative language, word relationships and nuances in word meanings.
		L.4.5c	Demonstrate understanding of words by relating them to their opposites (antonyms) and to words with similar but not identical meanings (synonyms).
		L.5.5c	Use the relationship between particular words (e.g., synonyms, antonyms, homographs) to better understand each of the words.
	Write About Characters	CCRA.W.2	Write informative/explanatory texts to examine and convey complex ideas and information clearly and accurately through the effective selection, organization, and analysis of content.
		CCRA.W.10	Write routinely over extended time frames (time for research, reflection, and revision) and shorter time frames (a single sitting or a day or two) for a range of tasks, purposes, and audiences.

Common Core State Standards, continued

Language and Content

SE Pages	Lesson	Code	Standards Text
157	**Success in Language Arts: Learn About Myths**	• CCRA.R.2	Determine central ideas or themes of a text and analyze their development; summarize the key supporting details and ideas.
		• CCRA.R.7	Integrate and evaluate content presented in diverse media and formats, including visually and quantitatively, as well as in words.
		• CCRA.R.10	Read and comprehend complex literary and informational texts independently and proficiently.
158–159	**Build Background and Vocabulary**	• CCRA.R.7	Integrate and evaluate content presented in diverse media and formats, including visually and quantitatively, as well as in words.
		• CCRA.SL.1	Prepare for and participate effectively in a range of conversations and collaborations with diverse partners, building on others' ideas and expressing their own clearly and persuasively.
		• CCRA.L.6	Acquire and use accurately a range of general academic and domain-specific words and phrases sufficient for reading, writing, speaking, and listening at the college and career readiness level; demonstrate independence in gathering vocabulary knowledge when encountering an unknown term important to comprehension or expression.
			Determine or clarify the meaning of unknown and multiple-meaning words and phrases based on grade-level reading and content, choosing flexibly from a range of strategies.
		• L.1.4a • L.2.4a • L.3.4a	Use sentence-level context as a clue to the meaning of a word or phrase.
		• L.4.4a	Use context (e.g., definitions, examples, or restatements in text) as a clue to the meaning of a word or phrase.
160–167	**Listen and Read Along: "Stories from Greece"**	• CCRA.R.2	Determine central ideas or themes of a text and analyze their development; summarize the key supporting details and ideas.
		• CCRA.R.4	Interpret words and phrases as they are used in a text, including determining technical, connotative, and figurative meanings, and analyze how specific word choices shape meaning or tone.
		• CCRA.R.9	Analyze how two or more texts address similar themes or topics in order to build knowledge or to compare the approaches the authors take.
		• CCRA.R.10	Read and comprehend complex literary and informational texts independently and proficiently.
		• CCRA.L.6	Acquire and use accurately a range of general academic and domain-specific words and phrases sufficient for reading, writing, speaking, and listening at the college and career readiness level; demonstrate independence in gathering vocabulary knowledge when encountering an unknown term important to comprehension or expression.
168	**Check Your Understanding**	• CCRA.R.2	Determine central ideas or themes of a text and analyze their development; summarize the key supporting details and ideas.
		• CCRA.R.3	Analyze how and why individuals, events, or ideas develop and interact over the course of a text.
	Review Vocabulary	• CCRA.R.4	Interpret words and phrases as they are used in a text, including determining technical, connotative, and figurative meanings, and analyze how specific word choices shape meaning or tone.

Language and Content, continued

SE Pages	Lesson	Code	Standards Text
168	**Write About Myths**	• CCRA.W.3	Write narratives to develop real or imagined experiences or events using effective technique, well-chosen details and well-structured event sequences.
		• CCRA.W.10	Write routinely over extended time frames (time for research, reflection, and revision) and shorter time frames (a single sitting or a day or two) for a range of tasks, purposes, and audiences.

Writing Project

SE Pages	Lesson	Code	Standards Text
169	**Model Study: Short Story**	• CCRA.R.5	Analyze the structure of texts, including how specific sentences, paragraphs, and larger portions of the text (e.g., a section, chapter, scene, or stanza) relate to each other and the whole.
170	**Prewrite**	• CCRA.W.4	Produce clear and coherent writing in which the development, organization, and style are appropriate to task, purpose, and audience.
171	**Draft**	• CCRA.W.3	Write narratives to develop real or imagined experiences or events using effective technique, well-chosen details and well-structured event sequences.
171	**Revise**	• CCRA.W.4	Produce clear and coherent writing in which the development, organization, and style are appropriate to task, purpose, and audience.
		• CCRA.W.5	Develop and strengthen writing as needed by planning, revising, editing, rewriting, or trying a new approach.
172	**Edit and Proofread**	• CCRA.W.5	Develop and strengthen writing as needed by planning, revising, editing, rewriting, or trying a new approach.
		• CCRA.L.2	Demonstrate command of the conventions of standard English capitalization, punctuation, and spelling when writing.
			Demonstrate command of the conventions of standard English capitalization, punctuation, and spelling when writing.
		• L.2.2e • L.3.2g	Consult reference materials, including beginning dictionaries, as needed to check and correct spellings.
		• L.3.2c	Use commas and quotation marks in dialogue.
		• L.4.2d • L.5.2e	Spell grade-appropriate words correctly, consulting references as needed.
173	**Publish, Share, and Reflect**	• CCRA.W.10	Write routinely over extended time frames (time for research, reflection, and revision) and shorter time frames (a single sitting or a day or two) for a range of tasks, purposes, and audiences.
		• CCRA.SL.4	Present information, findings, and supporting evidence such that listeners can follow the line of reasoning and the organization, development, and style are appropriate to task, purpose, and audience.
		• CCRA.SL.6	Adapt speech to a variety of contexts and communicative tasks, demonstrating command of formal English when indicated or appropriate.

Unit 6 Personal Best

Language Development

SE Pages	Lesson	Code	Standards Text
174–175	**Unit Launch**	• CCRA.SL.2	Integrate and evaluate information presented in diverse media and formats, including visually, quantitatively, and orally.

Common Core State Standards, continued

Language Development, continued

SE Pages	Lesson	Code	Standards Text
176	**Language:** **Ask for and Give Information**	• CCRA.SL.1	Prepare for and participate effectively in a range of conversations and collaborations with diverse partners, building on others' ideas and expressing their own clearly and persuasively.
		• CCRA.L.6	Acquire and use accurately a range of general academic and domain-specific words and phrases sufficient for reading, writing, speaking, and listening at the college and career readiness level; demonstrate independence in gathering vocabulary knowledge when encountering an unknown term important to comprehension or expression.
177	**Grammar:** **Present Tense Verbs**	• CCRA.W.2	Write informative/explanatory texts to examine and convey complex ideas and information clearly and accurately through the effective selection, organization, and analysis of content.
		• CCRA.SL.1	Prepare for and participate effectively in a range of conversations and collaborations with diverse partners, building on others' ideas and expressing their own clearly and persuasively.
			Demonstrate command of the conventions of standard English grammar and usage when writing or speaking.
		• L.1.1e	Use verbs to convey a sense of past, present, and future (e.g., *Yesterday I walked home; Today I walk home; Tomorrow I will walk home*).
		• L.3.1d	Form and use regular and irregular verbs.
		• L.3.1e	Form and use the simple (e.g., *I walked; I walk; I will walk*) verb tenses.
		• L.5.1c	Use verb tense to convey various times, sequences, states, and conditions.
178	**Vocabulary:** **Sports**	• CCRA.W.4	Produce clear and coherent writing in which the development, organization, and style are appropriate to task, purpose, and audience.
	Language: **Express Thanks**	• CCRA.W.10	Write routinely over extended time frames (time for research, reflection, and revision) and shorter time frames (a single sitting or a day or two) for a range of tasks, purposes, and audiences.
		• CCRA.L.6	Acquire and use accurately a range of general academic and domain-specific words and phrases sufficient for reading, writing, speaking, and listening at the college and career readiness level; demonstrate independence in gathering vocabulary knowledge when encountering an unknown term important to comprehension or expression.
179	**Grammar:** **Pronouns**	• CCRA.W.2	Write informative/explanatory texts to examine and convey complex ideas and information clearly and accurately through the effective selection, organization, and analysis of content.
			Demonstrate command of the conventions of standard English grammar and usage when writing or speaking.
		• L.1.1d	Use personal, possessive, and indefinite pronouns (e.g., *I, me, my; they, them, their, anyone, everything*).
		• L.3.1f	Ensure subject-verb and pronoun-antecedent agreement.
180	**Listen and Read Along:** ***Body Works***	• CCRA.R.4	Interpret words and phrases as they are used in a text, including determining technical, connotative, and figurative meanings, and analyze how specific word choices shape meaning or tone.
		• CCRA.R.10	Read and comprehend complex literary and informational texts independently and proficiently.

Language Development, continued

SE Pages	Lesson	Code	Standards Text
180	**Listen and Read Along:** *Body Works,* continued		With guidance and support from adults, demonstrate understanding of word relationships and nuances in word meanings.
		• L.1.5a	Sort words into categories (e.g., colors, clothing) to gain a sense of the concepts the categories represent.
181	**Comprehension: Identify Main Idea and Details**	• CCRA.R.2	Determine central ideas or themes of a text and analyze their development; summarize the key supporting details and ideas.
		• CCRA.R.5	Analyze the structure of texts, including how specific sentences, paragraphs, and larger portions of the text (e.g., a section, chapter, scene, or stanza) relate to each other and the whole.
		• CCRA.SL.4	Present information, findings, and supporting evidence such that listeners can follow the line of reasoning and the organization, development, and style are appropriate to task, purpose, and audience.

Language and Literacy

SE Pages	Lesson	Code	Standards Text
182–183	**High Frequency Words**		Know and apply grade-level phonics and word analysis skills in decoding words.
		• RF.K.3c	Read common high-frequency words by sight (e.g., *the, of, to, you, she, my, is, are, do, does*).
		• RF.1.3g • RF.2.3f	Recognize and read grade-appropriate irregularly spelled words.
			Demonstrate command of the conventions of standard English capitalization, punctuation, and spelling when writing.
		• L.1.2d	Use conventional spelling for words with common spelling patterns and for frequently occurring irregular words.
		• L.3.2e	Use conventional spelling for high-frequency and other studied words and for adding suffixes to base words (e.g., *sitting, smiled, cries, happiness*).
		• L.4.2d • L.5.2e	Spell grade-appropriate words correctly, consulting references as needed.
184–185	**Reading and Spelling: Variant Vowels and Consonants**		Know and apply grade-level phonics and word analysis skills in decoding words.
		• RF.K.3a	Demonstrate basic knowledge of one-to-one letter-sound correspondences by producing the primary sound or many of the most frequent sounds for each consonant.
		• CCRA.L.1	Demonstrate command of the conventions of standard English grammar and usage when writing or speaking.
			Demonstrate command of the conventions of standard English capitalization, punctuation, and spelling when writing.
		• L.1.2d	Use conventional spelling for words with common spelling patterns and for frequently occurring irregular words.
186–189	**Read on Your Own: "Summer Games Are a Big Hit"**	• CCRA.R.10	Read and comprehend complex literary and informational texts independently and proficiently.
			Know and apply grade-level phonics and word analysis skills in decoding words.
		• RF.1.3g • RF.2.3f	Recognize and read grade-appropriate irregularly spelled words.

Common Core State Standards, continued

Language and Literacy, continued

SE Pages	Lesson	Code	Standards Text
186–189	Read on Your Own: "Summer Games Are a Big Hit," continued	RF.1.4a RF.2.4a	Read with sufficient accuracy and fluency to support comprehension. Read grade-level text with purpose and understanding.
		RF.1.4b RF.2.4b	Read grade-level text orally with accuracy, appropriate rate, and expression on successive readings.
190	Check Your Understanding	CCRA.W.9	Draw evidence from literary or informational texts to support analysis, reflection, and research.
	Expand Vocabulary	CCRA.L.6	Acquire and use accurately a range of general academic and domain-specific words and phrases sufficient for reading, writing, speaking, and listening at the college and career readiness level; demonstrate independence in gathering vocabulary knowledge when encountering an unknown term important to comprehension or expression.
	Write About Sports	CCRA.W.2	Write informative/explanatory texts to examine and convey complex ideas and information clearly and accurately through the effective selection, organization, and analysis of content.
		CCRA.W.10	Write routinely over extended time frames (time for research, reflection, and revision) and shorter time frames (a single sitting or a day or two) for a range of tasks, purposes, and audiences.

Language and Content

191	Success in Social Science: Learn About Captions	CCRA.R.5	Analyze the structure of texts, including how specific sentences, paragraphs, and larger portions of the text (e.g., a section, chapter, scene, or stanza) relate to each other and the whole.
		CCRA.R.10	Read and comprehend complex literary and informational texts independently and proficiently.
192–193	Build Background and Vocabulary	CCRA.R.7	Integrate and evaluate content presented in diverse media and formats, including visually and quantitatively, as well as in words.
		CCRA.SL.1	Prepare for and participate effectively in a range of conversations and collaborations with diverse partners, building on others' ideas and expressing their own clearly and persuasively.
		CCRA.L.6	Acquire and use accurately a range of general academic and domain-specific words and phrases sufficient for reading, writing, speaking, and listening at the college and career readiness level; demonstrate independence in gathering vocabulary knowledge when encountering an unknown term important to comprehension or expression.
		L.1.4a L.2.4a L.3.4a	Determine or clarify the meaning of unknown and multiple-meaning words and phrases based on grade-level reading and content, choosing flexibly from a range of strategies. Use sentence-level context as a clue to the meaning of a word or phrase.
		L.4.4a	Use context (e.g., definitions, examples, or restatements in text) as a clue to the meaning of a word or phrase.

Language and Content, continued

SE Pages	Lesson	Code	Standards Text
194–201	Listen and Read Along: "Action Shots"	• CCRA.R.2	Determine central ideas or themes of a text and analyze their development; summarize the key supporting details and ideas.
		• CCRA.R.7	Integrate and evaluate content presented in diverse media and formats, including visually and quantitatively, as well as in words.
		• CCRA.R.10	Read and comprehend complex literary and informational texts independently and proficiently.
		• CCRA.L.6	Acquire and use accurately a range of general academic and domain-specific words and phrases sufficient for reading, writing, speaking, and listening at the college and career readiness level; demonstrate independence in gathering vocabulary knowledge when encountering an unknown term important to comprehension or expression.
202	Check Your Understanding	• CCRA.R.3	Analyze how and why individuals, events, or ideas develop and interact over the course of a text.
		• CCRA.R.2	Determine central ideas or themes of a text and analyze their development; summarize the key supporting details and ideas.
		• CCRA.SL.1	Prepare for and participate effectively in a range of conversations and collaborations with diverse partners, building on others' ideas and expressing their own clearly and persuasively.
	Review Vocabulary	• CCRA.R.4	Interpret words and phrases as they are used in a text, including determining technical, connotative, and figurative meanings, and analyze how specific word choices shape meaning or tone.
	Write About Sports	• CCRA.W.2	Write informative/explanatory texts to examine and convey complex ideas and information clearly and accurately through the effective selection, organization, and analysis of content.
		• CCRA.W.4	Produce clear and coherent writing in which the development, organization, and style are appropriate to task, purpose, and audience.
		• CCRA.W.10	Write routinely over extended time frames (time for research, reflection, and revision) and shorter time frames (a single sitting or a day or two) for a range of tasks, purposes, and audiences.

Writing Project

SE Pages	Lesson	Code	Standards Text
203	Model Study: Procedure	• CCRA.R.5	Analyze the structure of texts, including how specific sentences, paragraphs, and larger portions of the text (e.g., a section, chapter, scene, or stanza) relate to each other and the whole.
204	Prewrite	• CCRA.W.4	Produce clear and coherent writing in which the development, organization, and style are appropriate to task, purpose, and audience.
205	Draft	• CCRA.W.2	Write informative/explanatory texts to examine and convey complex ideas and information clearly and accurately through the effective selection, organization, and analysis of content.
205	Revise	• CCRA.W.4	Produce clear and coherent writing in which the development, organization, and style are appropriate to task, purpose, and audience.
		• CCRA.W.5	Develop and strengthen writing as needed by planning, revising, editing, rewriting, or trying a new approach.

Common Core State Standards, continued

Writing Project, continued

SE Pages	Lesson	Code	Standards Text
206	Edit and Proofread	• CCRA.W.5	Develop and strengthen writing as needed by planning, revising, editing, rewriting, or trying a new approach.
		• L.1.1d	Demonstrate command of the conventions of standard English grammar and usage when writing or speaking. Use personal, possessive, and indefinite pronouns (e.g., *I, me, my; they, them, their, anyone, everything*).
		• L.2.2e • L3.2g • L.4.2a • L.4.2d • L.5.2e	Demonstrate command of the conventions of standard English capitalization, punctuation, and spelling when writing. Consult reference materials, including beginning dictionaries, as needed to check and correct spellings. Use correct capitalization. Spell grade-appropriate words correctly, consulting references as needed.
207	Publish, Share, and Reflect	• CCRA.W.10	Write routinely over extended time frames (time for research, reflection, and revision) and shorter time frames (a single sitting or a day or two) for a range of tasks, purposes, and audiences.
		• CCRA.SL.4	Present information, findings, and supporting evidence such that listeners can follow the line of reasoning and the organization, development, and style are appropriate to task, purpose, and audience.
		• CCRA.SL.5	Make strategic use of digital media and visual displays of data to express information and enhance understanding of presentations.
		• CCRA.SL.6	Adapt speech to a variety of contexts and communicative tasks, demonstrating command of formal English when indicated or appropriate.

Unit 7   This Land is Our Land

Language Development

SE Pages	Lesson	Code	Standards Text
208–209	Unit Launch	• CCRA.SL.2	Integrate and evaluate information presented in diverse media and formats, including visually, quantitatively, and orally.
210	Language: Ask and Answer Questions	• CCRA.SL.1	Prepare for and participate effectively in a range of conversations and collaborations with diverse partners, building on others' ideas and expressing their own clearly and persuasively.
		• CCRA.SL.6	Adapt speech to a variety of contexts and communicative tasks, demonstrating command of formal English when indicated or appropriate.
211	Grammar: Questions With *How?* And *Why?*	• CCRA.SL.1	Prepare for and participate effectively in a range of conversations and collaborations with diverse partners, building on others' ideas and expressing their own clearly and persuasively.
		• L.3.1h	Demonstrate command of the conventions of standard English grammar and usage when writing or speaking. Use coordinating and subordinating conjunctions.

Language Development, continued

SE Pages	Lesson	Code	Standards Text
212	**Vocabulary: Landforms and Bodies of Water**	• CCRA.W.2	Write informative/explanatory texts to examine and convey complex ideas and information clearly and accurately through the effective selection, organization, and analysis of content.
	Language: Give Directions	• CCRA.W.10	Write routinely over extended time frames (time for research, reflection, and revision) and shorter time frames (a single sitting or a day or two) for a range of tasks, purposes, and audiences.
		• CCRA.SL.1	Prepare for and participate effectively in a range of conversations and collaborations with diverse partners, building on others' ideas and expressing their own clearly and persuasively.
		• CCRA.L.6	Acquire and use accurately a range of general academic and domain-specific words and phrases sufficient for reading, writing, speaking, and listening at the college and career readiness level; demonstrate independence in gathering vocabulary knowledge when encountering an unknown term important to comprehension or expression.
213	**Grammar: Capitalization: Proper Nouns**		Demonstrate understanding of the organization and basic features of print.
		• RF.1.1a	Recognize the distinguishing features of a sentence (e.g., first word, capitalization, ending punctuation).
			Demonstrate command of the conventions of standard English grammar and usage when writing or speaking.
		• L.1.1b	Use common, proper, and possessive nouns.
			Demonstrate command of the conventions of standard English capitalization, punctuation, and spelling when writing.
		• L.2.2a	Capitalize holidays, product names, and geographic names.
214	**Listen and Read Along:** *All Across America*	• CCRA.R.4	Interpret words and phrases as they are used in a text, including determining technical, connotative, and figurative meanings, and analyze how specific word choices shape meaning or tone.
		• CCRA.R.10	Read and comprehend complex literary and informational texts independently and proficiently.
		• CCRA.L.6	Acquire and use accurately a range of general academic and domain-specific words and phrases sufficient for reading, writing, speaking, and listening at the college and career readiness level; demonstrate independence in gathering vocabulary knowledge when encountering an unknown term important to comprehension or expression.
			With guidance and support from adults, demonstrate understanding of word relationships and nuances in word meanings.
		• L.1.5a	Sort words into categories (e.g., colors, clothing) to gain a sense of the concepts the categories represent.
215	**Comprehension: Classify**	• CCRA.R.2	Determine central ideas or themes of a text and analyze their development; summarize the key supporting details and ideas.
		• CCRA.SL.1	Prepare for and participate effectively in a range of conversations and collaborations with diverse partners, building on others' ideas and expressing their own clearly and persuasively.

Common Core State Standards, continued

Language and Literacy

SE Pages	Lesson	Code	Standards Text
216–217	High Frequency Words		Know and apply grade-level phonics and word analysis skills in decoding words.
		• RF.K.3c	Read common high-frequency words by sight (e.g., *the, of, to, you, she, my, is, are, do, does*).
		• RF.1.3g • RF.2.3f	Recognize and read grade-appropriate irregularly spelled words.
			Demonstrate command of the conventions of standard English capitalization, punctuation, and spelling when writing.
		• L.1.2d	Use conventional spelling for words with common spelling patterns and for frequently occurring irregular words.
		• L.3.2e	Use conventional spelling for high-frequency and other studied words and for adding suffixes to base words (e.g., *sitting, smiled, cries, happiness*).
		• L.4.2d • L.5.2e	Spell grade-appropriate words correctly, consulting references as needed.
218–219	Reading and Spelling: Multisyllabic Words		Know and apply grade-level phonics and word analysis skills in decoding words.
		• RF.K.3a	Demonstrate basic knowledge of one-to-one letter-sound correspondences by producing the primary sound or many of the most frequent sounds for each consonant.
		• RF.1.3d	Use knowledge that every syllable must have a vowel sound to determine the number of syllables in a printed word.
		• RF.1.3e	Decode two-syllable words following basic patterns by breaking the words into syllables.
			Demonstrate command of the conventions of standard English capitalization, punctuation, and spelling when writing.
		• L.1.2d	Use conventional spelling for words with common spelling patterns and for frequently occurring irregular words.
220–223	Read on Your Own: *Deep Canyon*	• CCRA.R.10	Read and comprehend complex literary and informational texts independently and proficiently.
			Know and apply grade-level phonics and word analysis skills in decoding words.
		• RF.1.3e	Decode two-syllable words following basic patterns by breaking the words into syllables.
		• RF.1.3g • RF.2.3f	Recognize and read grade-appropriate irregularly spelled words.
			Read with sufficient accuracy and fluency to support comprehension.
		• RF.1.4a • RF.2.4a	Read grade-level text with purpose and understanding.
		• RF.1.4b • RF.2.4b	Read grade-level text orally with accuracy, appropriate rate, and expression on successive readings.
		• RF.1.4c • RF.2.4c	Use context to confirm or self-correct word recognition and understanding, rereading as necessary

Language and Literacy, continued

SE Pages	Lesson	Code	Standards Text
224	**Check Your Understanding**	• CCRA.SL.1	Prepare for and participate effectively in a range of conversations and collaborations with diverse partners, building on others' ideas and expressing their own clearly and persuasively.
		• CCRA.W.9	Draw evidence from literary or informational texts to support analysis, reflection, and research.
	Expand Your Vocabulary	• CCRA.L.6	Acquire and use accurately a range of general academic and domain-specific words and phrases sufficient for reading, writing, speaking, and listening at the college and career readiness level; demonstrate independence in gathering vocabulary knowledge when encountering an unknown term important to comprehension or expression.
	Write About a Visit to the Grand Canyon	• CCRA.W.3	Write narratives to develop real or imagined experiences or events using effective technique, well-chosen details and well-structured event sequences.
		• CCRA.W.10	Write routinely over extended time frames (time for research, reflection, and revision) and shorter time frames (a single sitting or a day or two) for a range of tasks, purposes, and audiences.

Language and Content

SE Pages	Lesson	Code	Standards Text
225	**Success in Social Science: Learn About Regions of the U.S.**	• CCRA.R.10	Read and comprehend complex literary and informational texts independently and proficiently.
		• CCRA.SL.2	Integrate and evaluate information presented in diverse media and formats, including visually, quantitatively, and orally.
		• CCRA.L.6	Acquire and use accurately a range of general academic and domain-specific words and phrases sufficient for reading, writing, speaking, and listening at the college and career readiness level; demonstrate independence in gathering vocabulary knowledge when encountering an unknown term important to comprehension or expression.
226–227	**Build Background and Vocabulary**	• CCRA.R.7	Integrate and evaluate content presented in diverse media and formats, including visually and quantitatively, as well as in words.
		• CCRA.SL.1	Prepare for and participate effectively in a range of conversations and collaborations with diverse partners, building on others' ideas and expressing their own clearly and persuasively.
		• CCRA.L.6	Acquire and use accurately a range of general academic and domain-specific words and phrases sufficient for reading, writing, speaking, and listening at the college and career readiness level; demonstrate independence in gathering vocabulary knowledge when encountering an unknown term important to comprehension or expression.
			Determine or clarify the meaning of unknown and multiple-meaning words and phrases based on grade-level reading and content, choosing flexibly from a range of strategies.
		• L.1.4a • L.2.4a • L.3.4a	Use sentence-level context as a clue to the meaning of a word or phrase.
		• L.4.4a	Use context (e.g., definitions, examples, or restatements in text) as a clue to the meaning of a word or phrase.
228–235	**Listen and Read Along: "The Big Southwest"**	• CCRA.R.2	Determine central ideas or themes of a text and analyze their development; summarize the key supporting details and ideas.

Common Core State Standards, continued

Language and Content, continued

SE Pages	Lesson	Code	Standards Text
228–235	**Listen and Read Along: "The Big Southwest,"** continued	• CCRA.R.4	Interpret words and phrases as they are used in a text, including determining technical, connotative, and figurative meanings, and analyze how specific word choices shape meaning or tone.
		• CCRA.R.7	Integrate and evaluate content presented in diverse media and formats, including visually and quantitatively, as well as in words.
		• CCRA.L.6	Acquire and use accurately a range of general academic and domain-specific words and phrases sufficient for reading, writing, speaking, and listening at the college and career readiness level; demonstrate independence in gathering vocabulary knowledge when encountering an unknown term important to comprehension or expression.
		• L.1.5a	With guidance and support from adults, demonstrate understanding of word relationships and nuances in word meanings. Sort words into categories (e.g., colors, clothing) to gain a sense of the concepts the categories represent.
236	**Check Your Understanding**	• CCRA.R.2	Determine central ideas or themes of a text and analyze their development; summarize the key supporting details and ideas.
		• CCRA.R.5	Analyze the structure of texts, including how specific sentences, paragraphs, and larger portions of the text (e.g., a section, chapter, scene, or stanza) relate to each other and the whole.
	Review Vocabulary	• CCRA.R.4	Interpret words and phrases as they are used in a text, including determining technical, connotative, and figurative meanings, and analyze how specific word choices shape meaning or tone.
	Write About a U.S. Region	• CCRA.W.1	Write arguments to support claims in an analysis of substantive topics or texts using valid reasoning and relevant and sufficient evidence.
		• CCRA.W.10	Write routinely over extended time frames (time for research, reflection, and revision) and shorter time frames (a single sitting or a day or two) for a range of tasks, purposes, and audiences.

Writing Project

SE Pages	Lesson	Code	Standards Text
237	**Model Study: Biography**	• CCRA.R.5	Analyze the structure of texts, including how specific sentences, paragraphs, and larger portions of the text (e.g., a section, chapter, scene, or stanza) relate to each other and the whole.
238	**Prewrite**	• CCRA.W.4	Produce clear and coherent writing in which the development, organization, and style are appropriate to task, purpose, and audience.
		• CCRA.W.6	Use technology, including the Internet, to produce and publish writing and to interact and collaborate with others.
239	**Draft**	• CCRA.W.2	Write informative/explanatory texts to examine and convey complex ideas and information clearly and accurately through the effective selection, organization, and analysis of content.
239	**Revise**	• CCRA.W.4	Produce clear and coherent writing in which the development, organization, and style are appropriate to task, purpose, and audience.
		• CCRA.W.5	Develop and strengthen writing as needed by planning, revising, editing, rewriting, or trying a new approach.
		• CCRA.SL.1	Prepare for and participate effectively in a range of conversations and collaborations with diverse partners, building on others' ideas and expressing their own clearly and persuasively.

Writing Project, continued

SE Pages	Lesson	Code	Standards Text
240	Edit and Proofread	● CCRA.W.5	Develop and strengthen writing as needed by planning, revising, editing, rewriting, or trying a new approach.
		● CCRA.L.2	Demonstrate command of the conventions of standard English capitalization, punctuation, and spelling when writing.
			Demonstrate command of the conventions of standard English capitalization, punctuation, and spelling when writing.
		● L.1.2c	Use commas in dates and to separate single words in a series.
		● L.2.2a	Capitalize holidays, product names, and geographic names.
		● L.2.2e ● L.3.2g	Consult reference materials, including beginning dictionaries, as needed to check and correct spellings.
		● L.4.2d ● L.5.2e	Spell grade-appropriate words correctly, consulting references as needed.
241	Publish, Share, and Reflect	● CCRA.W.10	Write routinely over extended time frames (time for research, reflection, and revision) and shorter time frames (a single sitting or a day or two) for a range of tasks, purposes, and audiences.
		● CCRA.SL.4	Present information, findings, and supporting evidence such that listeners can follow the line of reasoning and the organization, development, and style are appropriate to task, purpose, and audience.
		● CCRA.SL.5	Make strategic use of digital media and visual displays of data to express information and enhance understanding of presentations.
		● CCRA.SL.6	Adapt speech to a variety of contexts and communicative tasks, demonstrating command of formal English when indicated or appropriate.

Unit 8   Harvest Time

Language Development

SE Pages	Lesson	Code	Standards Text
242–243	Unit Launch	● CCRA.SL.2	Integrate and evaluate information presented in diverse media and formats, including visually, quantitatively, and orally.
244	Language: Buy or Sell an Item	● CCRA.SL.1	Prepare for and participate effectively in a range of conversations and collaborations with diverse partners, building on others' ideas and expressing their own clearly and persuasively.
245	Vocabulary: Farming	● CCRA.SL.1	Prepare for and participate effectively in a range of conversations and collaborations with diverse partners, building on others' ideas and expressing their own clearly and persuasively.
	Language: Give Information	● CCRA.L.6	Acquire and use accurately a range of general academic and domain-specific words and phrases sufficient for reading, writing, speaking, and listening at the college and career readiness level; demonstrate independence in gathering vocabulary knowledge when encountering an unknown term important to comprehension or expression.
		● CCRA.W.2	Write informative/explanatory texts to examine and convey complex ideas and information clearly and accurately through the effective selection, organization, and analysis of content.
246–247	Grammar: Subjects, Predicates, and Word Order	● CCRA.W.2	Write informative/explanatory texts to examine and convey complex ideas and information clearly and accurately through the effective selection, organization, and analysis of content.

Common Core State Standards, continued

Language Development, continued

SE Pages	Lesson	Code	Standards Text
246–247	**Grammar: Subjects, Predicates, and Word Order,** continued	● CCRA.SL.1	Prepare for and participate effectively in a range of conversations and collaborations with diverse partners, building on others' ideas and expressing their own clearly and persuasively.
			Demonstrate command of the conventions of standard English grammar and usage when writing or speaking.
		● L.3.1f	Ensure subject-verb and pronoun-antecedent agreement.
248	**Listen and Read Along:** *Crops*	● CCRA.R.4	Interpret words and phrases as they are used in a text, including determining technical, connotative, and figurative meanings, and analyze how specific word choices shape meaning or tone.
		● CCRA.R.10	Read and comprehend complex literary and informational texts independently and proficiently.
			With guidance and support from adults, demonstrate understanding of word relationships and nuances in word meanings.
		● L.1.5a	Sort words into categories (e.g., colors, clothing) to gain a sense of the concepts the categories represent.
249	**Comprehension: Make Comparisons**	● CCRA.R.1	Read closely to determine what the text says explicitly and to make logical inferences from it; cite specific textual evidence when writing or speaking to support conclusions drawn from the text.
		● CCRA.R.2	Determine central ideas or themes of a text and analyze their development; summarize the key supporting details and ideas.
		● CCRA.SL.1	Prepare for and participate effectively in a range of conversations and collaborations with diverse partners, building on others' ideas and expressing their own clearly and persuasively.
			With guidance and support from adults, demonstrate understanding of word relationships and nuances in word meanings.
		● L.1.5a	Sort words into categories (e.g., colors, clothing) to gain a sense of the concepts the categories represent.

Language and Literacy

SE Pages	Lesson	Code	Standards Text
250–251	**High Frequency Words**		Know and apply grade-level phonics and word analysis skills in decoding words.
		● RF.K.3c	Read common high-frequency words by sight (e.g., *the, of, to, you, she, my, is, are, do, does*).
		● RF.1.3g ● RF.2.3f	Recognize and read grade-appropriate irregularly spelled words.
			Demonstrate command of the conventions of standard English capitalization, punctuation, and spelling when writing.
		● L.1.2d	Use conventional spelling for words with common spelling patterns and for frequently occurring irregular words.
		● L.3.2e	Use conventional spelling for high-frequency and other studied words and for adding suffixes to base words (e.g., *sitting, smiled, cries, happiness*).
		● L.4.2d ● L.5.2e	Spell grade-appropriate words correctly, consulting references as needed.

Language and Literacy, continued

SE Pages	Lesson	Code	Standards Text
252–253	**Reading and Spelling: Prefixes and Suffixes**		Know and apply grade-level phonics and word analysis skills in decoding words.
		• RF.K.3a	Demonstrate basic knowledge of one-to-one letter-sound correspondences by producing the primary sound or many of the most frequent sounds for each consonant.
		• RF.2.3d	Decode words with common prefixes and suffixes.
		• CCRA.L.1	Demonstrate command of the conventions of standard English grammar and usage when writing or speaking.
		• CCRA.L.4	Determine or clarify the meaning of unknown and multiple-meaning words and phrases by using context clues, analyzing meaningful word parts, and consulting general and specialized reference materials, as appropriate.
			Demonstrate command of the conventions of standard English capitalization, punctuation, and spelling when writing.
		• L.1.2d	Use conventional spelling for words with common spelling patterns and for frequently occurring irregular words.
		• L.3.2e	Use conventional spelling for high-frequency and other studied words and for adding suffixes to base words (e.g., *sitting, smiled, cries, happiness*).
			Determine or clarify the meaning of unknown and multiple-meaning words and phrases based on grade 2 reading and content, choosing flexibly from a range of strategies.
		• L.2.4b	Determine the meaning of the new word formed when a known prefix is added to a known word (e.g., *happy/unhappy, tell/retell*).
254–257	**Read on Your Own: "Many Places to Plant a Plant"**	• CCRA.R.10	Read and comprehend complex literary and informational texts independently and proficiently.
			Know and apply grade-level phonics and word analysis skills in decoding words.
		• RF.1.3g • RF.2.3f	Recognize and read grade-appropriate irregularly spelled words.
		• RF.2.3d	Decode words with common prefixes and suffixes.
			Read with sufficient accuracy and fluency to support comprehension.
		• RF.1.4a • RF.2.4a	Read grade-level text with purpose and understanding.
		• RF.1.4b • RF.2.4b	Read grade-level text orally with accuracy, appropriate rate, and expression on successive readings.
			Determine or clarify the meaning of unknown and multiple-meaning words and phrases based on grade 2 reading and content, choosing flexibly from a range of strategies.
		• L.2.4b	Determine the meaning of the new word formed when a known prefix is added to a known word (e.g., *happy/unhappy, tell/retell*).
			Demonstrate command of the conventions of standard English capitalization, punctuation, and spelling when writing.
		• L.3.2e	Use conventional spelling for high-frequency and other studied words and for adding suffixes to base words (e.g., *sitting, smiled, cries, happiness*).

Common Core State Standards, continued

Language and Literacy, continued

SE Pages	Lesson	Code	Standards Text
258	**Check Your Understanding**	• CCRA.W.9	Draw evidence from literary or informational texts to support analysis, reflection, and research.
		• CCRA.SL.1	Prepare for and participate effectively in a range of conversations and collaborations with diverse partners, building on others' ideas and expressing their own clearly and persuasively.
	Expand Your Vocabulary	• CCRA.L.6	Acquire and use accurately a range of general academic and domain-specific words and phrases sufficient for reading, writing, speaking, and listening at the college and career readiness level; demonstrate independence in gathering vocabulary knowledge when encountering an unknown term important to comprehension or expression.
		• L.2.4d	Determine or clarify the meaning of unknown and multiple-meaning words and phrases based on grade 2 reading and content, choosing flexibly from a range of strategies. Use knowledge of the meaning of individual words to predict the meaning of compound words (e.g., *birdhouse, lighthouse, housefly; bookshelf, notebook, bookmark*).
	Write More Comparisons	• CCRA.W.2	Write informative/explanatory texts to examine and convey complex ideas and information clearly and accurately through the effective selection, organization, and analysis of content.
		• CCRA.W.10	Write routinely over extended time frames (time for research, reflection, and revision) and shorter time frames (a single sitting or a day or two) for a range of tasks, purposes, and audiences.
		• L.1.5a	With guidance and support from adults, demonstrate understanding of word relationships and nuances in word meanings. Sort words into categories (e.g., colors, clothing) to gain a sense of the concepts the categories represent.

Language and Content

SE Pages	Lesson	Code	Standards Text
259	**Success in Science: Learn About Plants**	• CCRA.R.2	Determine central ideas or themes of a text and analyze their development; summarize the key supporting details and ideas.
		• CCRA.R.4	Interpret words and phrases as they are used in a text, including determining technical, connotative, and figurative meanings, and analyze how specific word choices shape meaning or tone.
		• CCRA.R.10	Read and comprehend complex literary and informational texts independently and proficiently.
		• CCRA.L.4	Determine or clarify the meaning of unknown and multiple-meaning words and phrases by using context clues, analyzing meaningful word parts, and consulting general and specialized reference materials, as appropriate.
260–261	**Build Background and Vocabulary**	• CCRA.R.7	Integrate and evaluate content presented in diverse media and formats, including visually and quantitatively, as well as in words.
		• CCRA.SL.1	Prepare for and participate effectively in a range of conversations and collaborations with diverse partners, building on others' ideas and expressing their own clearly and persuasively.
		• CCRA.L.6	Acquire and use accurately a range of general academic and domain-specific words and phrases sufficient for reading, writing, speaking, and listening at the college and career readiness level; demonstrate independence in gathering vocabulary knowledge when encountering an unknown term important to comprehension or expression.

Language and Content, continued

SE Pages	Lesson	Code	Standards Text
260–261	**Build Background and Vocabulary,** continued		Determine or clarify the meaning of unknown and multiple-meaning words and phrases based on grade-level reading and content, choosing flexibly from a range of strategies.
		• L.1.4a • L.2.4a • L.3.4a	Use sentence-level context as a clue to the meaning of a word or phrase.
		• L.4.4a	Use context (e.g., definitions, examples, or restatements in text) as a clue to the meaning of a word or phrase.
262–269	**Listen and Read Along: "Plant Power"**	• CCRA.R.2	Determine central ideas or themes of a text and analyze their development; summarize the key supporting details and ideas.
		• CCRA.R.4	Interpret words and phrases as they are used in a text, including determining technical, connotative, and figurative meanings, and analyze how specific word choices shape meaning or tone.
		• CCRA.R.7	Integrate and evaluate content presented in diverse media and formats, including visually and quantitatively, as well as in words.
		• CCRA.L.6	Acquire and use accurately a range of general academic and domain-specific words and phrases sufficient for reading, writing, speaking, and listening at the college and career readiness level; demonstrate independence in gathering vocabulary knowledge when encountering an unknown term important to comprehension or expression.
270	**Check Your Understanding**	• CCRA.R.2	Determine central ideas or themes of a text and analyze their development; summarize the key supporting details and ideas.
		• CCRA.SL.1	Prepare for and participate effectively in a range of conversations and collaborations with diverse partners, building on others' ideas and expressing their own clearly and persuasively.
	Review Vocabulary	• CCRA.R.4	Interpret words and phrases as they are used in a text, including determining technical, connotative, and figurative meanings, and analyze how specific word choices shape meaning or tone.
	Write About Plants	• CCRA.W.2	Write informative/explanatory texts to examine and convey complex ideas and information clearly and accurately through the effective selection, organization, and analysis of content.
		• CCRA.W.10	Write routinely over extended time frames (time for research, reflection, and revision) and shorter time frames (a single sitting or a day or two) for a range of tasks, purposes, and audiences.

Writing Project

SE Pages	Lesson	Code	Standards Text
271	**Model Study: Report**	• CCRA.R.5	Analyze the structure of texts, including how specific sentences, paragraphs, and larger portions of the text (e.g., a section, chapter, scene, or stanza) relate to each other and the whole.
272	**Prewrite**	• CCRA.W.4	Produce clear and coherent writing in which the development, organization, and style are appropriate to task, purpose, and audience.
		• CCRA.W.7	Conduct short as well as more sustained research projects based on focused questions, demonstrating understanding of the subject under investigation.
		• CCRA.W.8	Gather relevant information from multiple print and digital sources, assess the credibility and accuracy of each source, and integrate the information while avoiding plagiarism.

Common Core State Standards, continued

Writing Project, continued

SE Pages	Lesson	Code	Standards Text
273	Draft	• CCRA.W.2	Write informative/explanatory texts to examine and convey complex ideas and information clearly and accurately through the effective selection, organization, and analysis of content.
273	Revise	• CCRA.W.4	Produce clear and coherent writing in which the development, organization, and style are appropriate to task, purpose, and audience.
		• CCRA.W.5	Develop and strengthen writing as needed by planning, revising, editing, rewriting, or trying a new approach.
274	Edit and Proofread	• CCRA.W.5	Develop and strengthen writing as needed by planning, revising, editing, rewriting, or trying a new approach.
		• L.1.1b	Demonstrate command of the conventions of standard English grammar and usage when writing or speaking. Use common, proper, and possessive nouns.
		• L.2.2a	Demonstrate command of the conventions of standard English capitalization, punctuation, and spelling when writing. Capitalize holidays, product names, and geographic names.
		• L.2.2e • L.3.2g	Consult reference materials, including beginning dictionaries, as needed to check and correct spellings.
		• L.4.2a	Use correct capitalization.
		• L.4.2d • L.5.2e	Spell grade-appropriate words correctly, consulting references as needed.
275	Publish, Share, and Reflect	• CCRA.W.10	Write routinely over extended time frames (time for research, reflection, and revision) and shorter time frames (a single sitting or a day or two) for a range of tasks, purposes, and audiences.
		• CCRA.SL.5	Make strategic use of digital media and visual displays of data to express information and enhance understanding of presentations.
		• CCRA.SL.6	Adapt speech to a variety of contexts and communicative tasks, demonstrating command of formal English when indicated or appropriate.

Unit 9   Superstars

Language Development

SE Pages	Lesson	Code	Standards Text
276–277	Unit Launch	• CCRA.SL.2	Integrate and evaluate information presented in diverse media and formats, including visually, quantitatively, and orally.
278	Language: Agree and Disagree	• CCRA.SL.1	Prepare for and participate effectively in a range of conversations and collaborations with diverse partners, building on others' ideas and expressing their own clearly and persuasively.
279	Grammar: Future Tense Verbs and Contractions	• CCRA.W.2	Write informative/explanatory texts to examine and convey complex ideas and information clearly and accurately through the effective selection, organization, and analysis of content.
		• CCRA.W.10	Write routinely over extended time frames (time for research, reflection, and revision) and shorter time frames (a single sitting or a day or two) for a range of tasks, purposes, and audiences.

Language Development, continued

SE Pages	Lesson	Code	Standards Text
279	**Grammar:** **Future Tense Verbs** **and Contractions,** continued		Demonstrate command of the conventions of standard English grammar and usage when writing or speaking.
		● L.1.1e	Use verbs to convey a sense of past, present, and future (e.g., *Yesterday I walked home; Today I walk home; Tomorrow I will walk home*).
		● L.3.1e	Form and use the simple (e.g., *I walked; I walk; I will walk*) verb tenses.
		● L.5.1c	Use verb tense to convey various times, sequences, states, and conditions.
			Demonstrate command of the conventions of standard English capitalization, punctuation, and spelling when writing.
		● L.2.2c	Use an apostrophe to form contractions and frequently occurring possessives.
280	**Vocabulary:** **Space**	● CCRA.W.3	Write narratives to develop real or imagined experiences or events using effective technique, well-chosen details and well-structured event sequences.
	Language: **Give Information**	● CCRA.SL.1	Prepare for and participate effectively in a range of conversations and collaborations with diverse partners, building on others' ideas and expressing their own clearly and persuasively.
		● CCRA.L.6	Acquire and use accurately a range of general academic and domain-specific words and phrases sufficient for reading, writing, speaking, and listening at the college and career readiness level; demonstrate independence in gathering vocabulary knowledge when encountering an unknown term important to comprehension or expression.
281	**Grammar:** **Verb Tenses**	● CCRA.W.2	Write informative/explanatory texts to examine and convey complex ideas and information clearly and accurately through the effective selection, organization, and analysis of content.
		● CCRA.W.10	Write routinely over extended time frames (time for research, reflection, and revision) and shorter time frames (a single sitting or a day or two) for a range of tasks, purposes, and audiences.
		● CCRA.SL.1	Prepare for and participate effectively in a range of conversations and collaborations with diverse partners, building on others' ideas and expressing their own clearly and persuasively.
			Demonstrate command of the conventions of standard English grammar and usage when writing or speaking.
		● L.1.1e	Use verbs to convey a sense of past, present, and future (e.g., *Yesterday I walked home; Today I walk home; Tomorrow I will walk home*).
		● L.3.1e	Form and use the simple (e.g., *I walked; I walk; I will walk*) verb tenses.
		● L.5.1c	Use verb tense to convey various times, sequences, states, and conditions.
282	**Listen and Read Along:** ***Sunny and Moonshine***	● CCRA.R.4	Interpret words and phrases as they are used in a text, including determining technical, connotative, and figurative meanings, and analyze how specific word choices shape meaning or tone.
		● CCRA.R.10	Read and comprehend complex literary and informational texts independently and proficiently.
			With guidance and support from adults, demonstrate understanding of word relationships and nuances in word meanings.
		● L.1.5a	Sort words into categories (e.g., colors, clothing) to gain a sense of the concepts the categories represent.

Common Core State Standards, continued

Language Development, continued

SE Pages	Lesson	Code	Standards Text
283	Comprehension: Identify Goal and Outcome	• CCRA.R.3	Analyze how and why individuals, events, or ideas develop and interact over the course of a text.
		• CCRA.R.5	Analyze the structure of texts, including how specific sentences, paragraphs, and larger portions of the text (e.g., a section, chapter, scene, or stanza) relate to each other and the whole.
		• CCRA.SL.1	Prepare for and participate effectively in a range of conversations and collaborations with diverse partners, building on others' ideas and expressing their own clearly and persuasively.

Language and Literacy

SE Pages	Lesson	Code	Standards Text
284–285	High Frequency Words		Know and apply grade-level phonics and word analysis skills in decoding words.
		• RF.K.3c	Read common high-frequency words by sight (e.g., *the, of, to, you, she, my, is, are, do, does*).
		• RF.1.3g • RF.2.3f	Recognize and read grade-appropriate irregularly spelled words.
		• CCRA.L.4	Determine or clarify the meaning of unknown and multiple-meaning words and phrases by using context clues, analyzing meaningful word parts, and consulting general and specialized reference materials, as appropriate.
			Demonstrate command of the conventions of standard English capitalization, punctuation, and spelling when writing.
		• L.1.2d	Use conventional spelling for words with common spelling patterns and for frequently occurring irregular words.
		• L.3.2e	Use conventional spelling for high-frequency and other studied words and for adding suffixes to base words (e.g., *sitting, smiled, cries, happiness*).
		• L.4.2d • L.5.2e	Spell grade-appropriate words correctly, consulting references as needed.
			Determine or clarify the meaning of unknown and multiple-meaning words and phrases based on grade 2 reading and content, choosing flexibly from a range of strategies.
		• L.2.4a	Use sentence-level context as a clue to the meaning of a word or phrase.
286–287	Reading and Spelling: Multisyllabic Words		Know and apply grade-level phonics and word analysis skills in decoding words.
		• RF.K.3a	Demonstrate basic knowledge of one-to-one letter-sound correspondences by producing the primary sound or many of the most frequent sounds for each consonant.
		• RF.1.3f	Read words with inflectional endings.
		• RF.2.3d	Decode words with common prefixes and suffixes.
		• CCRA.L.1	Demonstrate command of the conventions of standard English grammar and usage when writing or speaking.
			Demonstrate command of the conventions of standard English capitalization, punctuation, and spelling when writing.
		• L.1.2d	Use conventional spelling for words with common spelling patterns and for frequently occurring irregular words.

Language and Literacy, continued

SE Pages	Lesson	Code	Standards Text
288–291	Read on Your Own: "Fifth Moon's Story"	CCRA.R.10	Read and comprehend complex literary and informational texts independently and proficiently.
		RF.K.3a	Know and apply grade-level phonics and word analysis skills in decoding words. Demonstrate basic knowledge of one-to-one letter-sound correspondences by producing the primary sound or many of the most frequent sounds for each consonant.
		RF.1.3g RF.2.3f	Recognize and read grade-appropriate irregularly spelled words.
		RF.1.4a RF.2.4a	Read with sufficient accuracy and fluency to support comprehension. Read grade-level text with purpose and understanding.
		RF.1.4b RF.2.4b	Read grade-level text orally with accuracy, appropriate rate, and expression on successive readings.
		CCRA.L.4	Determine or clarify the meaning of unknown and multiple-meaning words and phrases by using context clues, analyzing meaningful word parts, and consulting general and specialized reference materials, as appropriate.
292	Check Your Understanding	CCRA.W.9	Draw evidence from literary or informational texts to support analysis, reflection, and research.
		CCRA.SL.1	Prepare for and participate effectively in a range of conversations and collaborations with diverse partners, building on others' ideas and expressing their own clearly and persuasively.
	Expand Your Vocabulary	CCRA.L.6	Acquire and use accurately a range of general academic and domain-specific words and phrases sufficient for reading, writing, speaking, and listening at the college and career readiness level; demonstrate independence in gathering vocabulary knowledge when encountering an unknown term important to comprehension or expression.
	Write About the Sun	CCRA.W.2	Write informative/explanatory texts to examine and convey complex ideas and information clearly and accurately through the effective selection, organization, and analysis of content.
		CCRA.W.10	Write routinely over extended time frames (time for research, reflection, and revision) and shorter time frames (a single sitting or a day or two) for a range of tasks, purposes, and audiences.

Language and Content

SE Pages	Lesson	Code	Standards Text
293	Success in Science: Learn About Outer Space	CCRA.R.2	Determine central ideas or themes of a text and analyze their development; summarize the key supporting details and ideas.
		CCRA.R.4	Interpret words and phrases as they are used in a text, including determining technical, connotative, and figurative meanings, and analyze how specific word choices shape meaning or tone.
		CCRA.R.10	Read and comprehend complex literary and informational texts independently and proficiently.
		CCRA.L.4	Determine or clarify the meaning of unknown and multiple-meaning words and phrases by using context clues, analyzing meaningful word parts, and consulting general and specialized reference materials, as appropriate.

Common Core State Standards, continued

Language and Content, continued

SE Pages	Lesson	Code	Standards Text
294–295	**Build Background and Vocabulary**	• CCRA.R.7	Integrate and evaluate content presented in diverse media and formats, including visually and quantitatively, as well as in words.
		• CCRA.SL.1	Prepare for and participate effectively in a range of conversations and collaborations with diverse partners, building on others' ideas and expressing their own clearly and persuasively.
		• CCRA.L.6	Acquire and use accurately a range of general academic and domain-specific words and phrases sufficient for reading, writing, speaking, and listening at the college and career readiness level; demonstrate independence in gathering vocabulary knowledge when encountering an unknown term important to comprehension or expression.
			Determine or clarify the meaning of unknown and multiple-meaning words and phrases based on grade-level reading and content, choosing flexibly from a range of strategies.
		• L.1.4a • L.2.4a • L.3.4a	Use sentence-level context as a clue to the meaning of a word or phrase.
		• L.4.4a	Use context (e.g., definitions, examples, or restatements in text) as a clue to the meaning of a word or phrase.
296–303	**Listen and Read Along: "Exploring Space"**	• CCRA.R.2	Determine central ideas or themes of a text and analyze their development; summarize the key supporting details and ideas.
		• CCRA.R.4	Interpret words and phrases as they are used in a text, including determining technical, connotative, and figurative meanings, and analyze how specific word choices shape meaning or tone.
		• CCRA.R.7	Integrate and evaluate content presented in diverse media and formats, including visually and quantitatively, as well as in words.
		• CCRA.R.9	Analyze how two or more texts address similar themes or topics in order to build knowledge or to compare the approaches the authors take.
		• CCRA.L.6	Acquire and use accurately a range of general academic and domain-specific words and phrases sufficient for reading, writing, speaking, and listening at the college and career readiness level; demonstrate independence in gathering vocabulary knowledge when encountering an unknown term important to comprehension or expression.
304	**Check Your Understanding**	• CCRA.R.2	Determine central ideas or themes of a text and analyze their development; summarize the key supporting details and ideas.
		• CCRA.SL.1	Prepare for and participate effectively in a range of conversations and collaborations with diverse partners, building on others' ideas and expressing their own clearly and persuasively.
	Review Vocabulary	• CCRA.R.4	Interpret words and phrases as they are used in a text, including determining technical, connotative, and figurative meanings, and analyze how specific word choices shape meaning or tone.
	Write About Outer Space	• CCRA.W.3	Write narratives to develop real or imagined experiences or events using effective technique, well-chosen details and well-structured event sequences.
		• CCRA.W.4	Produce clear and coherent writing in which the development, organization, and style are appropriate to task, purpose, and audience.

Language and Content, continued

SE Pages	Lesson	Code	Standards Text
304	**Write About Outer Space,** continued	• CCRA.W.10	Write routinely over extended time frames (time for research, reflection, and revision) and shorter time frames (a single sitting or a day or two) for a range of tasks, purposes, and audiences.

Writing Project

SE Pages	Lesson	Code	Standards Text
305	**Model Study: Diamante Poem**	• CCRA.R.5	Analyze the structure of texts, including how specific sentences, paragraphs, and larger portions of the text (e.g., a section, chapter, scene, or stanza) relate to each other and the whole.
306	**Prewrite**	• CCRA.W.4	Produce clear and coherent writing in which the development, organization, and style are appropriate to task, purpose, and audience.
307	**Draft**	• CCRA.W.2	Write informative/explanatory texts to examine and convey complex ideas and information clearly and accurately through the effective selection, organization, and analysis of content.
307	**Revise**	• CCRA.W.4	Produce clear and coherent writing in which the development, organization, and style are appropriate to task, purpose, and audience.
		• CCRA.W.5	Develop and strengthen writing as needed by planning, revising, editing, rewriting, or trying a new approach.
		• CCRA.SL.1	Prepare for and participate effectively in a range of conversations and collaborations with diverse partners, building on others' ideas and expressing their own clearly and persuasively.
308	**Edit and Proofread**	• CCRA.W.5	Develop and strengthen writing as needed by planning, revising, editing, rewriting, or trying a new approach.
			With guidance and support from adults, demonstrate understanding of word relationships and nuances in word meanings.
		• L.1.5d	Distinguish shades of meaning among verbs differing in manner (e.g., *look, peek, glance, stare, glare, scowl*) and adjectives differing in intensity (e.g., *large, gigantic*) by defining or choosing them or by acting out the meanings.
		• L.2.5b	Distinguish shades of meaning among closely related verbs (e.g., *toss, throw, hurl*) and closely related adjectives (e.g., *thin, slender, skinny, scrawny*).
			Demonstrate command of the conventions of standard English capitalization, punctuation, and spelling when writing.
		• L.2.2e • L.3.2g	Consult reference materials, including beginning dictionaries, as needed to check and correct spellings.
		• L.4.2d • L.5.2e	Spell grade-appropriate words correctly, consulting references as needed.
309	**Publish, Share, and Reflect**	• CCRA.W.4	Produce clear and coherent writing in which the development, organization, and style are appropriate to task, purpose, and audience.
		• CCRA.W.10	Write routinely over extended time frames (time for research, reflection, and revision) and shorter time frames (a single sitting or a day or two) for a range of tasks, purposes, and audiences.
		• CCRA.SL.4	Present information, findings, and supporting evidence such that listeners can follow the line of reasoning and the organization, development, and style are appropriate to task, purpose, and audience.

Common Core State Standards, continued

Handbook			

Strategies for Learning Language

SE Pages	Lesson	Code	Standards Text
312–313	Strategies for Learning Language	• CCRA.SL.1	Prepare for and participate effectively in a range of conversations and collaborations with diverse partners, building on others' ideas and expressing their own clearly and persuasively.
		• CCRA.SL.6	Adapt speech to a variety of contexts and communicative tasks, demonstrating command of formal English when indicated or appropriate.
		• CCRA.L.3	Apply knowledge of language to understand how language functions in different contexts, to make effective choices for meaning or style, and to comprehend more fully when reading or listening.

Grammar

SE Pages	Lesson	Code	Standards Text
314–316	Sentences	• CCRA.L.1	Demonstrate command of the conventions of standard English grammar and usage when writing or speaking.
			Demonstrate command of the conventions of standard English capitalization, punctuation, and spelling when writing.
		• L.2.2c	Use an apostrophe to form contractions and frequently occurring possessives.
317–319	Punctuation Marks	• CCRA.L.3	Apply knowledge of language to understand how language functions in different contexts, to make effective choices for meaning or style, and to comprehend more fully when reading or listening.
			Demonstrate command of the conventions of standard English capitalization, punctuation, and spelling when writing.
		• L.1.2b	Use end punctuation for sentences.
		• L.1.2c	Use commas in dates and to separate single words in a series.
		• L.2.2b	Use commas in greetings and closings of letters.
		• L.3.2b	Use commas in addresses.
		• L.3.2c	Use commas and quotation marks in dialogue.
		• L.4.2b	Use commas and quotation marks to mark direct speech and quotations from a text.
		• L.5.2a	Use punctuation to separate items in a series.
		• L.5.2d	Use underlining, quotation marks, or italics to indicate titles of works.
320–322	Capital Letters		Demonstrate command of the conventions of standard English capitalization, punctuation, and spelling when writing.
		• L.1.2a	Capitalize dates and names of people.
		• L.2.2a	Capitalize holidays, product names, and geographic names.
		• L.3.2a	Capitalize appropriate words in titles.
		• L.4.2a	Use correct capitalization.

Grammar, continued

SE Pages	Lesson	Code	Standards Text
323–327	**Nouns**		Demonstrate command of the conventions of standard English grammar and usage when writing or speaking.
		• L.1.1b	Use common, proper, and possessive nouns.
		• L.2.1b	Form and use frequently occurring irregular plural nouns (e.g., *feet, children, teeth, mice, fish*).
		• L.3.1a	Explain the function of nouns, pronouns, verbs, adjectives, and adverbs in general and their functions in particular sentences.
		• L.3.1b	Form and use regular and irregular plural nouns.
		• L.3.1c	Use abstract nouns (e.g., *childhood*).
328–329	**Pronouns**		Demonstrate command of the conventions of standard English grammar and usage when writing or speaking.
		• L.1.1d	Use personal, possessive, and indefinite pronouns (e.g., *I, me, my; they, them, their, anyone, everything*).
		• L.3.1a	Explain the function of nouns, pronouns, verbs, adjectives, and adverbs in general and their functions in particular sentences.
330–334	**Adjectives**		Demonstrate command of the conventions of standard English grammar and usage when writing or speaking.
		• L.1.1f	Use frequently occurring adjectives.
		• L.3.1a	Explain the function of nouns, pronouns, verbs, adjectives, and adverbs in general and their functions in particular sentences.
335–339	**Verbs**		Demonstrate command of the conventions of standard English grammar and usage when writing or speaking.
		• L.1.1e	Use verbs to convey a sense of past, present, and future (e.g., *Yesterday I walked home; Today I walk home; Tomorrow I will walk home*).
		• L.2.1d	Form and use the past tense of frequently occurring irregular verbs (e.g., *sat, hid, told*).
		• L.3.1a	Explain the function of nouns, pronouns, verbs, adjectives, and adverbs in general and their functions in particular sentences.
		• L.3.1d	Form and use regular and irregular verbs.
		• L.3.1e	Form and use the simple (e.g., *I walked; I walk; I will walk*) verb tenses.
		• L.4.1b	Form and use the progressive (e.g., *I was walking; I am walking; I will be walking*) verb tenses.

Handwriting

SE Pages	Lesson	Code	Standards Text
340–347	**Writing Letters, Words, and Sentences**		Demonstrate command of the conventions of standard English grammar and usage when writing or speaking.
		• L.1.1a	Print all upper- and lowercase letters.

Common Core State Standards, continued

The Writing Process

SE Pages	Lesson	Code	Standards Text
348–349	Prewrite	• CCRA.W.5	Develop and strengthen writing as needed by planning, revising, editing, rewriting, or trying a new approach.
	Collect Ideas, Choose a Topic, and Plan Your Writing	• CCRA.W.7	Conduct short as well as more sustained research projects based on focused questions, demonstrating understanding of the subject under investigation.
	Gather Details and Get Organized	• CCRA.W.8	Gather relevant information from multiple print and digital sources, assess the credibility and accuracy of each source, and integrate the information while avoiding plagiarism.
350–352	Draft and Revise Edit and Proofread	• CCRA.W.5	Develop and strengthen writing as needed by planning, revising, editing, rewriting, or trying a new approach.
353	Publish	• CCRA.W.6	Use technology, including the Internet, to produce and publish writing and to interact and collaborate with others.

Using Information Resources

SE Pages	Lesson	Code	Standards Text
354–355	How to Find Information	• CCRA.R.7	Integrate and evaluate content presented in diverse media and formats, including visually and quantitatively, as well as in words.
		• CCRA.W.8	Gather relevant information from multiple print and digital sources, assess the credibility and accuracy of each source, and integrate the information while avoiding plagiarism.
356–359	Dictionary and Thesaurus	• CCRA.L.4	Determine or clarify the meaning of unknown and multiple-meaning words and phrases by using context clues, analyzing meaningful word parts, and consulting general and specialized reference materials, as appropriate.
360–361	Parts of a Book	• CCRA.R.5	Analyze the structure of texts, including how specific sentences, paragraphs, and larger portions of the text (e.g., a section, chapter, scene, or stanza) relate to each other and the whole.
362–363	Atlas: Maps	• CCRA.R.7	Integrate and evaluate content presented in diverse media and formats, including visually and quantitatively, as well as in words.
364–367	Internet	• CCRA.W.8	Gather relevant information from multiple print and digital sources, assess the credibility and accuracy of each source, and integrate the information while avoiding plagiarism.